The Laurel Classical Drama has as its purpose the presentation of a representative selection of the major tragedies and comedies of ancient Greece and Rome. The masterpieces of Aeschylus, Sophocles, Euripides, Aristophanes, Menander, Plautus, Seneca, and Terence appear in translations chosen for their freshness and readability.

Robert W. Corrigan is Dean of the School of the Arts and Professor of Dramatic Literature at New York University. Previously he was Andrew Mellon Professor of Drama and Head of the Department of Drama at Carnegie Institute of Technology. Having taught at Tulane, Carleton, and Minnesota, Professor Corrigan was the founder and editor of the *Tulane Drama Review*. He is the editor of several anthologies of the drama and dramatic criticism, including *The Modern Theatre, Theatre in the 20th Century*, the Delta *New Theatre of Europe* series, as well as the forthcoming British Drama (6 vols.) now being published in the Dell Laurel Editions.

Roman Drama

The Laurel Classical Drama

Plautus

THE MENAECHMI

THE MERCHANT

Terence

PHORMIO

THE BROTHERS

Seneca

MEDEA

and the ARS POETICA by *Horace*

*in modern translations
edited, with an introduction, by Robert W. Corrigan*

Published by DELL PUBLISHING CO., INC.
750 Third Avenue, New York, N.Y. 10017
© *Copyright 1966, by Dell Publishing Co., Inc.*
Laurel ® *TM 674623, Dell Publishing Co., Inc.*
First printing: August, 1966
Printed in U.S.A.

Grateful acknowledgment to the following for the
translations used in this volume:

Chandler Publishing Company for THE MENAECHMI, *translated*
by Palmer Bovie.
Copyright © *1962 by Chandler Publishing Company.*
Reprinted by permission.

Arthur R. Wilmurt for his translation of THE MERCHANT.
Copyright © *1966 by Arthur Wilmurt. All rights reserved.*
This play in its printed form is designed for the reading public
only. All dramatic rights are fully protected by copyright and
no public or private performance may be given without written
permission. All applications for performance should be addressed
to Arthur Wilmurt, Department of Drama, Carnegie Institute
of Technology, Pittsburgh, Pa.

Lionel Casson for his translation of PHORMIO.
Reprinted with permission of The Macmillan Co., from MASTERS
OF ANCIENT COMEDY, *edited and translated by Lionel Casson.*
Copyright © *1960 by Lionel Casson.*

Warren H. Held for his translation of THE BROTHERS.
Copyright © *1963 by Literary Discoveries, Inc.*
Reprinted by permission of the translator.

The Bobbs-Merrill Company, Inc., for MEDEA, *translated by*
Moses Hadas.
Copyright © *1956 by Bobbs-Merrill Company, Inc.*

Norman J. DeWitt for his translation of ARS POETICA.
Copyright © *1961 by Norman J. DeWitt*

Introduction 7

Plautus

THE MENAECHMI 25
Translated by Palmer Bovie

THE MERCHANT 119
Adapted by Arthur Wilmurt

Terence

Contents

PHORMIO 179
Translated by Lionel Casson

THE BROTHERS 263
Translated by Warren H. Held

Seneca

MEDEA 327
Translated by Moses Hadas

Horace

ARS POETICA 361
Translated and introduced by
Norman J. DeWitt

Introduction

Some Thoughts on Roman Drama

Robert W. Corrigan

I. THE THEATRE IN OUR FIRST GREAT SOCIETY

On Monday, June 14, 1965, President and Mrs. Johnson were hosts to America's first National Arts Day. Better than 400 artists—some famous, most nearly so—gathered at the White House for a thirteen-hour marathon session of poetry reading, chamber music, sculpture on the lawn, abstract painting in the halls, and some snippets from the best of Broadway and Hollywood. The gala event was brought to a close with a concert by Mr. Edward K. Ellington (no Dukes were invited) and his band, and as the guests took the A train home we could all relax—after all these years the Arts had finally had their day.

It's all over, at least for another year, and now we begin to ponder. Just what did it mean? Why was Robert Lowell's absence more significant than the presence of his 400 other colleagues? Wasn't the whole affair somewhat like being religious by going to church only on Christmas and Easter? Why do the sciences have advisory councils to the President, rather than National Science Days? Instead of all the hoop-la, why didn't the President and his wife commission a symphony or two, buy a few paintings, or set up a theatre somewhere? One could go on asking questions, but one thing is certain: we now have Official Art.

The whole affair had an Augustan quality to it; in fact, it was Roman through and through. Only in self-consciously "great" societies are the arts institutionalized in this fashion. So it is understandable if the occasion prompts one to wonder about the arts of the first great society. What kind of art was produced under the Caesars in an age of public life, public virtue, public welfare, and public works? Great stadiums and grand public buildings were built; an impressive, patriotically inspired epic poem was written, as were numerous essays and philosophical treatises, not to mention some ribald fiction and licentious verse; a great deal of imitative sculpture was produced, and next to no drama worth remembering. We seem to do a little better today, but given the same conditions, how much better would we have done over the same span of time? Idle speculation, perhaps; but not beside the point. This is particularly true of the theatre.

The Roman theatre in its first days was one of the most vital the world has ever known. It knew and drew upon the established traditions of the Greeks; there existed in many parts of Italy lively popular customs which were theatrical in nature; numerous theatrical troupes traveled and regularly performed throughout most of the country; and early in its development (the second half of the third century B.C.), a playwright of great talent had emerged to assist the theatre in its growth. Only the English theatre of the fifteenth and sixteenth centuries had conditions anywhere near comparable. But here the similarities cease: the England of Elizabeth gave us Shakespeare, Marlowe and Jonson; the Romans—well, Seneca. Ironically, as the Romans gave the theatre more official patronage they destroyed the popular tradition which had been the source of its vitality. The virile Atellan farces were replaced by gaudy circuses. The riotous comedy of Plautus gave way to the pretentious moralizing of would-be tragedians. Soon the histrionic sensibility went underground, and only emerged in the form of a Terence who wrote for the cultivated members of the Scipionic Circle, or a Seneca who wrote mostly for himself. The Roman audience—apparently one of the best history has ever known—was transformed into a passive Public, and the theatre ceased being entertainment (a meaningful tension between a performer and his audience—*inter:* between and *tenere:* to hold) and soon became only a diversion. Great theatre always has a sense of mystery about it; no such quality existed in the Roman drama of the first century.

There are many reasons that such promising beginnings bore so little fruit, but certainly one of the most important causes for the rapid decline of this theatre was the need on the part of the Roman leaders to take every spontaneous popular involvement and turn it into a public attitude.

Perhaps our apprehensions about conditions today are unwarranted, but it is worth recalling that when Julius, Augustus and Tiberius Caesar were building the first of history's "great" societies, they honored Roman artists publicly, albeit briefly, and then went back to more important matters such as war or tribute. We remember Pericles and Sophocles, Elizabeth and Shakespeare, Louis and Molière, Weimar and Goethe. Then there is Caesar and ——!

II. FANTASY AND FARCE

When reading the plays of Plautus, one very quickly becomes conscious of what a remarkable sense of the theatre that early Roman playwright had. He seems to have known every theatrical trick, and what's more, he knew how to use them. There is something in his work which would be sure to appeal to every level of sophistication and every social class. As could be expected, much has been written about Plautus and his theatre (unquestionably the best book being George Duckworth's *The Nature of Roman Comedy*, Princeton: Princeton University Press, 1952), and there isn't much we don't know about his sources, his techniques, and the conventions of the theatre of his time. But somehow this isn't enough. None of the magistral studies ever seems to get to the heart of things. Everyone admits that Plautus was a great farceur, and after describing the external characteristics and so-called conventions of farce—usually in a deprecatory manner— the subject is dropped. Q.E.D. But this is the key subject; this is what Plautus was really up to and, if one is ever to understand the spirit which courses through the plays of Plautus, he must also understand something about the nature of farce. Now, farce isn't quite a dirty word in critical parlance, but it certainly hasn't been given very much attention by our serious critics and theorists. At least not until Eric Bentley turned his fine mind to the subject; and as so often is the case, Bentley is right. Attention must be paid!

Farce, like a curse, is the expression of repressed wishes. We in the United States lack the colorful curses of Europe, particularly those of the staunchly Catholic countries such as Spain and Italy: When a Spaniard says, "I'll defecate in your mother's milk" or calls another a "son of a whore," he is in effect committing murder. (Indeed, after he says such things, he may actually be murdered in return.) All such phrases are expressions of the wish to destroy the existence of a person. Farce works in much the same way. As Bentley points out in his *The Life of Drama*, farces are much like dreams in that they "show the disguised fulfillment of repressed wishes." I believe Professor Bentley is right in this, but I believe it would be more fruitful to use a less limiting and more inclusive idea—namely, fantasy. Dreams certainly are assertions on the part of the unconscious to express many things which our consciousness represses. But farce also concerns itself with the materials and images of our conscious fantasies. We know that fantasy and repression are inextricably linked in a dynamic tension, and the rhythm of farce is— to use a forced image—that of the cat of fantasy chasing its tail of repression. And our pleasure in witnessing farce is that our wildest fantasies can be acted out, without— as Bentley reminds us—our having to suffer the consequences. In technique it is like psychiatric therapy: the doctor urges the patient to tell all of his fantasies within the safe confines of the office, so he will not feel so compelled to act them out in more destructive ways elsewhere.

This relationship leads us to one of the central misunderstandings about farce. Just as so many discussions of psychoanalysis are invariably reduced to the psychopathology of sex, so, too, the literature on farce—such as it is—is invariably concerned with farce as an expression of our sexual fantasies. Hence "bedroom" is the adjective most commonly associated with this whole form of drama. There is certainly some justification for this, but when we read (or even better, see) Plautus' plays, we become increasingly conscious of the fact that, although sex is present, so too are many other subjects. Think of Molière's one-act farces, or Chekhov's riotous early plays. Or think of the best known of our modern farceurs: Chaplin, Buster Keaton, the Marx Brothers, Abbott and Costello, Laurel and Hardy. Sex and slapstick have always been combined, but never exclusively, except in the old-time burlesque routines. Farce's spirit of violence and rebellion is also directed to other situations and standards of value such as wealth, social class, life in the city, and even the arts.

The essential condition for the creation of farce is the

existence of strong publicly shared values and standards of behavior. The last really big-hit bedroom farce on Broadway was *The Seven Year Itch,* and I believe it is significant that it was first produced in 1952. The sexual taboos and rigid standards of sexual behavior have been dissolving (or at least are changing profoundly) so rapidly in the past couple of decades, that the old-fashioned bedroom farce has just about disappeared. The *Up in Mabel's Room* and *Getting Gertie's Garter* of my youth just don't make it today, and even such a blatantly lewd piece as the more recent *Pajama Tops* was most successful in the boondocks and to my knowledge was never brought into New York. The sex farce undoubtedly still has some appeal, but usually to less sophisticated and more parochial audiences. (In this regard, it is worth noting that many so-called bedroom comedies can do very badly in New York, and still be counted upon to make money in community theatres around the country.) The Hollywood film is still a pretty hospitable medium for the sex farce, as *The Apartment* and *Some Like It Hot* will attest, but even here things seem to be changing.

Eric Bentley is certainly correct in his explanation of why bedroom farce appeals to audiences. He writes:

> Farce in general offers a special opportunity: shielded by delicious darkness and seated in warm security, we enjoy the privilege of being totally passive while on stage our most treasured, unmentionable wishes are fulfilled before our eyes by the most violently active human beings that ever sprang from the human imagination. In that application of the formula which is bedroom farce, we savor the adventure of adultery, ingeniously exaggerated in the highest degree, and all without taking the responsibility or suffering the guilt. Our wives may be with us leading the laughter.[1]

But as more liberal sexual attitudes develop, farce has tended to move to other realms.

Not too long ago I was talking to some of my students about the subject of farce, and I discovered that they did not find the bedroom variety very funny. Sex, they said,

---

[1] *The Life of the Drama* (New York: Atheneum Publishers, 1964), p. 229.

was increasingly a take it or leave it matter for most of
their generation, and they were neither outraged nor titil-
lated by it when it was represented in the theatre. They
even went on to admit that they had actually acted out
most of their sexual fantasies—or at least all of those
which, with even a modicum of taste, could ever be presented on the stage. Money, business, bureaucratic power,
IBM-ization, and the system—these, they insisted, were
the widely held values of our time, and hence the more appropriate subject matter for farce. One then thinks of the
popularity of *How To Succeed in Business Without Really
Trying* and *Dr. Strangelove, A Hard Day's Night* and the
films featuring Jean-Paul Belmondo, or such farcical contemporary novels as *Up the Down Staircase* and *Catch-22.*
Perhaps the younger generation is right.

The real point, however, is that farce can and does have
many masks. The theatre of Plautus is one of the first in
the Western world to reveal this fact. Sex and the family,
money and social caste, accomplishment and pride, are
just some of the materials that this first farceur used. He
seemed, instinctively, to understand the cathartic nature
of fantasy. He also knew—and equally as well—that fantasy
is both preceded and followed by repression.

III. THE TEMPO OF FARCE

Whenever stage directors talk about the problems of producing farce, inevitably the first matter mentioned is the
question of pace. Farce, they say, must be played at break-
neck speed. So everything is speeded up, only to discover,
more often than not, that what has been created is not
art at all—only confusion. This chaos usually stems from
the director's failure to understand the inner dynamics
of farce. But directors are not the only guilty parties; the
critics and scholars have been just as far off the mark,
and nowhere is this fact more apparent than in the studies
of Roman comedy.

Even those critics well-disposed to Plautus cannot help
but approach his plays with an air of slight superiority.
We must like Plautus, they imply, because it is our cultural duty to do so; but they then go on to admit in con-
fidential tones that his plays are really pretty thin. This
prejudice against farce in general and Plautus in particu-

lar is inevitably revealed when the critics begin discussing the tempo of his plays. Farce, they say, deals with "amusing confusions rather than psychological complications." They go on to say that there is no real conflict in farce and the characters have little stature and practically no significance. Being only a drama of situation, it is peopled with passive characters who in no way determine the course of events. Finally, they argue that, since the characters lack complexity and the situations exist only to be superficially exploited, these situations have no other meaning than confusion and embarrassment for their own sake. Hence the conclusion: if a situation has no intrinsic meaning, then the playwright must depend upon variety, novelty, and uniqueness if he is to ever achieve the proper theatrical effects. Rapidity of pace is seen, then, as a means of compensating for the script's obvious insignificance. Plautus is praised as a farceur because of his ability to move from situation to situation, incident to incident, so fast that the audience never has the time to question the implausibiliy of what is taking place on the stage, nor to be bored by what is essentially only cotton-candy fluff. However, interspersed in the midst of all of this are numerous kind references to the author's earthy sense of humor and his boisterous animal spirits.

Such well-intentioned criticism could not be more wrong!

Farce is a surrealistic art. Like the fairy tale and the dream, it is an art of flat surfaces. It is also an art of images. Like a giant collage, it is composed of violent juxtapositions, short, bright flashes, and disparate patterns having no apparent continuity. As a result, through all the external hilarity, we become aware of the childlike truth of its nature and the mysterious quality of its means. Both in its techniques and in our responses to them, the dynamics of farce are much like those of the Punch-and-Judy shows. Since the laws of logical cause and effect do not exist in such a world, the facts of our daily existence are presented in what seems to be a distorted fashion. But, as Bentley has pointed out so persuasively, farce is "always faithful to the inner experience."

"That's the way it is; that's the way it *really* is!" So the saying goes, and so it goes in farce. We may never have literally experienced the trials and tribulations of the Brothers Menaechmus, but our most profound psychic dramas certainly includes an Erotium and a wife, an irate father-in-law and a Brush, and above all an alter ego among its cast of characters.

Farce, then, appeals directly to our senses and our psyche and not to our ratiocinative faculties. And this accounts for the unique rapidity of its pace. It is not a question of plausibility or implausibility; it has a quick tempo because in the world of fantasy the laws of logic have been suspended and everything that happens occurs more directly, and hence more quickly.

No other form of drama makes such great demands on the actor, and Plautus, being an actor, must have been well aware of it. This fact, probably more than any other, accounts for the great disparity which exists between the audience's enthusiastic response to farce and the scholar's general lack of regard for it. Its most important qualities cannot be gotten inside the covers of a book. Farce is always acted. For its effects it concentrates on the actor's body—on his facial expressions, his mimicries, and his physical gestures. (Bentley, to quote him yet again, put it beautifully when he wrote: "The dialogue of farce is sound and movement.") The critics' problem is to capture the physics of performance. This is next to impossible to do except through performance itself. But what the critics can do is to make directors and actors aware of the fact that the tempo of farce is not an external compensatory technique; it is not something a George Abbott can come in and impose upon a production that won't get off the ground. To do Plautus—or the plays of any farceur—well one must first enter into fantasy's magic realm; once there, the buoyant and violent spirit of that world will provide all the other necessary directions.

IV. A FUNNY THING HAPPENED ON THE WAY TO THE FORUM

When *A Funny Thing Happened on the Way to the Forum,* starring Zero Mostel, opened on May 8, 1962, many people were surprised to learn that this successful musical was actually a pastiche of scenes from Plautine farce. How amazing, many of them thought, that the works of an old Roman could have such vitality and be so much fun. They shouldn't have been surprised, for the authors were doing little more than updating essentially Plautine techniques. In fact, Plautus is history's first know

writer of musical comedy and it is no accident that countless musicals *(Fanny, The Boys From Syracuse* and *A
Funny Thing,* to name a few) have been based on his
plays.

Because musical comedy is not generally respected in
academic circles, most scholars have not paid much attention to this aspect of Plautus's work. They do discuss his
practice of *contamnatio* (the technique of stealing and
piecing together scenes from several plays by the writers
of the Greek New Comedy), and then go on to talk about
the puns, racy obscenities, the many comic-coined words,
and the general exuberance of his language. But the most
significant aspects of Plautine theatre are the songs and
the dance routines.

From the more than 130 plays which we know Plautus
wrote, we have close to sixty songs still remaining. And it
is clear from these texts that the typical Plautus play was
composed of forty percent songs and another twenty percent was probably chanted or recited to a flute, *à la* Rex
Harrison in *My Fair Lady.* (One play, *Epidicus,* was eighty
percent musical.)

The clue to this is the great variety of meter to be
found in any one of Plautus's plays. All Roman comedy
was composed in verse, but no other playwright used so
many different kinds of meter and, more important, used
them in such wild combinations. Terence, for instance,
almost always used regular iambic meters and only occasionally shifted to regular trochees. Plautus, on the
other hand, used not only highly irregular iambic and
trochaic meters, but the extremely colloquial proceleus-
matic and the rarely used anapestic meters as well. Even
the Roman critics tended to denigrate Plautus for such
impurity. Quintillian considered Terence a better playwright because he wrote with greater consistency of style
rather than in the hodgepodge style of his predecessor.
Horace complained of Plautus's fame, using many of the
same arguments that the academic detractors of musical
comedy use today. But at least one critic of great repute
was on Plautus's side. At the playwright's death, Varro
wrote in *De Poetis:*

> After the death of Plautus, comedy mourned, the
> stage was deserted, and laughter, sport, jest, and
> countless numbers all shed tears of sorrow.

The "countless numbers" *(numeri innumeri)* was a direct reference to both the songs and the polymetry of Plautine farce.

This raises a difficult question: it is generally believed that the source of Roman comedy was the Greek New Comedy, especially the plays of Menander. But polymetry is not a characteristic of Greek New Comedy. We find shifts of meter only in the choruses, and these follow a very consistent pattern. It is more likely that Plautus borrowed his plots from the Greeks and then infused them with the musical-comedy techniques of the Italian popular theatre, especially those of the Etruscan *satura* and the Fescenine verses of Etruria. Whatever the explanation, the medieval editor put it just right when he wrote on a Plautine manuscript, *"mutatis modis cantica."* (Songs in changing measures).

It is this quality which makes Plautus's plays so devilishly hard to translate. There are frequent elisions (or else hiatuses); synizesis—the running together of separate vowel sounds within a word to create a pun or other comic effects—is common; and the songs themselves are filled with unnatural accents, obviously necessary to create the proper rhythms of song. In short, only if approached as a musical text will a Plautine play make much sense.

So, in reading Plautus, we must realize that we are reading a musical-comedy script. Not much is there. This fact certainly explains why a literary playwright like Terence became more influential than Plautus in the Augustan period and also later on in both the Middle Ages and early Renaissance. But the Renaissance theatre of both England and Spain had no real vitality until its writers began to discover Plautus; or, if not Plautus himself, at least the buoyant spirit of musical comedy that dominates his plays.

V. THE BEGINNINGS OF THE COMMEDIA TRADITION

Probably the most penetrating, brief description of the peculiar genius of the Italian theatre can be found in Pirandello's essay, "Introduction to the Italian Theatre." [2] The

[2] "Introduzione al teatro italiano," translated by Anne Paulucci, in *The Genius of the Italian Theatre*, (N.Y.: Mentor Books) Eric Bentley, Editor.

great playwright writes about many aspects of his country's theatre, but he is at his best when he accounts for the development and describes the nature of the *Commedia dell'arte*. One passage in particular is worth noting here:

> The *Commedia dell'arte* emerged, little by little, precisely from theatrical personalities . . . who, as actors, knew the pulse of the public and, as authors, also indulged their own personal tastes and ambitions. . . . But they were also well acquainted with the output of the *litterati*, and as producers took out options on those works, performing them with their own, or revising them to suit their purposes. It is absurd to imagine in this an accidental discovery of mere actors. Anyone having even the slightest acquaintance with the way an actor works on stage, with the precise directions he requires if he is to take a step to the right instead of the left, will readily see that the idea of improvising their performances could never have occurred to actors.
>
> The *Commedia dell'arte* is born, on the contrary, out of authors who are so deeply involved in the Theatre, in the life of the Theatre, as to become, in fact, actors; who begin by writing the comedies they later perform, comedies at once more theatrical because not written in the isolated study of the man of letters but in the presence, as it were, of the warm breath of the public; who then take up the task of adapting for their own performance and that of their troupe the comedies of other authors, old and new, in order to supply the pressing need for repertory, constantly revising these adaptations, after having tried out on their audiences the effectiveness of certain flourishes added as an outlet and vehicle for the particular talents of some actor of the company. And as their fellow actors gradually become skilled in keeping up the already-familiar repartee of the middle episodes, they will write only the exits and the outline of the action.
>
> In other words those authors must have lost all their serious artistic pretensions; the transitory, impassioned life of the Theatre must have taken such full possession of them that the only interest left to them was that of the spectacle itself—a complete ab-

sorption in the quality of the performance and communication with the audience.

They are no longer authors; but they are no longer even actors, in the true sense of the word.

What are they, then?

By now each one of them has become a *type*, with a completely defined stage life of its own; so that finally a theatrical convention is established whereby with ten of them, ten such types—no more, no less— a complex and varied spectacle can be put on that will provide full satisfaction for the audience—an audience already familiar with these conventions, with the rules of the game, and passionately interested in how their favorites carry on, how far each succeeds in giving prominence to his part.

Pirandello then goes on to point out that the *Commedia* is uniquely Italianate in spirit. There is no doubt he is right about this; the traditions of the *Commedia* are as old as Italy itself. But one might have wished that Pirandello had broadened his perspective a bit more, for no man of the Italian theatre embodied those traditions more fully than Titus Maccius Plautus. He even had a *Commedia* name.

The popular Italian theatre has always been imbued with the spirit of *Commedia* and the particular genius of Plautus is that he was the first to incorporate it into his plays. The first known theatrical performances in Italy were the *Fabulae Atellanae*, developed by the Oscans in the town of Atella in Campagna. The *Fabulae* were short (300 lines) satiric parodies of life in the country. They had such titles as "The Sick Boar" or "Daddy, the Farmer," and occasionally they were parodies of heroic figures, as can be gathered by a title like "Hercules, the Tax Collector." These sketches were filled with riddles and obscenities and were played by companies of touring actors. It is interesting to note that the actors played them *"planipes,"* with bare feet, and not in the *cothurni* of tragedy nor in the *socci* of comedy; indicating that, from the beginning, the *fabulae* were farcical in nature.

However, the most significant thing about them was the fact that their casts were composed entirely of the "stock" or type characters which Pirandello referred to in his essay. The first records tell us of only four characte͏ͭ

(*Maccus,* the clown; *Bucco,* the glutton or braggart; *Pappus,* the foolish old man; and *Dossemus,* the hunchback trickster), but this number was gradually increased, and by the middle of the third century B.C. there were at least eight. And all of them can be found in the plays of Plautus.

Plautus began as an actor, and from his name it is obvious that he played the clown. He was not the first known Roman dramatist (both Livius Andronicus and Gnaeus Naevius are known to have preceded him), but it is clear that he was the first to incorporate the native comic traditions of the *Fabulae* into the framework of the literary comedy which his predecessors had borrowed from the Greeks. And very soon Plautine farce came to dominate the Roman theatre.

The first thing one notices about Plautus's plays is how insignificant the plots are. In fact, the plot is usually revealed in the prologue. The audience was not concerned with what happened; their interest was in how things were worked out and the form of the performance itself. For this reason, type characters are ideally suited for Plautine drama. A type character is one who needs no explaining and whose future is predictable no matter what his situation might be. Such a character is, as Bentley describes him, a creature of habit, and he brings a great energy to the theatre. He has the characteristics essential for farce; these also happen to be the same qualities which Pirandello ascribed to the characters of *Commedia.*

No one, to my knowledge, has ever referred to Plautus as the father of the *Commedia dell'arte;* and one would probably be in error to do so now. But the *Commedia* did not come into being *de novis* either. Ruzzante and his colleagues may not have known it, but Titus the clown was out there on the platform with them.

VI. THE LIMITATIONS OF UNDERSTANDING

It seems almost inevitable that, when we discuss authors of the past—especially classical authors—we tend to link together writers who have so little in common that, if we were to do it with our own contemporaries, we would be dismissed with derision. Such, however, has nearly always been the case with Plautus and Publius Terentius Afer, better known as Terence. True, they lived at approximately the same time (Plautus: *c.*254–184 B.C., Terence: *c.*195–159 B.C.), and they both wrote comedies based upon the plots of Greek New Comedy. But the similarities stop there, and our understanding of how the Roman theatre developed (or, perhaps, failed to develop) has been severely limited by our failure to realize how different in style, tone, and technique these two dramatists actually are. Plautus, as I have indicated, was a man of the theatre. His plays are imbued with that sense of immediacy which popular performance demands. He was no *littérateur*, but a theatre craftsman who knew what his boisterous audiences liked and wanted, and he happily gave it to them. Terence, on the other hand, was first and always a writer—a writer who happened to write plays. His work belongs in the library and is best appreciated when read. (I know of no major revivals of a Terence play in the twentieth century.) The vast difference between these two writers is certainly one of temperament and sensibility, but it is also much more than that.

Unlike his predecessor, Terence wrote his plays to be read (and occasionally performed) for the cultivated members of the Scipionic Circle. I doubt if there have been many literary circles in all of Western history whose membership could be compared to that of this august group. (Dr. Johnson's circle is the only one which readily comes to mind.) Regularly, the members of the Circle would meet at Scipio's to discuss ways in which the Roman language and literature could be refined and improved. Terence was an important member of this group, and his plays reflect its linguistic interests much more than they reveal any sense of theatrical vitality.

Today, Terence is best known for his numerous neat and polished maxims, and it is certainly true that without his plays *Bartlett's Familiar Quotations* would be much impoverished. One immediately thinks, for example, of such lines as: "A word to the wise is sufficient," "Fortune favors the brave," "The very flower of youth," and "The quarrels of lovers are the renewal of love." But quotable lines, although many of them have been used by playwrights, are not the stuff out of which great plays are made, and Terence as a great writer was not much of a playwright.

Actually the cause of his failure can probably be attributed to the most famous of his maxims: "*Homo sum*·

humani nil a me alienum puto" (I am a man: I consider nothing human foreign to me). This is a profound view of life, and it is no doubt true that a playwright (not to mention all other men) must be receptive to all of man's possibilities. But when, as it is in Terence's case, this capacity for understanding is carried to the point of absolute compassion, to that point where the playwright can "forgive all" that his characters may do, it becomes exceedingly dangerous. The limitations of the stage, and more particularly the demands of comedy, require that the dramatist have a partial view of life in his attitude toward his characters. This Terence did not have. His characters are always attractive, his plots are intricate and carefully worked out, and the dialogue is polished to a glossy brightness; but somehow as a whole his plays lack substance. Like Chinese food, they are never fully satisfying. We can admire his wisdom, respect his compassion for his fellowmen, and praise him as a master of literary style, but as a writer of plays Terence was too gentle and kind to exist for long in the knockabout and violently partial world of the theatre. His work has long been a source of inspiration for other playwrights, but his natural habitat was, and still is, the library.

VII. AN ECSTASY OF MADNESS

Whenever something intended to have great dramatic significance takes place in one of Seneca's plays, it is sure to be either preceded or followed by the stage direction, "In an ecstasy of madness." Scholars usually explain this direction by going on at great length about Seneca's belief in the supernatural and its role as the motivating force in his plays. While such an interpretation may well be correct, it is not the whole story. The long history of tragic drama shows us that, when the most important events in a play do not spring from the characters themselves, it is a sure sign that the playwright has not presented a dramatic action, but only a recounting of dramatic deeds. Such is the case with Seneca. For all of his concern with dramatic motivation—both natural and supernatural, the characters in a play like *Medea* have little or no life of their own. They are flat and two-dimensional; and, like pawns in a grandiose stage chess game, they have no choice but to move forward. Psychological explanations are not enough to make a play, as many of our contemporary playwrights have discovered, especially if, in its crucial moments, we do not believe the characters are responsible for what they do.

T. S. Eliot, in his important essay, "The Three Voices of Poetry," reminds us that the fact that lines in a play are spoken by many characters does not necessarily make them dramatic. To be dramatic, characters must speak for themselves; and it is the playwright's job to extract the language out of the characters rather than impose it on them. Nor is complexity of character essential, so long as we believe that communication between the characters is taking place. In the end, drama is concerned only with human relationships, with what men do to each other. Aeschylus' characters in the *Oresteia*, for instance, are not very well developed psychologically; in fact, they are so simple they could be described as monolithic. But we always believe them as characters, because they are individuated parts of an action. They have an existence independent of the playwright—within the action. We do not experience Seneca's characters in this way; rather, we feel that he—much like Browning—was always speaking for himself through the characters.

This failure to achieve a dramatic idiom is in large measure due to the fact that, as far as we know, Seneca composed his plays for private readings rather than public performances on the stage. But it can also be explained in terms of the entrenched Roman oratorical tradition, which we know had a strong influence not only on Seneca's style, but on his whole approach to the dramatic event. The most revealing evidence of this influence is to be found in Seneca's continued use of *sententiae* (wise sayings) in his dialogue. These pat verbal solutions and moral clichés first appeared in the plays of Euripides, but there is some justification for the Greek tragedian's use of them. There were some problems and dramatic issues which Euripides could not resolve, nor did he believe they ever could be resolved; the meaning of several of his plays resides in this very lack of a resolution. However, since the play as a theatre piece had to come to an end, Euripides resorted to the use of the *deus ex machina* (a plot device) and the *sententiae* (a device of language) as means of resolution. There is no doubt that this is a shortcoming in Euripides' work, but it is an understandab'

and even justifiable, one. But in the Roman drama the
use of *sententiae* was not a strategy of despair. Because
of the state-oriented nature of Roman life, virtue, and
artistic expression, its writers were not given to private
utterance. And the *sententiae* were an essential part of
Rome's long and well-established oratorical tradition.
Every great speaker from Demosthenes and Cicero to
Kennedy and Stevenson is considered effective because of
his ability to express complex issues in a meaningful but
brief statement. (Loftiness of tone is another essential
characteristic of great oratory, and it is interesting to note
that the early investigations on the sublime were seldom
concerned with the drama.) But the substitution of statement, no matter how apt or lofty, for dramatic process inevitably reduces the range of the theatre. Nowhere in the
history of drama can this reduction be more clearly observed than in the plays of Seneca. He consistently aborted
his dramatic situations with the persistent maxim. Note
for example:

> MEDEA [*My crimes*] are yours, they are yours, in-
> deed! The one who profits by a crime is guilty of it.

and in Act V:

> MESSENGER: Ruin, total ruin! Our royalty is annihi-
> lated. Daughter and father are one low heap of ashes.
> CHORUS: How are they trapped?
> MESSENGER: As kings regularly are, by gifts.

A similar debilitating tendency can be found in the
bloody images Seneca uses to describe death. For all the
gore, these passages are purely ornamental. They are a
substitute for both dramatic and moral significance, and
while they may be horrifying they are never horrible.
They lack the sharp bite of a conscience which is involved in human suffering. The passion of these rolling
speeches is only a *declared* passion; it does not involve
developed feelings. It is merely a pose, a passion of attitude.

Again, the public nature of Roman life at the time of
the Caesars may account for this tendency in Seneca's
drama (Eliot, for one, argues that "the ethic of Seneca's
plays is that of an age which supplied the lack of moral

habits by a system of moral attitudes and poses"), but it must finally be attributed to Seneca's failure to understand the demands of the theatre. In the plays of Seneca everything is in the word, but his words are not supported by any other concrete reality. They neither require nor imply an actor, a stage, or a specific emotional actuality. His plays, as Eliot observed, are, in effect, radio plays "full of statements useful only to an audience which sees nothing." Such plays are not without qualities, but they are qualities which find the stage an inhospitable medium.

Thus, in reading Seneca today, we cannot help but feel his significance is only of an historical nature. This does not mean his plays do not have value. They do, for instance, embody—probably better than anything else in Roman literature—the qualities of Roman Stoicism. Also, there is no doubt that the rhythms of his language especially as they were translated into English in the sixteenth century, had a profound influence on the development of the blank verse which reached its fullest flower in Elizabethan drama. No one should deny the importance of these facts; but, finally, Seneca has been kept alive by the scholars and not by the theatre. And one cannot help but wonder if this is not one of the reasons that classical literature has declined as a meaningful force in the imaginative lives of modern men.

Plautus

THE MENAECHMI

Translated by Palmer Bovie

Characters   *Peniculus [Brush], a parasite*

Menaechmus I, a young gentleman living in Epidamnus

Menaechmus II [Sosicles], a young gentleman of Syracuse

Désirée [Erotium], a courtesan

Mixmaster [Cylindrus], her cook

Messenio, slave of Menaechmus II [Sosicles]

Maid, in the service of Désirée

Wife, wife of Menaechmus I

Old Man, father-in-law of Menaechmus I

A Doctor

Whipster I

Whipster II

Prologus in Person

Ladies and gentlemen, and everybody else, I announce
  In the first fine foremost and friendly words I pronounce,
  Myself! How are you all out there? Do let me greet you.
  It's a particular pride and personal privilege to meet you,
  And present to you Plautus in person, that is as he looks
  When he speaks in his very own words; I don't mean
      in books
  When you read what he says, but here on the stage
      where he *is*.
  Won't you lend us your ears and put yourselves quite
      at ease,
  Tune in on our logic, and turn your minds to the plot
  I now go over in a very few words, not a lot?
        Oh yes . . . poets often insist, more often than not
  In their comedies, "It's an action in Athens," it takes
      place
  Where you're expected to find it most charming, in
      Greece. [*Irish pronunciation.*]
        But I'm not the underhanded sort who is willing
            to say
  It takes place somewhere it doesn't, or . . . anyway
  Nowhere except *when* it does occur there. And today
  While I grant that our play bubbles up through Greek
      grounds,
  It's distilled in Sicilian, not acted in Attic towns.
  So your Prologue expounds the preface to his foreword.
      He pounds
  In the plot now, not a little, but a lot; it's scoops of
      synopsis
  To ladle out. I'll shovel on now, and bury my worries,
  In view of the generous way you hear out our stories.
        A certain old man was a merchant in Syracuse.
  To him twin sons were born, identical youths

So alike in appearance the wet nurse could never get used

To telling them apart when she popped up to offer her breasts;

Their own mother didn't know which was which, she just guessed.

Well . . . at least, that's what someone who saw these boys once told me:

I don't want you thinking *I* went there and saw them, you see.

Now one day when both boys were seven, their father loaded up

A huge cargo ship full of goods to be sold, and toted up

One of the boys on the boat. Then off they went

To the market together being held in the town of Tarentum;

The other son, of course, he left back home with the mother.

And when they got to Tarentum, the father and the other,

There was some sort of fair going on, with hundreds of games,

And hundreds of people to watch them, which quickly explains

How the boy wandered off in the crowd, away from his dad.

A merchant from Epidamnus latched on to the lad

And snatched him off home. And then when the father discovered

He'd lost his son, sick at heart, he never recovered

From the fatal depression that carried him right to his grave

In Tarentum a few days later on. When the messenger arrived

At Syracuse with this grisly news of how the father lay dead

At Tarentum, and twin number one was completely mislaid,

The affectionate grandfather promptly took it in his head

To rename the Syracuse son in honor of the other,

And call him Menaechmus from now on, after his brother;

So dear to the grandfather's heart was that boy and his name:

The grandfather's own, as a matter of fact, was the
  same.
I remember that name *Menaechmus* all right, all the
  better
Because I'm sure I've seen it stuck up somewhere in
  Big Letters.
Isn't that just like us? "Hmmm, *Menaechmus* . . ."
  we say,
Funny how it strikes us . . . "Haven't I seen that
  somewhere today?"
But, not to lead you astray,
I hereby officially announce, pronounce, and relay
The fact that both twins henceforth have identical
  names.
     Now, my feet must head Epidamnuswards, for the
       claims
Of this complicated plot I must measure by the foot;
  this explains,
I hope, how metricalloused my rhythmic diet may be.
To survey this plot I must personally run on and see
Where it happens to be ambling along itself, iambically.
And if any of you out there have something you'd like
  me to do
At Epidamnus for you, speak up and let me know.
Don't forget what things cost, though; I'll need some
  dough.
If you don't tip you're bound to be rooked, even though
When you do tip you'll also be had, for the money
  will flow
Even farther; the less you hold on to, the more you
  let go.
     Anyway, here I am back where I started. I stand as
I originally did when I came out and ran on. Epidamnus
Is the name of the place, you remember the merchant
  of which
Kidnaped the twin other brother. Being very rich,
But childless, he adopted the boy to add interest to
  his life,
And invested as well for his son in a suitable wife
With a juicy dowry, to marry, and arranged his whole
  life
By making Menaechmus his heir, when he passed away.
Not bad for a lad whose dad was a thief, wouldn't
  you say?

And curiously enough, that end came around rather
    soon;
For the merchant was out in the country, not far from
    town
On a day it had rained very hard, and started across
    a river.
Darned if that body-snatching sliver of a river didn't
    deliver
The kidnaper himself into the hands of his jailer forever,
And clap the chap off the scene in death's unseen trap.
Menaechmus promptly inherited a fortune; although
    kidnaped,
He is very well off in Epidamnus. He feels quite at ease
And at home with his funds. And guess now, just who
    would breeze
Into town just today with his slave on the run right
    behind him?
Menaechmus (you like this?) to search for his brother,
    and find him,
Perhaps . . . we'll see about that. *Twins Billed to Appear*
At Epidamnus today. Of course, they wouldn't be here
Not a bit of it, if our plot didn't admit of it, but *there*
Wherever the story demanded, and in that case I'd steer
You to the right destination and make the situation clear.
    In the acting profession things tend to change:
        the town
The play's in, the actor's part, the lines handed down
He has to say. That house front behind me, for instance,
Depends for its very existence on the playwright's
    insistence
In installing inside it the characters he would provide it
With, and let live a moment; not even reside, it
Appears, but multiply or divide there. Shifty as the
    truth,
It houses an oldster, kings, beggars, gangsters, a youth;
A sharp-witted bellyaching sponger, any kind of quack
You can think of, the real one, the fake. Our profession
    is kind,
And makes room for all. Like me, the actors will remind
You of the double dealings dwelling anon in our comedy.
I'm off and away now, just going down on one knee
To hope you'll applaud us: smile on poor Plautus
    And Not Frown on Me!

Act One

scene one

[PENICULUS.

Peniculus

    The boys all call me Peniculus, which may sound ridiculous

    But just means *Table Duster* and shows *How Able an Adjuster*

    I am to dinner and meticulous in clearing off the table:

    You can call me Soft Hairbrush: It seems to be my fate

    To be famous as a famished feaster and wear such a tail plate.

        You know, some men chain down their captives, and they shackle

    The legs of runaway slaves. I think *that's* ridiculous,

    To load still worse weight on a badly enough burdened crate.

    If you put pressure on him, the underdog *wants* to get up

    And take off, and never do another stroke of work.

    Somehow, they'll always wriggle loose, file off the link

    Or knock the lock to bits with a rock. Are chains worth the pains?

    If you'd like to rope someone in, so he doesn't feel

    Like escaping, snare him with wine and a meal!

    You're putting a ring through his nose when you take him to dinner.

    And as long as you keep him well stocked with food and liquor,

    Regularly and the way he likes it, he'll stick with you,

    Even though he's under heavy sentence. He'll want to serve you;

    As long as you're bound to give him food, he's bound to eat it.

The nets and meshes of food are remarkably strong
And elastic, and squeeze even tighter when they get
 long.
I'm off to Menaechmus' at the moment, where I've
 signed on
To appear for dinner. I volunteer gaily for a jail
Like his, especially at meals. He doesn't feed, he deals
With his guests, increasing their status; like a good
 restauranteur
He doesn't diagnose, he offers a cure. This sharp epicure
Puts out a very fine spread, he doesn't spare the courses;
He builds up skyscrapers of dishes—you see something
 delicious
And have to stand up on the couch and stretch out to
 reach it
Over all the other things that look nearly as luscious.
I've been out of commission for quite a long intermission,
Not in the preferred position at Menaechmus' house,
 but at home,
Domiciled and dominated by my own little sweetmeats.
 Those treats
I provide for myself and my near ones have proved
 dear ones,
Thanks to my expensive tastes—and they all go to waist.
So I'm drumming myself out of those ranks, not burning
 up money
Trooping in with food for the group. Instead, I'm turning
 tummy
To Menaechmus' place. He may just embrace my com-
 pany. Here he comes now
Flouncing out of the house—looks like they've had a row.

scene two

[PENICULUS *and* MENAECHMUS I.

Menaechmus I
If you weren't such a mean, prying snoop,
You stoop, you'd see that when I blow up
It's *your* fault. You'd better stop, or
I'll pack you right back to your papa,
Drooping out-of-doors, divorced, good and proper.
 Every time I go for a walk, you let go a squawk

And assault me with questions. Where am I going?
What's doing? Where? What's *that* I've got there?
I didn't bring home a wife, I brought home a hawk-
Eyed customs inspector, an unconscientious objector
To everything I do. One who makes me *declare*
Everything I've got in mind. Oh woemankind!
Personal effects, you defect detective. Oh, the heck
    with it!
I guess I've spoiled you with too much attention
And turned this into a house of detention.
From now on, things will be different. I'm here to
    mention
What I expect or else from your lie detector: shelves
    full of silence;
No more prying, my high-powered Highness; absolute,
    utter compliance.
I gave you money and clothes,
Robes and dresses, domestics;
I've been pretty good and elastic
In meeting your demands.
You keep your hands, and your nose,
Out of my business. That's the best trick
To play if you want to stay on good terms with me.
Why look over, inspect, and go right on shaking
The man who's made you a major in his own
    homemaking?
To prove that you can't fence me in, I've promised today
To take a girl out to dinner and reward you that way.

Peniculus

Taking it out on his wife? Taking that line
Won't ruin his wife but will leave me out on a limb.

Menaechmus I

Ah now, by God, and good show! I've finally told my
    wife where to go:
Inside, and to leave me alone. Now where are you
    uxorious types, all of you
Out there, you who ought to be oozing up front to
    shower your thanks
On me for fighting the good fight? And look what I've
    done, each and every one
Of you, my fellow sufferers. I've taken this delicate
    mantilla-dress

Out of my wife's most favorite chest, to present to
  my girl.
An excellent trick, don't you think, to reward the
  warden
By stealing something right from under her nose? I
  propose
A subject for congratulations: this beautifully planned,
Charming little crime, dutifully and well carried out:
Converting a legalized loss to a preferable self-ruination.
Diverting the loot from the foe's hands to those of our
  allies.

Peniculus
I say there, young fellow, what share in the prize can I
Hope to realize?

Menaechmus I
God! I've dropped into a trap!

Peniculus
Not at all, a fortified position.

Menaechmus I
                                Who in perdition
Are you?

Peniculus
Fine, thanks, who are you? I'm me, as a matter of fact.

Menaechmus I
Oh, you. My most modern convenience, you beautifully
  timed supergadget!

Peniculus
Greetings.

Menaechmus I
What are you doing at the moment?

Peniculus
                                Fervently latching
Onto the hand of my right-hand man.

Menaechmus I
                        You couldn't be stringing along
At a better time than this that's bringing you on into
  my orbit.

Peniculus

That's how I usually time my launching forth in search
of a luncheon.

I've studied, got the thing down pat, I don't just play
my hunches.

Menaechmus I

Want to feast your eyes on a sparkling treat I've
completed

The arrangements for?

Peniculus

It'll look less crooked to me when I see

Who's cooked it up. If there's been any slip-up in
preparing this fête

I'll know when I see what's left untouched on the plate.

Menaechmus I

Say, you've seen the famous painting plastered against
a wall

Showing the eagle ferrying off that handsome sort of
fancy-bred boyfriend

To his handler in the sky? Or the one that shows Venus'
and Adonis'

Bare . . . ?

Peniculus

Kneeness? Sure, lots of times, but what do I care
about art?

Menaechmus I

Just look at me? Don't I do that part to perfection?

Peniculus

Cahn't sigh I'm accustomed to a costume . . . what the
hell is that you're wearing?

Menaechmus I

Aren't I the apple of your eye, your Prince Charming?
Come on, say it.

Peniculus

Not until I know what time dinner is and whether
I'm invited.

Menaechmus I

Why not be so disarming as to admit what I ask you to?

Peniculus

All right, all right, Prince, you're charming.

Menaechmus I

Anything else
You'd like to add voluntarily?

Peniculus

Well, that's a fairly airily merrily
Wingspread you've got there.

Menaechmus I

More, more! Makes me *soar!*

Peniculus

Damned if I'll say any more, by God in heaven, until
I get some whiff
Of what my reward will be if. You've had a row with
your wife.
I'd better look out warily carefully, my life is in danger.

Menaechmus I

Incidentally, my wife hasn't a clue about where we're
going to do
The town today. We're going to set the hot spots on
fire.

Peniculus

Well, thank heavens, now you make sense. How soon
do I light the pyre?
The day's half used up already, dead down to the navel.

Menaechmus I

You're slowing up the show, interrupting with that
drivel.

Peniculus

Knock out my eye, Menaechmus, dig it into the ground,
bash it
Back and below till it comes out my ankle, if I ever
make a sound
From now on, except to say what you order me to.

Menaechmus I

Just step over here, away from my door.

Peniculus

How's this for size?

Menaechmus I

A little farther, please.

Peniculus

It's a breeze. How's this? Far enough?

Menaechmus I

Now, step out, like a man safe out of reach of the
lion's den.

Peniculus

By God in heaven, if you wouldn't make the best
jockey.

Menaechmus I

How come?

Peniculus

You keep looking back over your shoulder to see
If your wife isn't thudding up behind you.

Menaechmus I

You're telling me?

Peniculus

I'm telling you? Well, fellow, I'm not telling you
anything,
Let's get that clear; just what you want to hear, or
you don't.
That much I'll say, or I won't. I'm your best yes man yet.

Menaechmus I

All right, let's have a guess, then, at what you can
make of
This garment I'm exposing to your nose. What sort of
scent
Does it put you on the trail of . . . ? Why get pale
and shove it out of range?

Peniculus

Strange, it doesn't put me on the trail of, it pins me
to the tail of . . .
Look here, old boy, you know as well as I do, men
shouldn't try to
Imbibe the fragrance of feminine apparel except from
up near the top
Of same dainty. Down lower the unwashed part makes
you feel fainty.

Menaechmus I

All right, Peniculus, try this part over here; tickle
your nose
With this wholesome whiff. Aha! Now you make like
truffles.

Peniculus

Sure, it suits my snuffles.

Menaechmus I

Oh, puffle, come on and say,
Say what it tells you. What sort of smells you deduce.

Peniculus

Phew, what a naral escape! I'm glad to produce my
solution.
This is my diagnosis: You steal a *jeune fille* for a meal;
You purloin a *fräulein* for some sirloin; you flirt with
a skirt
And alert your tastebuds to a smorgasbord; a distress
And theft, and this dress is left for your mistress to
drape round
Her; gleaming napery; conjugal japery, all very vapory.
The whole deal,
From my point of view, leads straight toward an
excellent meal, and I'm joining you.

Menaechmus I

Don't! I'm not coming apart. But you've hit
The female suggestion on the head, no question, and
orated convincingly.
For I've pretty winsomely sneaked this dress from
my wife
And am spiriting it off to the niftiest mistress of mine,
Désirée. I'm ordering a banquet, this very day
For you and me, a treat at her place.

Peniculus

Oh, I say!

Menaechmus I

We'll drink from now till tomorrow's morning star
puts out
This night so bibulous.

Peniculus

I say, you *are* fabulous. Shall I knock
At Désirée's door?

Menaechmus I
Sure, go ahead. No, better knock off.
Hold it! I said.

Peniculus
You're the one that's holding it: my head
Wants to get at that bottle, not back off a mile in the
distance.

Menaechmus I
Knock very gently.

Peniculus
The door, evidently, 's the consistency
Of papyrus.

Menaechmus I
Knock off, I insist, do desist! God in heaven!
Lay off or I'll knock your block off! And besides, rub
your eyes:
Can't you see? Here she comes out, herself, free and
easy. Her body
Eclipses the sun. An excellent exit, dancing
Into view like this; she wins more acclaim than the
flame
Of the sun. He goes quite blind, when I find her so
entrancing.

scene three

[DÉSIRÉE, PENICULUS, *and* MENAECHMUS I.

Désirée
Oh, my dear, *dear* Menaechmus, how *are* you today?

Peniculus
Hey, say!
What about me? Don't I rate a greeting?

Désirée
Zero, you cipher.

Peniculus
Well, a soldier has to get used to being a serial
number, I guess.

Menaechmus I
Now darling look here, I would love to have you go
and fix up . . .

Peniculus

Ohhh, fray can you see? Let's have us a mix-up: you
  be the smorgas
And I'll come aboard you. We'll fight it out all day;
  ohhh, I say . . .
Till the dawn's early light, which of us battlers is the
  heavier weight
When it comes to hitting the bottle. Daisy, you can be
  the general,
And feel free to choose which company you'll spend
  the duration
Of this dark operation with. Let's hope your proper
  ration is . . . me.

Menaechmus I

Sweet and lovely! How loathly my wife appears in
  my eyes
When they light on you.

Peniculus

                    Meanwhile you put on her things
And wifey still clings to you.

Désirée

                              What in the world . . . ?

Menaechmus I

                                        I'm unfurled.
My dear girl. Here's the dress I deprive my wife of
  and provide
You with. You look better in her clothes than she does
  without them,
My rose.

Désirée

Touché or not touché, I must say I must give way
To so super-sartorial an assault on my virtue. You win
  the day.

Peniculus

Listen to the mistress whisper sweet somethings, as
  long as
She sees he's bringing her that gay thing for nothing.
  Now is
The time, if you love her, to have what you want of her
In the form of some toothsome kisses.

Menaechmus I

                        Oh, hang up, Brush Face.
I've only done just what I swore I would with this
    garment: placed
It on the altar of her grace.

Peniculus

                     By God in heaven, I give in!
Listen, *twist* in it, won't you? I can see you in the
    ballet, like a fine
Boy, a dear for the dance, with the veil trailing behind
    your tight pants.

Menaechmus I

Dance, me? By God in heaven, you're crazy.

Peniculus

                            Me, crazy?
I'd say, easy does it, *you* may be *that* way instead, in
    your head.

Désirée

If you're not going to wear it, take it off then. And
    stop saying
"By God in heaven!"

Menaechmus I

                 After all, I won this today by playing
A pretty dangerous game; I stole it.

Peniculus

              On the whole, it's even more fraying
To the nerves than Hercules (or "heavenly God," if
    you please)
Swerving round those curves to steal Hippolyta's girdle
    and sneak off swaying.
I'd say you were in more mortal danger than that
    thievish stranger
Ever ran into, even though he was stronger.

Menaechmus I

                       I can no longer
Hold back this offer I proffer to you, Désirée. So do
    have it,
You wonderful girl, sole creature alive sympathetic to
    my wants.

Désirée

This is the true-hearted sort of fervor nature should
always transplant

In the souls of romancers whose desires are their
favorite haunts.

Peniculus

Or at least sharp sparks going broke at full speed
chasing spooks.

Menaechmus I

I bought it for my wife last year. $85.00.

Peniculus

We can close the books on that sum and kiss it good-by.

Menaechmus I

And now can you guess what I want to do?

Désirée

                                        Yes, I know

And what's more, I'll do what you want.

Menaechmus I

                                        Dinner for three,

Chez Daisy. Order this done and I'll be pleased.

Peniculus

                                        And say, see

While you're at it that whoever goes to buy the food at
the forum

Picks out something specially tasty; a perfect little
pork filet

Or savory thin-sliced prosciutto, ham recherché,

Like a succulent half-section head of a pig—let's do it
the big way,

And have that ham so well cooked that I can pounce
on the table like a hawk

Who knows what he likes, and then strikes. And let's
make it quick.

Désirée

                                        By Jiminy, yes! You're on!

Menaechmus I

                                        That's very nice, the way you didn't

Say "By God in heaven." Me and old slothful here,
we're heading down-

Town to hang around the forum and see what's up.
    We'll be right back.
While dinner's cooking, we'll start with the drinking.

Désirée

Come on
Along whenever you want. Things will be ready.

Menaechmus I

But do get a steady move on.
Now let's go, and let's you keep up.

Peniculus

By God in heaven, how true!
I'll follow you all right and I'll slave for you too. If I
    lost you
Today and got all the wealth in heaven, I wouldn't
    break even.

[*Exeunt* MENAECHMUS I *and* PENICULUS.

Désirée
[*Alone.*]
    I wonder why they always say "God in heaven"?
    Where else could he be?
    You, girls in there! Call out Mixmaster, the head cook,
    And tell him to come outside here. I need him this
        minute.
[*Enter* MIXMASTER.]
    Take this shopping basket, my man, and, yes, here's
        some money;
    Let's see . . . $9.63.

Mixmaster

Right you are, miss.

Désirée

Now scoot, Sonny-boy
And get on with your catering. Buy enough for three
    people only,
No more, no less.

Mixmaster

Who's coming?

Désirée

Menaechmus, and that lonely
Crowd of his, Soft Hair, the never-to-be-brushed off,
    plus me.

Mixmaster

Well, Miss, that's three *times* three plus one, actually:
Peniculus eats enough for eight, and you both make
two.

Désirée

I've given out the guest list. The rest of this is up
to you.

Mixmaster

Right you are, Miss. The dinner is as good as all done.
You can all take your places. Won't you all please
sit down?

Désirée

Get going now, you fix-faster, and hurry right back
from town.

Mixmaster

I'll be back here so soon you won't even know I've
been gone.

Act Two

scene one

[MENAECHMUS II *and* MESSENIO.

Menaechmus II

Messenio, I tell you, there's no greater source of delight
For sailors than to look out across the deep water and
sight
The land they're heading for.

Messenio

                    I couldn't be more
In agreement, provided the land you refer to is home.
Therefore,
Why in hell, I implore you, are *we* in Epidamnus?

Do you plan to act like the ocean and noisily slam us
Against every damned piece of land we can touch?

Menaechmus II

As much
As I need to cover to locate my own twin, my brother.

Messenio

But how much longer do we have to keep looking for
him?
It's six years now since we started. When we departed
You didn't say we'd try everywhere, moseying to
Marseilles,
Skirting around Spain, bounding back to menace Venice,
And do the whole coastal *bit* from Trieste to Dubrovnik
to Split,
Or skim the whole rim of Italy, littorally. As the sea
Goes, that's where we rows. My point is—a haystack
With the well-known needle in it . . . you'd have found
it. But we lack
The object to bring our search to a head. He's quite
dead,
The man you're after, while you ransack the land of
the living
If he were anywhere around you'd have found him.

Menaechmus II

I won't give in
Until I've found out for sure from someone I have to
believe in
Who'll say that he knows that my brother is dead. And
when that day
Arrives, our travels are over. But I *won't* stop pursuing
My other half, and I know what I'm doing: he means
Everything to me.

Messenio

You're looking for a knot in a marshmallow reed.
We won't go home until we've gone round the world,
then, as fellow
Travelers, and written a book about what it looks like?

Menaechmus II

I doubt it.
But see here, my boy, you just do as you're told; don't
be too bold;

Eat your food; be good; don't be a bother. It's not your good
That matters in this expedition.

Messenio

Take that definition
Of a typical slave's condition. I know who I am now, all right.
He couldn't have put a bigger proposition in many fewer words,
Or in so clear a light. Still and all, I just can't keep stalling
Around; I can't just stop talking. You listening, Menaechmus?
My purse, I mean, our purse, now that I look at it,
Has too much vacation space; our wardrobe there looks quite scanty,
Are we going in for summer sports? By God in heaven, you'll groan,
Exhausted by the search for your twin, unless you turn back home.
They'll *wham* us in Epidamnus, positive; Dubrovnik us to clinkers.
The town's chock full of nuts, fast-living long-range drinkers,
Go-between wheedlers, middlemen who take you, the stinkers,
In to be cleaned and doused by the masters of the house,
I mean mistresses, who whisper sweet slopniks to you,
And profit from your losses in the process. That's what they do,
Damn us strangers in this town. No wonder it's called, up and down,
Epidamnus; every damn one of us innocents in Greece
Gets introduced here to the golden fleece, before he's released,
Enormously decreased in value.

Menaechmus II

Take it easy. Hand me that greasy
Wallet.

Messenio

What do you want with it?

Menaechmus II

Your speech has haunted
Me. I'm panicked by your frantic appeal to the facts
of life.

Messenio
Afraid, why afraid for me? . . .

Menaechmus II

You'll whammy us both in Epidamnus.
You're a great lady's man, Messenio: I know you. And I?
I'm a man of many moods, all of which prompt me
to fly
Off the handle in a hurry. And since I'm the furious sort,
And you the luxurious sport, always in pursuit of a skirt,
I'll manage both crises nicely, and simply divert
The money into my control. Then you won't waste the
whole
Thing on women; and I won't get mad when you do;
or even peeved.

Messenio
Take it and keep it then, do. I'm somewhat relieved.

scene two

[MIXMASTER, MENAECHMUS II, *and* MESSENIO.

Mixmaster
I've shopped very shrewdly and well, if I say so myself:
I'll spread a fine feast in front of these dauntless diners.
Oh, oh, Menaechmus, already! I'll bet I'm in for a
beating:
The guests have arrived and here I've just gotten back
From the market. They're walking around in front of
the house;
I'll go up and greet them. Menaechmus, good afternoon!

Menaechmus II
Best wishes, old chap, whoever you happen to be.

Mixmaster
Whoever I'm . . . ? You don't say, Menaechmus, you
don't know?

Menaechmus II
Oh God in heaven, you know I don't.

Mixmaster

But where
Are the rest of our guests?

Menaechmus II

What guests?

Mixmaster

Your parasite, for one.

Menaechmus II
My parasite? Obviously this fellow is quite off his nut.

Messenio
Didn't I tell you this town was lousy with scroungers?

Menaechmus II
Which parasite of mine did you mean, young man?

Mixmaster
Why that peachy little Peniculus, the fuzzy table duster.

Messenio
Oh *him*, peenie brush? He's safe all right, here in
    our bag.

Mixmaster
Menaechmus, you've come along a bit soon for dinner:
I'm just getting back from buying the food.

Menaechmus II
Listen here,
How much does a good box of sure-fire tranquilizers cost
In this town?

Mixmaster

$1.98 for the economy size.

Menaechmus II
Here's $3.96. Get yourself a double prescription.
I can see you're quite out of control, making trouble
    like this
For someone like me you don't even know, whoever
    you are.

Mixmaster
I'm Mixmaster: that's not complicated, and don't
    say you don't know it.

Menaechmus II
You can be Mixmaster, or Sizzling Ham Steak

With Cloves En Brochette,
I couldn't care less. I've never seen you before today
And now that I have, I'm not at all very pleased to
    meet you.

Mixmaster
Your name's Menaechmus.

Menaechmus II
                  You seem to be talking sense
At the moment, since you call me by name, but where
    did you learn
Who I am?

Mixmaster
Who you are? When I work for your mistress right
    in this house?
Désirée?

Menaechmus II
By God, she's *not* my mistress and I *do not*
Know you.

Mixmaster
Don't know *me*, who pours you out drink after drink
    when you come here
For dinner?

Messcnio
        I wish I could lay hands on something to bat this
        nut with.

Menaechmus II
You mix drinks and pour them for *me*, for *me*,
Who never even came this way, much less saw
    Epidamnus
Before today?

Mixmaster
        Never even saw it, you say?

Menaechmus II
Yes; I mean *no*, dear God in heaven, so help
    me, *no!*

Mixmaster
I suppose you don't really live in that house over
    there?

Menaechmus II

 May the gods cave the roof in hard on whoever
  does!

Mixmaster

 Stark, raving loony. Wishing himself such bad luck.
 Can you hear me, Menaechmus?

Menaechmus II

  Depends on what you're saying.

Mixmaster

 Now look, take my advice. Remember that $3.96
 You offered to give me a minute ago for the pills?
 Go spend it on yourself; you're the one who needs it
  the most,
 And the soonest, calling down curses, by God in
  heaven,
 On your very own head. You're just not *all there*,
  Menaechmus.
 If you've any brains left you'll send out at once for the
  medicine;
 There's a new triple-dose thing out, The Three Little
  Big Tranquilizers,
 Frightens off all kinds of weird wolves.

Menaechmus II

  He sure talks a lot.

Mixmaster

 Of course, Menaechmus always teases me, like this;
  he's a joker
 When his wife's not around. What's that you're saying
  Menaechmus?

Menaechmus II

 I beg your pardon, Mixmaster, did you say something?

Mixmaster

 How does this stuff look? Like enough for dinner for
  three?
 Or shall I go out and buy more for the girlfriend
  and you
 And your parasite pal?

Menaechmus II

  Women? Parasite? Pals? What
 women, what parasites, pal?

Messenio

Look here, old boy, what terrible crime is weighing on
  your mind
And making you pester him so?

Mixmaster

                    Stranger boy, you stay out
Of my business; I'll conduct that with the person I know
And am talking to.

Messenio

        Oh God in . . . I give up; except for the fact
That I'm sure as can be that this cook is completely
  cracked.

Mixmaster

Well, now, I'll just get busy with these things. I can
  promise you
Some succulent results, very soon. You'll stay around
  the house,
Menaechmus, I hope. Anything else you can think of?

Menaechmus II

I can think of you as one real upside-down cake.
  You're baked.

Mixmaster

Oh by God in . . . somewhere or other, I could swear
  it's you
Who are the mixed-up master. I wish you would go . . .
  lie down
Somewhere until you feel better, while I take this stuff
And commit it to the fire-breathing forces of Vulcan.
  I'll tell
Désirée you're out here. She'll want to ask you in, I
  feel sure.

[*Goes into the house.*

Menaechmus II

Gone, has he? God, how right I see your words were
When you talked about this place.

Messenio

                    Mark my words further.
One of those fast-working, loose-jointed women lives
  here, you can bet,

As sure as that crackpot cook who went in there said she did.

Menaechmus II
I do wonder, though, how he came by my name?

Messenio
That's easy.
Why, that's a cinch. The women have it all worked out.
They send their slave boys or housemaids down to the docks.
When a strange ship comes in, they ask the passenger's name,
And find out where he's from. Later on, they pick him up casually
And stick close to him. If their charms have the right effect
They ship him back home plucked quite clean of his money.[*Pointing to* DÉSIRÉE's *house.*]
And right over there rocks a fast little pirate sloop at anchor:
We'd better look out for her, and look sharp, Commander.

Menaechmus II
Damned if I don't think you're right.

Messenio
I'll know what you think
For sure when I see what preeeeecautions you're taking.

Menaechmus II
Just a moment.
I hear the door swinging open; let's see who comes out.

Messenio
I'll drop our seabag right here. Heave ho, my bellboys!
You fleet runners, shift this gear into neutral for a while.

scene three

[DÉSIRÉE, MENAECHMUS II, *and* MESSENIO.

Désirée
[*Singing gaily.*]
Open the doors, open wide: I don't want them shut.

You in there, look to it, come here and do it,
What has to be done:
Couches to be hung with fine drapes;
Tables adorned; some incense burned;
Lights set blazing; the place made amazing.
To dazzle and delight your bright lover's heart
Is to play with skill your gay charming part,
And importune at his expense while you make your
    fortune.
        Where is he though? A moment ago, my cook
        said I'd find him standing
Around by the door . . . oh there he is, the one I adore
    when he's handing
His money over freely. I'll ask him in now for the meal
    he wanted made ready
And get him started on the drinks, to keep him from
    staying too steady.
I'll just slip over and speak to him first.
Oh my favorite fellow, my poor heart will burst
If you keep standing here outside
When the doors to our house are open wide
To take you in. It's much more your place,
This house, than your own home is, an embrace,
A bright smile on its face just for you, and a kiss
On that most generous of mouths. This really is your
    house.
And now all is prepared just the way you wanted
And shortly we'll serve you your dinner and pour out
    the wine. [*Pause.*]
I said, the meal's all in order, just as you commanded;
Whenever you're ready, come on in now, honey, any
    time.

Menaechmus II
Who in the world does this woman think she's talking to?

Désirée
To you, that's who.

Menaechmus II
        But what business have I with you
At present, or what have I ever had to do with you up
    to now?

Désirée
Heavens! It's you that Venus has inspired me to prize

Over all the others, and you've certainly turned out to
>   be worth it.
Heavens above! You've set me up high enough with
>   your generous gifts!

Menaechmus II

This woman is surely quite crazy or definitely drunk,
Messenio, talking such intimate stuff to me
A man she doesn't even know.

Messenio

>   I told you so!
And now, it's only the leaves that are falling, just wait;
Spend three more days in this town and the trees
>   themselves
Will be crashing down down on your head. The women
>   are biased,
Buy us this, buy us that, and buzzing around for your
>   money.
But let me talk to her. Hey, sweetie, I'm speaking
>   to you.

Désirée

You're what?

Messenio

No, I'm not, I'm who. And while I'm at it, just *where*
Did you get to know the man here who's with me
>   so well?

Désirée

Why, right here in Epidamnus, where I've been for so
>   long.

Messenio

Epidamnus? A place he never set foot in before today?

Désirée

A *delicious* joke, you rascal. Now, Menaechmus, darling,
Won't you come in? You'll feel much cozier and settled.

Menaechmus II

By God, the woman's quite right to call me by my
>   own name.
Still I can't help wondering what's up.

Messenio

>   She's got wind of your moneybag,

The one you relieved me of.

Menaechmus II

                  And damned if you didn't alert me
To that very thing. Here, you'd better take it. That way,
I can find out for sure whether she's after me, or my
    money.

Désirée

Andiam', O caro bene! And we'll tuck right into that
    meal;
Mangiamo, igitur, et cetera.

Menaechmus II

                      Music to my ears,
And you're very nice to sing it, my dear. I only regret
I cannot accept.

Désirée

But why in the world did you tell me, a short while ago,
To have dinner ready for you?

Menaechmus II

                    I told *you* to have dinner ready?

Désirée

Of course, dinner for three, you, your parasite, and me.

Menaechmus II

Oh hell, lady, what the hell is all this parasite stuff?
God, what a woman! She's crazy as can be once again.

Désirée

Cookie duster Peniculus, C. D. Peniculus, the crumb
    devourer.

Menaechmus II

But I mean what kind of a peniculus? We all know
    that's a soft hair
Brush, but I don't know anyone *named* that. You mean
    my ridiculous
Little thing, the traveling shoebrush I carry for my suede
    sandals,
The better to buff them with? What peniculus hangs so
    close to me?

Désirée

You know I mean that local leech who just now came
    by with you

When you brought me that sweet silk dress you stole
from your wife.

Menaechmus II

I gave you a dress, did I? One I stole from my wife?
You're sure? I'd swear you were asleep, like a horse
standing up.

Désirée

Oh gosh, what's the fun of making fun of me and
denying
Everything you've done?

Menaechmus II

Just tell me what I'm denying.

Désirée

That you gave me today your wife's most expensive silk
dress.

Menaechmus II

All right, I deny that. I'm not married. And I've never
been married.
And I've never come near this port since the day I
was born,
Much less set foot in it. I dined on board ship, dis-
embarked,
And ran into you.

Désirée

Some situation! I'm nearly a wreck. What's that ship
You're talking about?

Menaechmus II

Oh, an old prewar propeller job,
Wood and canvas, patched in a million places;
transportation,
I guess, runs on force of habit. She's got so many pegs
Pounded in now, one right up against the next, she looks
like the rack
You see in a fur-seller's store where the strips are hung
all in a row.

Désirée

Oh, do stop now, please, making fun, and come on in
with me.

Menaechmus II

My dear woman, you're looking for some other man,
not me.

Désirée

I don't know you, Menaechmus? the son of Moschus,
Born at Syracuse in Sicily, when Agathocles ruled,
And after him, Phintia; then Leporello passed on the
power
After his death to Hiero, so that Hiero is now the man
in control?

Menaechmus II

Well, that information seems certainly accurate, Miss.

Messenio

By God Himself! Is the woman *from* Syracuse to have
This all down so pat?

Menaechmus II

By the various gods, I don't see
How I can now really decline that offer she's making.

Messenio

Please do, I mean *don't* step over that doorstep!
You're gone if you do.

Menaechmus II

Pipe down. This is working out well.
I'll admit to anything she says, if I can just take
advantage
Of the good time in store. Mademoiselle, a moment ago
I was holding back on purpose, afraid that my wife
might hear
About the silk dress and our dinner date. I'm all set
Now, anytime you are.

Désirée

You won't wait for Soft Hair?

Menaechmus II

No, let's brush *him* off; I don't care a whisker if he
never, . . .
And besides, when he does, I don't want him let in.

Désirée

Heavens to Castor!

I'm more than happy to comply with that one. But now,
Just one thing, darling, you know what I'd like you
    to do?

Menaechmus II

All you need do is name it.

Désirée

          That sweet silk dress: send it over
To the Persian's place, the embroiderer's shop. I want
It taken in, and a pattern I've specially designed added
    to it.

Menaechmus II

What a good idea! It won't look at all like the dress
I stole, if my wife should happen to meet you in town.

Désirée

Good. Take it with you, then, when you go.

Menaechmus II

                    Yes, of course.

Désirée

And now let's go on in.

Menaechmus II

          Right away. I've just got to speak
To him for a minute. Hey, Messenio, hop over here!

Messenio

What's cooking?

Menaechmus II

          Jump, boy.

Messenio

                  What's all the hurry?

Menaechmus II

We're all the hurry, that's what. I know what you'll say.

Messenio

You're a dope.

Menaechmus II

          Nope, I'm a fiend. I've already stolen some loot.
Real loot. This is a big deal: Operation Mix-up.
And I'm one up already without even throwing up
    earthworks.

Race off, fast as you can, and drape all those sea
   troops [*points to the sailors.*]
In the local bar, on the double. Stay where you are then,
Until just before sunset, when it's time to come pick
   me up.

Messenio

Really, Commander, you're not *on* to those call girls.

Menaechmus II

You manage your affairs, I'll handle mine, and you
Can hang up and stay there. If I get into trouble, it's me
Who'll suffer for it, not you. That girl isn't crazy, she's
   dumb
And doesn't know what's up, at least as far as I can see,
Or where could this high-priced, pretty little dress have
   come from?

[*Exit.*

Messenio

I give up. You've gone, have you? In there? You're
   gone,
And done for. The pirate ship's got the rowboat on
   the run,
And you'll end up in the drink, *Menaechmus on the
   rocks.*
But who am I, a dumb slave, to try to outfox
That woman, with my hopes of showing Menaechmus
   the ropes?
He bought me to listen to him: I'm not in command.
Come on, kids, let's do what he says. But I'll be on hand
Later on, as he wanted, and drag him out to dry land.

Act Three

scene one

[PENICULUS.

Peniculus

In all my born days—and it's more than thirty years'
   worth—I've never

Pulled a boner like this, I'm a trecherous fiend, and
this time
I guess I've really transgressed. Imagine my missing
a meal!
And why? I got involved in listening to a public speech
And while I stood around gawking, all open mouth
and ears,
Menaechmus made his getaway and got back to his girl,
And didn't want *me* along, I suppose. May the heavenly
gods
Crack down on whoever it was that thought up public
speeches,
That invented this out-of-doors way to use up people's
good time
Who haven't any. Shouldn't the audience consist only
of those
With time on their hands? And shouldn't they perhaps
be fined
If they fail to attend those meetings where someone
gets up
In public and starts sounding off? There are people
enough
With nothing much to do, who eat only one meal a
day,
Never dine out, or have guests in, and it's to them
the duty
To show up at meetings or official functions should be
assigned.
If I hadn't stuck around today to listen, I wouldn't
Have lost out on the dinner Menaechmus invited
Me to come to—and I do think he meant it, as sure
as I can see
I'm alive. I'll show up, anyway, on the off-chance
There's still something left; the mere hope makes
my mouth water.
What's this I see? Menaechmus *leaving,* well looped?
That means *dinner's over:* by God, my timing is perfect.
I'll hide over here and watch a bit to see what he does
Before I go up to my host and give him a buzz.

scene two

[MENAECHMUS II *and* PENICULUS.

Menaechmus II

Calm down in there, woman! I'll bring the dress back
soon enough,

Expertly, so charmingly changed you won't even
know it.

Peniculus

Dinner's done, the wine's all gone, the parasite's lost,
And *he's* off to the coutur*ier*, with that dress in tow.
Is *that* so? I'm not who I am if I take this last bit
In my stride, lying down. Watch how I handle that
garment worker.

Menaechmus II

I thank you, immortal gods, each and all of you.
On whom have you ever showered so many good gifts
As you have on me today? And who could have hoped
for them less?
I've dined, I've wined, I've reclined, and at very close
quarters,
With one of the most delicious daughters . . . well, I've
had it in the best sense
Of that past tense. And here I am at present, still gifted
With a precious piece of silk. No one else will inherit
These convertible goods, much less wear it. How high
am I, its
Heir—O!

Peniculus

Hell, I can't hear from over here—did he say "hair,"
though?
That's my cue to brush in, isn't it, and sweep up my
share?
Hair today and bald tomorrow . . . Drink to me only
with mayonnaise . . .
I'll demand re-dressing . . . I'll scrape something out of
this mess yet.

Menaechmus II

She said I stole it from my wife and gave it to her.
When I realized how wrong she was, of course I began
To agree with everything she said, as if we agreed
On whatever it was we were doing. Need I say more?
I never had so good a time for so little money.

Peniculus

Here I go; I'm raring to get in my licks.

Menaechmus II

Well, well, who's this comes to see me?

Peniculus

What's that you say,
You featherhead, you worst of all possible, good-for-
nothing . . . man?
Man? You're not even a mistake, you're a premeditated
crime,
That's what you are, you shifty little good-for-nothing
. . . I just said that . . .
So-and-so. And so you spirited yourself away
From me at the forum a while ago, and celebrated my
funeral
At this cheerful dinner your friend just couldn't attend?
Some nerve, when you said I was invited to share it
with you.

Menaechmus II

Look, kiddo, what's with it, with you and me, that
can make
You curse out a man you don't even know? Would you
like
A nice hole in the head in return for turning loose
your lip?

Peniculus

God damn it to God damn. That hole's already in my
stomach,
You gave my mouth the slip.

Menaechmus II

What's your name, kid,
Anyway? Spit that much out.

Peniculus

Still being funny,
As if you didn't know?

Menaechmus II

As far as I know, no.
God knows I never saw you before today, never knew
you,

Whoever you are. I do know, though, if you don't
Get funny with me I won't make it hard for you.

Peniculus
For heck's sake, Menaechmus, wake up!

Menaechmus II
For Hercules' sake,
I'm up and walking around. I'm completely convinced
of it.

Peniculus
But you don't recognize me?

Menaechmus II
If I did, I wouldn't say I didn't.

Peniculus
You don't know your old parasite pal?

Menaechmus II
It's your old paralyzed dome
That's slipped, or cracked. You'd better have it patched
up and fixed.

Peniculus
All right. Here's a question for you. Did you, or did
you not,
Sneak a dress out from under your own wife's nose
today,
And give it to dear Désirée?

Menaechmus II
For Hercle's sake, no.
I don't happen to be married, and I didn't happen to
Give it to Désirée, and I didn't happen to fasten onto
A dress. Are you quite sure you've got it in the head,
enough?

Peniculus
Well, that's that, I guess. *Caput! E pluribus* be none.
Of course I didn't meet you coming out of your house
and wearing
The dress, just a while ago?

Menaechmus II
Ohhhhh for *sex'* sake! [*Very effeminate sibilants.*]
You think we're all fairy fine fellows just because you're
such

A *native* dancer, in a perfect fright at what's under our
   tights?
You say I put on a dress, and I wore it?

Peniculus

Could of swore it, on Hercules' head.

Menaechmus II

                         Don't bring him up,
He was a he-man, but you aren't even a me-man:
You don't even know who you are or I am, you
   absolute nut.
You'd better take the cure; you're asking for trouble
   from the gods.

Peniculus

Yeee gods, that's it! Now nobody's going to stop me
   from going
Straight to your wife to spill the beans about you and
   your schemes.
You've creamed me, and I'm whipped. But banquet boy,
   just you wait
Until this stuff starts coming back at you. That dinner
   you ate
And I never got to, is going to give you bad dreams.

Menaechmus II

What's going on around here? Is everyone I see
Planted here on purpose to make fun of me? And
   what for?
And here comes another, whoever it is, out that door.

scene three

[MENAECHMUS II *and* MAID.

Maid

Menaechmus, Désirée would like you to take
This bracelet to the jeweler's, as long as you're going
   downtown
With the dress, and have this piece of gold worked
   into it.

Menaechmus II

Oh, glad to take care of both things, of course, and
   anything

Else you want done along those lines; you only need
    mention it.

Maid
You remember the bracelet, don't you?

Menaechmus II
                      It's just a gold bracelet.

Maid
But this is the one you sneaked out of your wife's
    jewel box
And stole from her.

Menaechmus II
           I don't do things like that, I'm damned sure.

Maid
Well, if you don't recognize it . . . look, you'd better
    give it back to me.

Menaechmus II
Hold on . . . I think I do remember it now. . . .
Yes, that's the one I gave her, that's it all right.
But where are the armlets I gave Désirée when I
    gave her
The bracelet?

Maid
             You never gave her no armlets at all.

Menaechmus II
Oh yes, that's right, it was just the bracelet, come
    to think of it.

Maid
Can I tell her you'll have this fixed up?

Menaechmus II
                Yes, I'll take care of it.

Maid
And look, be a dear, and have him design me some
    earrings,
Won't you, teardrop style, six dollars of gold work
    in each?
If you do, you'll be *persona* terribly *grata* to me, your
Obedient, co-operative servant, the next time you visit.

Menaechmus II

Why of course. Just give me the gold, and I'll stand the cost
Of having it set.

Maid

Oh, you furnish the gold, why don't you?
And I'll pay you back later.

Menaechmus II

No, no, after you, my fair lady.
You let me pay you back later, and I'll pay twice as much.

Maid

I don't have the gold at the moment.

Menaechmus II

When you get it, I'll take it.

Maid

Is there anything else, kind sir?

Menaechmus II

No, just say I'll handle this.

[*Exit* MAID.]

And make a quick turnover on the market value of the stuff.
She's gone in? Yes, I see she's closed the door.
The gods must be on my side the way they're helping me out,
Enriching me, and doing me favors. But why hang around
When now is my chance to get away and out of reach
Of these foxy and, I must say, sexy confidence women?
Come on, Menaechmus, my boy, my own likeness, enjoy
Your rapture; and pick up your feet, old chap, let those sandals slap.
Here goes the laurel lie for today [*throws it right*], but I think I'll go this way,
In case they come looking for me; they can follow this lead
In the wrong direction. I'll dash off and make enough speed
To head off my slave, I hope, and tell that good lad
The good news about the goods we've acquired. Won't he be glad?

Act Four

scene one

[WIFE of MENAECHMUS and PENICULUS.

Wife

I suppose I'm supposed to submit to total frustration
Because I married a man who steals everything in
the house
He can lay hands on and carts it off to his mistress?

Peniculus

Not so loud, please. You'll catch him with the goods,
I promise.
Come over here. Now look over there. He was taking
Your dress to the couturier; he was well looped and
weaving
Downtown with the same dress he snuck from your
closet today.
And look, there's the laurel loop he had on, lying on
the ground.
Now do you believe me? He must have gone in that
direction,
If you'd like to follow up his tracks. Hey, we're in luck:
Here he comes back, just this moment; but not with
the dress.

Wife

What should I do?

Peniculus

Oh, what you always do, start nagging,
Nag him to pieces; don't take it, let him have it, I say.
Meanwhile, let's duck over here on the sly and not
let him
See us. He'll tangle himself in the birdcatchers' net.

scene two

[WIFE, PENICULUS, *and* MENAECHMUS I.

Menaechmus I

This is some social system we've got going here,
The troublesome custom of patrons and clients:
Bothersome clients, and jittery patrons, who fear
They may not have a big enough following. Compliance
And conformity to habit require even the best of us
To just make the most of it; and as for the rest of those
Trapped in place in the status race, let's face it,
They're coming at us, pushing forward from the ends
To swell out the middle. And it isn't *fides*, it's *res*
That matters in the clientele deal, which depends,
Not on the client's value as man and as friend,
But simply on his assets. Money is what he's worth
And you must amass it to show off less dearth
Of a deficit than the next aristocrat. You give a wide
    berth
To the poor man who needs you, however fine he may
    seem,
But if some rich bastard shows up and wants you to use
Your influence, you're ready to go to any extreme
To hang onto him. That's the scheme, and does it
    confuse
Us poor patrons with a gang of fast-breaking scofflaws
To stand up for in court? Thereby hang the loss
And the profits for us poor patricians. The clients'
    position
Is: pressure on the middle. He's got the money,
We've got the rank, we need his dough and he needs
    our thanks.
It's only lucky the prolies don't rate either of any;
Thank heavens, they're not powerful, just many.
        I'm from a good family and entitled to go into court
And represent as I wish some client who's short
Of the necessary social credentials. And, confidentially,
I say a lot that I wish I didn't have to. A lawyer can
    manage
To do this pretty well if he concentrates on it; and
    damages

Are his principal concern: to collect for, to sue for,
     to affirm
What is said to be false, and deny what is said to be
     true for.
On behalf of some client whose character makes him
     squirm
He will bribe the witnesses or rehearse them in what
     to do.
When the client's case comes up on the calendar, of
     course
That's a day we have to be on hand too, and be
     resourceful
In speaking up professionally in defense of his actions,
     awful
And impossible to defend though they are.
It's either a private hearing at the bar;
Or a public proceeding before a jury with people in
     the congregation;
Or a third form it takes is what you would call
     arbitration,
When a mediator is appointed to decide this special
     situation.
Well, today a client of mine had me right on the ropes;
His case came up as a private hearing, and my hopes
Of doing what I'd planned to today, and doing
It with the person I wanted to, have drooped and
     dropped near to ruin;
He kept me and kept me; there was angle after angle.
He was obviously at fault, with his wrong, tangled
Illegal action, and I knew it when I went in.
So in arguing the case I laid it on pretty thin,
And pleaded *extenuating circumstances;* that's a logical
     maze
And a judge's jungle, but a lawyer's paradise.
I summed up the case in the most complicated terms
I could summon up, overstating, sliding words like
     worms
Off the track, leaving a lot out when the need
Of the argument indicated, and the magistrate agreed
To drop the proceedings; he granted permission
For a settlement by *sponsio.*
There's a legal ounce for you, of the words we pronounce
     in due process,

Full of awful, responsible-sounding phrases like: I promise

You this *sponsio* I owe you, et cetera. What it comes down to

Is that a civil hearing can be brought to an end by payment

Of a fixed fee known as a forfeit or *sponsio*, a defrayment

Of the expenses plus a sum added on: call it "costs

And considerations" if you will, in consideration for the lost

Time and money involved. What happened today was that I

Had worked hard and fast to convince the judge that my

Client should be allowed to settle for costs and considerations.

The judge came around; and I was set to leave for the celebration

Of a good time at Désirée's party, when what did my other smarty party

Of a client pull but an "Oh, well . . . I don't know about that *sponsio* . . .

I don't think I ought to flounce in with a lot of money all at once

You know . . . I'm not so sure I've even got it. Are you sure

That's the way we want it to go, the case, et cetera?" The totally pure

Imbecile, caught redhanded, absolutely without a legal leg to stand on

And three unimpeachable witnesses were waiting just to get their hands on

Him and wring his neck! He nearly let it come up for trial.

And that's where I've been all this while.
       May the gods, all the gods, blast that fool

Who wrecked my beautiful day

And they might as well, while they're at it, lay

Into me for thinking I could steal

Off to town and look the forum over that way

Without being spotted and tapped for something dutiful.

No doubt, I've messed up a day

That promised to be quite alluring

From the moment I told Désirée

To set things up nicely for dinner. All during

The time I've been detained, she's been waiting for me
And here I am at last, the first instant I could break free.
If she's angry, I suppose she has some reason to be.
But perhaps the dress I purloined from my wife won't
    annoy her
In the least, and I'll win this one too, as my own
    lawyer.

Peniculus
What do you say to that?

Wife
                     That I've made a bad marriage
With an unworthy husband.

Peniculus
            Can you hear well enough where you are?

Wife
All too well.

Menaechmus I
The smart thing for me is to go on in there
Where I can count on a pretty good time.

Peniculus
                       Just you wait,
Bad times are just around the corner.

Wife
[*Confronting him.*]
                   You think you got away
With it, do you? This time you'll pay up, with interest.

Peniculus
That's it, let him have it.

Wife
            Pulled a fast one on the sly, didn't you?

Menaechmus I
What fast one are you referring to, dear?

Wife
                    You're asking me?

Menaechmus I
Should I ask him, instead?

Wife
              Take your paws off me.

Peniculus
That's the way!

Menaechmus I
Why so cross?

Wife
You ought to know.

Peniculus
He knows, all right, he's just faking.

Menaechmus I
With reference to what?

Wife
To that dress, that's what.

Menaechmus I
That dress that's what what?

Wife
A certain silk dress.

Peniculus
Why is your face turning pale?

Menaechmus I
It isn't.

Peniculus
Not much paler than a thin silk dress, it isn't.
And don't think you can go off and eat dinner behind
my back.
Keep pitching into him.

Menaechmus I
Won't you hang up for a moment?

Peniculus
God damn it, no, I won't. He's shaking his head
To warn me not to say anything.

Menaechmus I
God damn it, yourself,
If I'm shaking my head, or winking or blinking or
nodding.

Peniculus
Cool! Shakes his head to deny he was shaking his head.

Menaechmus I

I swear to you, wife, by Jupiter, and all the other gods—
I hope that's reinforced strong enough to satisfy you—
I did *not* nod at that nut.

Peniculus

Oh, she'll accept that
On good faith. Now let's return to the first case.

Menaechmus I

What first case?

Peniculus

The case of the costly couturier's place.
The dress-fixer's.

Menaechmus I

Dress? What dress?

Peniculus

Perhaps I'd better bow out.
After all, it's my client who's suing for redress of
grievance
And now she can't seem to remember a thing she
wanted to ask you.

Wife

Oh dear, I'm just a poor woman in trouble.

Menaechmus I

Come on, tell me,
What is it? One of the servant's upset you by answering
back?
You can tell me about it; I'll see that he's punished.

Wife

Don't be silly.

Menaechmus I

Really, you're *so* cross. I don't like you that way.

Wife

Don't be silly.

Menaechmus I

Obviously, it's one of the servants you're mad at?

Wife

Don't be silly.

Menaechmus I
You're not mad at me, are you?

Wife
Now you're not being so silly.

Menaechmus I
But, for God's sake, I haven't done anything.

Wife
Don't start being silly
All over again.

Menaechmus I
Come on, dear, what is it that's wrong
And upsets you so?

Peniculus
Smooth husband, smooths everything over.

Menaechmus I
Oh, hang up, I didn't call you.

Wife
Please take your paw off me.

Peniculus
That's the way, lady, stick up for your rights. We'll teach him
To run off to dinner and not wait for me, and then stagger out
Afterwards and lurch around in front of the house still wearing
His wreath and having a good laugh on me.

Menaechmus I
Dear God in heaven,
If I've even eaten yet, much less gone into that house.

Peniculus
You don't say?

Menaechmus I
That's right, I don't say, you're damned right I don't.

Peniculus
God, that's some nerve. Didn't I see you over there just now,
In front of the house, standing there with a wreath on your head?

Didn't I hear you telling me I was way off my nut,
and insisting
You didn't know who I was, and were a stranger here
yourself?

Menaechmus I
But I left you some time ago, and I'm just getting back.

Peniculus
That's what you say. You didn't think I'd fight back,
did you?
Well, by God, I've spilled the whole thing to your wife.

Menaechmus I
Saying what?

Peniculus
How should I know? Ask her.

Menaechmus I
How about it, dear?
What all has this type told you? Come on, don't
repress it;
Won't you tell me what it is?

Wife
As if you didn't know,
You ask me.

Menaechmus I
If I knew, for God's sake, I wouldn't be asking.

Peniculus
This is really some man the way he fakes out. Look,
you can't
Keep it from her, she knows all about it. By God in
wherever he is,
I practically dictated it.

Menaechmus I
Dictated what?

Wife
All right. Since you seem not to have an ounce of
shame left,
And you won't own up, give me your undivided
attention.
This is why I'm upset and this is what he told me.
I repeat,

I'm not really "cross"; I'm double-crossed, and doubly
upset.
Someone sneaked one of my very best dresses right out
of my house.

Menaechmus I

A dress? Right out of my house?

Peniculus

                    Listen to that louse,
Trying to scratch his way into your affections. Look,
Menaechmus,
We're not playing matched towels in the doctor's
bathroom
Marked "Hisia" and "Hernia"; we're discussing a
valuable dress,
And its *hers* not yours, and she's lost it, at least for the
time being.
If *yours* were missing it would really be missing for
good.

Menaechmus I

Will you please disappear? Now dear, what's your
point of view?

Wife

The way I see it, one of my best silk dresses is not at
home.

Menaechmus I

I wonder who might have taken it.

Wife

                          I'm pretty sure
I know a man who knows who took it, because he did.

Menaechmus I

Who dat?

Wife

Welllll . . . I'd like us to think of a certain Menaechmus.

Menaechmus I

Some man, just like us! Isn't that the fancy one, that
man?
But he's a mean man. And who the hell are all the
men you mean
Named Menaechmus?

Wife

You, that's what I say, you.

Menaechmus I
Who accuses me to you?

Wife

I do, for one.

Peniculus
I do too. And I say you gave it to a dear little Daisy.

Menaechmus I
I? Me? I'm that mean aechmus who . . .

Wife

Yes, you, that's who,
You brute, *et tu.*

Peniculus
You who too too too . . .
What is this, the Owl Movement from the Bird
    Symphony?
My ears are feeling the strain of that to-who refrain.

Menaechmus I
I swear, wife, by Jupiter, and all other gods within
    hearing distance—
And I hope that's a strongly enough reinforced religious
    insistence—
That I did not *give* . . .

Peniculus
But *we* can appeal to Hercules and he's
Even stronger, that we're not exactly not telling the
    truth.

Menaechmus I
That technically I did not *give* it, I only *conveyed* it
To Daisy today; you see, she doesn't have it, she's just
    using it.

Wife
I don't go around lending out your jacket or cloak.
A woman ought to lend out women's clothes, a man
    men's.
You'll bring back the dress?

Menaechmus I

I'll see that that's done.

Wife

If you know what's good for you, you will, I'm here
    to assure you.
You won't get back in this house unless you're carrying
    that dress.
I'm going in.

Peniculus

        What about me and my work?

Wife

I'll pay you back when something is stolen from your
    house.

Peniculus

Oh God, that means never. There's nothing in my place
    worth stealing.
Well, Husband and Wife, may the gods do their very
    worst for you both!
I'll run along now, to the forum. It's quite plain to see
I've lost out, and lost my touch, with this family.
    [*Exit; never returns.*

Menaechmus I

My wife thinks she's making life hard for me, shutting
    me out
Of the house. As if I didn't have a much more pleasant
    place
To go into. Fallen from your favor, have I? I imagine
I'll bear up under that and prove pleasing to an even
    more desirable
Favorite. Désirée won't lock me out, she'll lock me in.
I guess I'll go in there and ask her to *lend* back the dress
I *conveyed* to her this morning, and buy her something
    much better.
Hey, where's the doorman? Open up, somebody,
    and tell
Désirée to come out; there's someone to see her.

scene three

[DÉSIRÉE *and* MENAECHMUS I.

Désirée

Who's calling me?

Menaechmus I

> A man who'd be his own enemy
> Before he'd be yours.

Désirée

> Menaechmus, *dahling*, come in!
> Why stand out there?

Menaechmus I

> I bet you can't guess why I'm here.

Désirée

> Oh, yes I can. You want something sweet from your
>   honey,
> And what's more you'll get it, you naughty little
>   tumblebee.

Menaechmus I

> As a matter of fact, or thanks heavens, or something . . .
> What I have to have is that silly dress back I gave you
> This morning. My wife's found out all about it.
> But I'll buy you one worth twice as much, whatever
>   kind you want,
> So be a good girl and romp in there and get it, won't
>   you?

Désirée

> But I just handed it over to you to take to the Persian's,
> Just a while ago, and gave you that bracelet to take
>   to the jeweler
> And have the gold added to it.

Menaechmus I

> The dress and a bracelet?
> I think you may find you did no such thing. I gave
> The dress to you and then went to the forum, and here
> I am looking at you for the first time again since I
>   left you.

Désirée

> Don't look at me, I'll look at you. I see
> Just what you're up to, and what I'm down to, for
>   that matter.
> You take the stuff off my two trusting hands and then
> Do me out of it and pocket the cash for yourself.

Menaechmus I

> I'm not asking for it to cheat you out of it, I swear.

I tell you, my wife's cracked the case.

Désirée

Well, I didn't ask

For it in the first place. You brought it of your own
free will,

And you gave it to me as a gift, you didn't *convey* it,
you shyster.

Now you want it back. I give up. You can have the stuff;

Take it away, wear it yourself if you want,

Or let your wife wear it, or lock the loot in your safe.

You're not setting foot in my house from this moment on,

Don't kid yourself about that. I deserve better treatment

From you than being jerked around and laughed at
like a clown.

I've been your friend, lover boy—but that's at an end.

From now on, it's strictly for cash, if and when.

Find some other doll to play with and then let her
down.

Menaechmus I

God damn it, don't get so God damn mad. Hey,
don't go

Off like that, wait a minute! Come back here. You won't?

Oh come on, Dee. Not even for me? You won't? So
I see.

She's gone in and locked the door too. And I guess that
makes me

Just about the most locked-out fellow in this town
today,

Most unwanted man, most unlikely to get in, much
less to say

Anything that a wife, or a mistress, might take to
be true.

I'll go ask my friends what they think I ought to do.

Act Five

scene one

[MENAECHMUS II *and* WIFE OF MENAECHMUS I.

Menaechmus II

It was really pretty dumb of me to put that purseful
of money
In Messenio's hands, the way I did. He's probably
holed up
In some dive, drinking it down, and looking them over.

Wife

I think I'll just take a look and see how soon husband
Wends his way home. There he is now. And all's well
for me:
He's got the dress with him.

Menaechmus II

Where in hell has Messenio wandered off to?

Wife

I'll go up and welcome him now in the terms he
deserves.
Aren't you ashamed to show up in my sight, you mistake
Of a man . . . I mean, you deliberate premeditated
crime,
Tricked out with that fancy gown?

Menaechmus II

I don't get it, do I?
What's on your mind, my good woman?

Wife

How dare you address me?
How dare you utter a single slimy syllable, you snake?

Menaechmus II

What have I done that's so bad I don't dare address you?

Wife

You must have cast-iron nerves to inquire about that.

Menaechmus II

I don't know if you read much, lady, but Hecuba:
The Greeks always called her a bitch. I suppose you
   know why?

Wife

As a matter of fact, no. I don't.

Menaechmus II

                              Because she acted the way
You're acting right now. She kept dumping insults and
   curses
On everyone she met, and snarling at, pitching into
   everyone
Her eyes lighted on. No wonder they called her a prime
   bitch.

Wife

I really can't take this kind of abuse any longer.
I'd much rather never have been married, than
   submit to
The kind of dirt you shovel on me the way you do now.

Menaechmus II

What's it to me whether you like being married or not,
Or want to leave your husband? Do all the people
   around here
Tell their stories to every new man that blows into
   town?

Wife

What stories? I simply won't take it any longer, I
   tell you.
I'd rather live all alone than put up with you.

Menaechmus II

For God's sake, then, live alone, as far as I care,
Or as long as Jupiter may decide to grant you the
   option.

Wife

A few moments ago you were insisting you hadn't
   sneaked off
That mantilla-dress of mine, but now you're waving it

In front of my eyes. Aren't you a tiny bit conscience-
stricken?

Menaechmus II

God only knows what kind of a squeeze play you're
pulling,
You whack, you brazen. . . . How dare you say I took
this,
When another woman gave it to me to take and have
altered?

Wife

By God (my God, this time), a statement like that
Makes me want to . . . and I'm going to send for my
father,
And tell him every single horrible thing you've done,
That's what I'll do. Hey, Decio, in there, come out,
And go find my father and ask him to come here
with you.
Tell him please to come quickly, I simply have to
see him.
I'll show him every single horrible thing you've done
to me.

Menaechmus II

Are you feeling all right? What single horrible thing?

Wife

You housebreaker-into! You steal my dress and my jewels
From my house and rob your wife of her goods to
throw at
The feet of or load in the arms of your girlfriend as loot.
Have I rehearsed the story accurately enough for your
ears to take in?

Menaechmus II

Lady, you ought to watch your prepositions; and while
you're at it
Could you mix me a sedative of half hemlock, half lime
juice?
You must have some hemlock around here. I must be
kept *quiet*
If I'm meant to sustain your attacks. I'm not sure I know
Exactly who you think I am. I may have known you
Long ago in the days of Hercules' father-in-law's father.

Wife

Laugh at me all you want, but your father-in-law
Won't stand for that. Here he comes now. Take a good
    look,
Won't you? Recognize somebody?

Menaechmus II

                    Oh, him? I may have known him . . .
Yes, I did . . . oh sure, I remember old George from the
    Trojan War:
He was our Chaplain, bless his old heart. No, I guess not.
I've never seen him before, just as I've never seen
You before either, either of you, before today.

Wife

You say, you don't know me, and you don't know my
    father?

Menaechmus II

You're right. And actually, if you produced your
    grandfather,
I'd say the same.

Wife

                    One joke after another. What a bother!

scene two

[OLD MAN, WIFE *and* MENAECHMUS II.

Old Man

Here I come, pushing one foot after the other,
As fast and as far as my age allows, and to meet
This crisis at my own pace, pushing these pedals,
    progressing
As best I can. Papa isn't planning to pretend,
Though, to anybody, that it's easy. He's not so spry
    any more.
I'm pretty darned pregnant with years, that's a fact;
    planted
With a crop of them, if you conceive of me carrying
    the burden
Of this body. And there's precious little power left.
    Oh, it's a bad deal,
This business of being old. We're stuck with the bulk

Of our unwanted goods. Maybe we get more than we
    bargained for
Out of life. Old age brings the most of the worst when
    it comes,
To the ones who want it the least. If I named every
    pain
It bestows on us oldsters, I'd be drawing up a long
    long list,
And you'd have too much to listen to.
                          I wonder why my daughter
Sent for me all of a sudden? It weighs on my mind
And tugs at my heart to know what's afoot that can
    bring me
Running over here to see her. She didn't say why she
    sent for me,
Or tell me what's up. I can figure it out pretty well,
Of course. A quarrel with her husband has sprung
    up, I bet.
That's the way wives behave who bring a big dowry,
Coming loaded into the marriage and expecting their
    husbands
To love, honor, and slave away for them. They can
    be rough.
Of course, the husbands are at fault themselves, every
    now and then.
But there's a point at which it's no longer dignified
For the husband to take it any longer. That dear
    daughter of mine,
Darn her, never sends for me unless they've both of them
    been doing
Something wrong and a quarrel has started or is
    definitely brewing.
Whatever it is, I'll find out. *Yup!* I'll get brought up on
    the news.
Here she is now in front of the house. I see how
    aroused
They both are. She must have lashed into him; he looks
Pretty dashed. *Yup!* Just as I thought. I'll go call to her.

Wife

I'll go greet father. Good afternoon, Dad. How are you?

Old Man

Fine, thank you dear, and you? I hope everything's all
    right.

You didn't send for me because you're in trouble? But
    you look
Pretty peaked. And why's he standing over there looking
    mad?
You both look as if you've been trading punches,
    exchanged a few blows
Just for size, to see how it goes. Fill me in on the facts.
Tell me who's to blame, and explain the whole situation.
But briefly, I implore you. Let's not have even one
    oration,
Much less two.

Wife

               I didn't do anything, Father,
Don't worry. But I can't live here any longer, I can't
Stick it out. Please take me back.

Old Man

                       How did this happen?

Wife

    I've become someone just to be laughed at.

Old Man

                              By whom?

Wife

                              By him,
The man, the husband you conferred me on.

Old Man

                          A fight, eh?
That's it, eh? How many times have I told you both
    of you
To watch out you don't come whining to me with
    your troubles?

Wife

How could I watch out, Father dear?

Old Man

                       You really ask that?

Wife

Only if you don't mind my asking.

Old Man

                    How often have I told you

To put up with your husband? Don't watch where he
    goes;
Don't see what he does; don't pry into what he's
    engaged in.

Wife

But he's crazy about this daisy of a flower girl; and
    she lives right next door.

Old Man

That's perfectly natural, and in view of the way you're
    so busy
Keeping an eye on his business, he'll get even dizzier
    about Daisy,
I just bet you.

Wife

            But he goes over there for drinks all the time.

Old Man

What's it to you whether he drinks over there? If he
    drinks,
He'll have to do it somewhere. And what's so terrible
    about that?
You might as well ask him to stop having dinner in
    town,
Or never bring anyone home for a meal. Are husbands
Supposed to take orders from you? Let them run the
    house then,
And order the maids around, hand out wool to be
    carded
And get on with their spinning and weaving.

Wife

                But Father, I ask you
To represent *me*, not to be *his* lawyer in this case.
You're standing here on my side, but you're taking his.

Old Man

Of course, if he's misbehaved, I'll get after him as much
As I've lit into you, in fact more so. But he seems to
    be taking
Pretty good care of you, giving you jewels, clothes,
Your servants, furnishing the food. You ought to take
    a practical,
More sensible view of the thing.

Wife

But he's rooked me by stealing
Jewels and dresses from my closet at home to sneak
off with,
My clothes, my jewels, to dress up that girl he calls
on on the sly with.

Old Man

That's some prep . . . I mean proposition, I mean some
imposition.
I mean, that's terrible if that's going on—if it isn't
Your supposition's as bad, putting an innocent man
under suspicion.

Wife

But Dad, he's got them there with him, the dress and
that *sweet*
Gold flexible bracelet. He took them to her
And now, since I've found out about it, he's bringing
them back.

Old Man

Well, now, we'll see about that. I'm going to find out
About that. I'm going right over there and ask him,
I am.
Oh say, Menaechmus, would you mind telling me, if
you don't
Mind, about the matter you've been . . . discussing
with her?
I'm curious to know. And why are you looking so down
In the mouth, old fellow? Why's my girl standing
over there
By herself, all alone, and so cross?

Menaechmus II

I summon all the gods,
And Jupiter Himself Supreme, as they are my
witnesses. . . .
Old boy, whoever you are, whatever your name
May happen to be.

Old Man

As they are your witnesses to what?
Why do you need such a cloud of high-ranking
witnesses?

Menaechmus II
That I have not done anything wrong to this woman
Who claims that I surreptitiously deprived her
Of this dress and carried it off under suspicious
    circumstances.

Wife
Well, that's a clear enough lie. He's perjured himself
    for sure.

Menaechmus II
If I have ever even set foot inside her house
May I be of all men the most terribly tremendously
    miserably.

Old Man
That's not a very bright thing to wish for, is it? You
    don't say
You've never set foot in the house there you live in,
    do you,
You stupid goop?

Menaechmus II
What's that you're saying about me
Living in that house, you goofy duffer? *I* live *there*?

Old Man
You deny it?

Menaechmus II
                Oh for Hercle's sake, of course I deny it.

Old Man
Oh for Hercle's sake right back, you lie if you do
Say you don't, I mean deny it. Unless you moved out
    last night.
Come here, Daughter, listen: You two haven't moved
Recently, have you?

Wife
                Heavens! Where to? Or why should we have?

Old Man
Well, of course, I couldn't know about that.

Wife
                                Don't you *get* it?
He's joking around with you.

Old Man

All right, Menaechmus, I've taken
Enough of your joking now. Come on, boy, let's get
down to business.

Menaechmus II

Je vous en prie! What the hell business have you got
with me?
In the first place, who the hell are you? And in the
second place
I don't owe you any money. Nor her, in the third
place.
Who's giving me all this trouble, in the next few places?

Wife

Look, do you notice how his eyes seem to be going
all green
All of a sudden? And there's a green tinge developing
on the skin
Around his temples and forehead. Look at his eyes
glowing red,
Or is it green?

Menaechmus II

I wonder if I'd better not pretend I *am* crazy
And scare them away by throwing a fit? They're the
ones
Who seem to be insisting on it.

Wife

His arms twitch, his jaw drops.
Oh, Father, what shall I do?

Old Man

Come here to your father,
My girl, stay as far away as you can from him.

Menaechmus II

Ho yo to yo! Tobacco Boy! Take me back to ya!
I hear ya callin' me out to that happy hunting ground
*Deep down in desegregated Damnasia (that's in the
Near East),*
*Callin' your boy to come on out huntin' with his hound
dogs!*
I hear ya, Bromie Boy, but I jes' cain come near ya.
*They won't let me loose from this toothpickin' witch-
huntin' northland.*

*They's an old foam-covered bitch and she's keeping
      watch
On my left. And right behind me here they's a goat,
An ole toothpickin' garlic-stinking but I mean old goat,
Who's been buttin' down innocent citizens all of his life
By bringing up things that ain't true against them
And then rounding up people to come listen to them
      refute them.*

Old Man

I'm afraid your mind's been affected.

Menaechmus II

                    I've just swallowed an oracle
Of Apollo that orders me instantly to start setting about
Finding two red-hot searchlights to put her eyes out
      with.

Wife

Goodness, what a prepositionous preposterous
      proposition,
Father. He's threatening to burn out my eyes in.

Menaechmus II

Touché, for me. They say I'm raving, but they
Are rather wild at the moment. The straitjacket's on the
      other foot.

Old Man

Oh, my poor girl.

Wife

          Yes, Father?

Old Man

                    What shall we do?
Suppose I send for the slaves in a hurry; I'll go
And bring them myself, to take him away and chain him
Safely at home before he starts getting more destructive.

Menaechmus II

Trapped! Strung up by my own guitar! If I don't
Improvise something soon they'll come on and cart me
      away.
*Yes I hear you, sugar Radiant Apollo! I'll follow through
With my fists (you insist?) and spare not the laying on
      of hands.*

*Punch that woman in the jaw, you say, according to
    your law,*
*Unless she disappears from my view and gets herself
    gone*
The holy hell and crucified crutch of a cross
Out of my way? Apollo, I'll do what you say!

Old Man

Scoot into the house, fast as poss, or he'll slug you.

Wife

                                        Scoot I go,
Father, *ergo*, soon I'll be out of the way. But please,
    Father,
Keep stalling him, don't let him slip out of reach. Don't
    you agree,
I'm a most put-upon specimen of woman to put up
    with that?

Menaechmus II

I've got rid of her: not bad. Now for dad. You slob,
Listen, you baggy-bearded, quavering long-since-past
    father,
You shriveled old, dried-up grasshopper—and besides
    your voice's changed,
Singing your Glorias Swansong soprano in your second
    childhood.
*What's that, Apollo? Thou sayest I should smashest
    his frame,*
*His bones, and the joints that hook them to same? I'm
    game.*
Smashomin, you say, with his owncluboff? Use his cane?

Old Man

There'll be trouble for you if you lay a finger on me,
Or move any closer.

Menaechmus II

                        Oh sir, Apollo? The following
Changes in wording? Take one each two-headed axe
*And split right down through the frame, through the
    guts to the bones,*
*And hack his back to bits and make slivers of his liver
    and his*
Whole intestinal tract, don't just cudgel the codger?

Roger to tower. Look at that geezer cower and run
    for cover.

Old Man

I suppose I'd better look to my laurels, what's left of
    them, withered
As an old man's may be. I'll look after me. He's a
    menace,
That's clear enough. He just may decide to take it
    out on my hide.

Menaechmus II

For god's sake, Apollo, what's this? Another message?
    The traffic's
Getting heavy. *Take four wild bucking broncos and
    hitch*
*Them up to a buckboard, and climb aboard and drive
    them over*
This lion, this bearded biped, this antique toothless
Gumclicking biped with bad breath? Roger, I'm
    mounted, oh joy
To Yoy, King Roy Apolloy. I'm holding that wagon's
    reins
And flicking the whip already. Up there, you double
    pair
Of quadruplets. Drum it out on the ground when you
    trample him down.
Bend your knees, noble steeds, be nimble as the breeze.
Pound you there, pound.

Old Man

                He's coming at me with two pairs
Of horses?

Menaechmus II

Whoa there! *Yes, Apollo, of course I hear you*
Telling me to launch my attack against him, yes, him
Over there, and murder him. Whoa there! Who's hauling
    me back
By the hair, and pulling me out of the chariot? Who
    does this
Reverses the very command and eeeeeeedict of Apollo.

Old Man

It's really this poor fellow who's having the attack,
    I would say.

And he's really having one, the full-scale deluxe one
    with nuts in it,
God save us all. Well, that's how it is, by God. Here's
    a fellow
Completely crackers, and a minute ago he was perfectly
    rational.
When that mad stuff hits you it lands hard all of a
    sudden.
I'll go ask the doctor to get here as soon as he can.

[*Exit.*

Menaechmus II

[*Alone, faces audience and addresses them across the
stagefront.*]

    Now I ask you, have those two at last gotten out of
      my sight,
Who forced me to play this mad role, when, as *you*
    know,
I'm perfectly well? This is my chance to pick up and go
Winging back to my ship, don't you think, quick as a
    wink,
While I'm still safe and sound? Listen, if you're still
    around
When the old man comes back, you won't tell—he'll
    be in a rage—
Where I went when I left the stage? You won't say
    where I can be found?

[*Exit.*

scene three

[OLD MAN *and* DOCTOR.

Old Man

My back's stiff with sitting, my eyes nearly worn out
    with looking,
Hanging around waiting for God darn that darn
    medicine man
To finish with his patients and meet this emergency.
Well *finally* he's pulled himself away—not much urgency
Either, from his victims. He's his own worst pain in
    the neck!
Such a specialist, in name-dropping at least, of who's
    on his list

Of big shots with big troubles only he can fix. When
    I insisted
He hike over here, he said "Right away," but first he
    must set
This broken leg, to the Greater Glory of Aesculapius,
And then put an arm back in place, On Behalf of Apollo.
Which half of Apollo beats the Belvedere out of me:
    but I see
Him racing over now, weaving down the track like
    an ant
With lumbago. It's just his ego slows him down, the
    hot airman.
Putting those pieces together! What is he, a repairman,
A tinker, a joiner at heart? Are his patients all coming
    apart?

Doctor

Now let us see, my man. . . . You described the case of
    the deseased
As *larvated, id est,* he sees actual, live, dead ghost
    spooks?
Or *cerebrated, id est,* perturbated footzled left lobar
    cavity?
Which is of course only a false hallucination and
    would show
Some degree of mental inquietude. Would you be
    so good
As to describe the condition again, so I can decide
What to prescribe or proscribe, indeed just how
    to proceed?
Did you mention a species of *Hibernating* coma, a
    kind of
Tendency to feel sleepy all the time? Or did you more
    plainly see
A subaqueous subcutaneous *slurpation,* like say, water
    on the knee?

Old Man

The reason I've brought you in on the case is to find out
From you just what's wrong and ask you to cure it.

Doctor

                        How true,
And I'll do it to perfection, never fear; upon my
    profession

I assure you he'll be quite well again.

Old Man

You'll give him
The most careful attention?

Doctor

First-class care, rest assured.
My word, Deluxe! Private room; personal visits from me.
I'll see him daily and ponder him most thoughtfully,
Heave hundreds of luxury sighs. He'll rate a thrill
Being ill; and so will you when you see the bill.

Old Man

Shh. Here's our man. Let's watch and see what he does.

scene four

[OLD MAN, DOCTOR, *and* MENAECHMUS I.

Menaechmus I

By God in heaven, if this hasn't been the worst
Of all possible days for me! Everything's gone blooey.
What I planned to do on the sly, that particular parasite,
Peniculus, brought to light, and flooded me with shame
and remorse
In the process. Some Ulysses type, doping out this
dirty deal
For his own best protector and patron. Why that . . .
sure as I live,
I'll do him right out of his ensuing existence, I'll unroll
His scroll for him. *His* existence? I'm a fool
To call *his* what's actually mine. I'm the one who
brought him up
By wining and dining him. It was my subsistence he
lived on:
All he ever managed was coexistence. I'll snuff out
That half of his light by cutting off the supplies.
As for that mercenary Daisy, all I can say is she
Acted quite in keeping with the character of a kept
woman,
And I suppose that's human, if meretricious. A very
meretricious
And a happy new year to her. When in doubt, just
give money.
All I did was ask her for the dress to return to my wife

And she claimed she'd already handed it over. Turned
it over,
I bet, to some dealer for cash. Crash! Oh God in heaven,
Did any man ever let himself in for this big a cave-in?

Old Man

You hear that?

Doctor

          He says he's unhappy.

Old Man

                  Go on up to him.

Doctor

Meeeeenaechmus, *ciao!* How are you? Why expose your
arm
That way? Exposure can aggravate your serious condition.

Menaechmus I

Why don't you go hang up, yourself, on the nearest
branch?

Old Man

Notice anything peculiar?

Doctor

              Anything? The whole thing,
That's what I notice. This case couldn't be kept under
control
By a mountain of Miltowns. Menaechmus, just a word
with you, please.

Menaechmus I

What's up, Doc?

Doctor

          You are. Answer a few questions, please,
And take them in order. First, what color wine do
you drink?
White wine, or red?

Menaechmus I

          Oh, my crucified crotch!
What's that to you?

Doctor

          I seem to detect a slight tendency
To rave, here.

Menaechmus I

Why not color-quiz me on bread?
Do I take purple, cerise, or golden red? As a rule,
Do I eat fish with their feathers or birds with their
    scales and all?

Old Man

I win! Ill, eh? Pu! Can't you hear he's delirious? Hurry
    up
With that sedative, can't you? Why wait for the fit to
    come on?

Doctor

Just hold on a bit. I've a few more questions to ask.

Old Man

You'll finish him off with the questions you keep
    inventing.

Doctor

Do your eyes ever feel like they're starting out of your
    head?

Menaechmus I

What do you take me for, you seahorse doctor, a
    lobster?

Doctor

Do your bowels rumble powerfully, as far as you can
    tell?

Menaechmus I

They're perfectly still when I'm full; when hungry,
    they grumble.

Doctor

Well now, that's a perfectly straightforward, digestible
    answer,
Not the word of a nut. You sleep until dawn, and
    sleep well?

Menaechmus I

I sleep right through, if I've paid all my bills. Listen,
    you
Special investigator, I wish to heaven the gods would
    crack down on you.

Doctor

Ah, now, to judge from that statement, he's being
    irrational.

Old Man

Oh no, that's a wise saying, worthy of Nestor, compared
To what he was saying a while back, when he called
his own wife
A stark raving bitch.

Menaechmus I

What's that you say I said?

Old Man

You're out of your head, that's what I say.

Menaechmus I

Who's out of what? Me?

Old Man

Yes, you, that's who. Boo! Threatening to flatten me out
With a four-horsepower chariot. I can swear to it.
I saw you with my own eyes. I charge you with it.

Menaechmus I

Ah, but here's what I know about you. You purloined
the crown
Of Jupiter, his sacred crown, and were locked up in jail.
That's what I know about you. And when they let
you out,
It was to put you under the yoke and whip you in public,
With birch rods. That's what I know about you. And
then, too,
You killed your own father and sold off your mother
as a slave,
That's what I know about you. Don't you think that
might possibly do
As a reasonably sound reply to the charges you're
letting fly?

Old Man

Oh hurry up, Doctor, for Hercle's sake, and do what
you ought to.
Can't you see, the man's *off?*

Doctor

You know what I think is best?
Have him brought over to my place.

Old Man

You're sure?

Doctor

Sure, why not?
I'll be able to treat him there by the very latest methods.

Old Man

Good. You know best.

Doctor

I assure you, Menaechmus, you'll lap up
Super tranquilizers for twenty days.

Menaechmus I

Is that medicine
Your madness? I'll gore you, hanging there, for thirty days.

Doctor
[*Aside.*]

Go call the help, to carry him over to my house.

Old Man
[*Aside.*]

How many men do we need?

Doctor
[*Aside.*]

At least four, to judge
From the way he's raving at present.

Old Man
[*Aside.*]

They're practically here.
I'll go run and get them. You stay right here, Doctor, do,
And keep a close eye on him.

Doctor
[*Aside.*]

No. As a matter of fact,
I think I'll be off for home, and make the preparations
To receive him. There's quite a lot to do. You go get
    the help;
Have them bring him to me.

Old Man
[*Aside.*]

He's as good as carried there already.

Doctor
I'm off.

Old Man

So am I.

Menaechmus I

Now I'm alone. That father-in-law
And that doctor have gone, somewhere or other. But
     what in God's name
Makes these men insist I'm insane? I've never been sick
A day in my life, and I'm not ailing now. I don't start
     fights,
Or dispute everything that comes up. I wish others well
When I meet them, quite calmly, I recognize people
     I know,
And speak to them civilly enough. I wonder if they,
Who absurdly declare that I'm mad, since they're in
     the wrong,
Aren't in fact crazy themselves? I wish I knew what
     to do.
I'd like to go home, but my wife won't allow it—as for
     that place [*points to* DÉSIRÉE'S *house*]
No one will let me in there, Well, it's all worked out
All right; worked me out of house and home. So I guess
I'll stick around here. I imagine, by the time night comes
I'll be welcome to enter the right one of these two homes.

scene five

[MESSENIO.

Messenio

God slave the king!
And of me I sing.
Or rather, the slave's the thing
I present and I represent.
The good slave, intent
On making his master content,
Looks after his master's affairs.
Arranging and planning, he never spares
Any effort in lavishing cares
On everything that needs being done.
When the master's away, he handles all alone
Problems that keep coming up, and he solves them
As well as the boss could, himself, all of them;
And sometimes manages the whole business better
     than master.

You need a good sense of balance, to fend off disaster
From your legs and your back. And you've got to
    remember
That your throat and your stomach are not the most vital
    members.
If you go off guzzling and eating, instead of performing,
When you come back you're in for a beating and a
    good body-warming.

        May I remind all the shiftless delinquents who
            keep hanging back
From doing their work, of the price all masters exact
From good-for-nothings, men they can't count on,
    in fact?

        Lashes, and chains;
        Turning those wheels at the mill
        Until you begin to feel
        Your brains churning loose and writhing
            like eels.
        You'll be starved and left out to sleep in the
            cold open fields.
        That's the wages of laziness.
        Not to fear earning that would be the worst
            sort of craziness.

Therefore, I've decided, for once and for all, to be good
And not bad. I'd rather be lashed by the tongue than
    the wood.
As for meal, I find it more pleasant to eat than to
    grind it.
Therefore, I always comply with the will of my lord
Calmly, and well I preserve it; and I can afford
To deserve whatever I get by way of reward.
Let others look after their interests; they'll find a good
    way.
But this is how to serve your man best. That's what
    I say.
Let me always be careful, and pretty darn prayerful
Not to get in any trouble, so that I'll always be there, full
Of energy, coming in on the double where he needs
    me most,
His assistant host. Slaves who keep themselves good
    and scared
When they're not in the wrong usually find that they
    are declared

Highly usable by their owners. The fearless ones are
    the goners;
When it comes time to face the music, these singsongers
Will be cheeping like jailbirds and wishing they weren't
    such gone-wrongers.
But I don't have to worry much longer, not me.
The time's almost here now when he promised to set
    me free.
That's how I slave and work well, and how I decide
To do the best thing and take the best care of my hide.
    Sooooo . . . now that I've seen all the baggage and
        the porters in their bedding
In the tavern downtown, as Menaechmus instructed,
    I'm heading
Back to meet him. Guess I'll knock on the door
So he'll know I'm out here and get up off the floor
Or at least let me pull him outside
From this den of iniquity, now that he's tried
To have a good time, and probably found out the cost.
I hope I'm not too late and that the battle's not already
    lost.

scene six

[OLD MAN, WHIPSTERS, MESSENIO, *and* MENAECHMUS I

Old Man

Now I tell you, by all that's human or holy, make sure
You carry out my orders just right as I ordered you to
And order you now. You're to heft that man on your
    shoulders
And hustle him off to the clinic, if you don't want
    your legs
And your back pounded in. And don't pay the least
    attention,
Any one of you, to anything he says. Well, don't just
    stand there.
What are you waiting for? You ought to be after him,
    lifting him.
I'll trot on over to the doctor's and be there when you
    pull in.

Menaechmus I

Well I'll be *God* damned! What's on the schedule now?

Why are these men rushing at me, what in the name
of . . . ?

What do you guys want? What's all the racket about?

Why are you closing in on me all of a sudden? What's
the hurry?

Where we going? Some rumble. Creepers! They're
giving me the tumble.

God *damn* us! Citizens all, of Epidamnus! To the rescue!

Save me, my fellow men! Help! Let go me, you
whipster bastards.

Messenio

Holy smoke! Creepers! What's this bunch of gypsters
think

They're gonna get away with? My master? Why those
hijacking lifters,

They've got him on their shoulders. Let's see who gets
the most blisters.

Menaechmus I

Won't *anyone* lend me a hand?

Messenio

           I will sir, at your command;

You brave Captain. Boy, this is gonna give Epidamnus
a black eye,

A mugging like this, right out in the open. *Epidam-
nee-ee-ee-I!*

My master's being towed away in broad daylight, a
free man

Who came to your city in peace, attacked on the
street. *Can*

Anybody help us? Stay off, you lugs. Lay off.

Menaechmus I

Hey, for God's sake, whoever you are, help me out,

Won't you? Don't let them get away with murder. You
can see

I'm in the right.

Messenio

        Quite. Of course I'll pitch in

And come to your defense and stand by you with all
my might.

I'd never let you go under, Commander, I'd sink first.

Now you sink your fist in that guy's eye . . . No, not
    that one,
The one who's got you by the shoulder. That's it. Now
    a bolder
Swipe at the ball, gouge it out for him. I'll start
    distributing
A crack in the puss here, a sock in the jaw there. I'm
    at liberty
To do so? By the heavyweight Hercules, you thugs
    are gonna lug
Him away like a carload of lead, today. You'll pay by
    the ounce
When you feel my fists bounce all over your faces. Let
    go his grace.

Menaechmus I
I've got this guy's eye.

Messenio
                    Make like it's just a hole in his head.
You're a bunch of bums, you body snatching, loot-latch-
    ing whipsters.

Whipster I
Hey, this wasn't what the doctor ordered, was it, or
    the old mister?

Whipster II
They didn't say we'd be on the receiving end, did
    they . . . ouch!
Gee Hercules, Jerkules, that hurt!

Messenio
                    Well, let him loose, then.

Menaechmus I
How dare this ape lay hands on me? Bongo him,
    jungle boy.

Messenio
Here we go, kids, you too; take off, fade out, monkey
    face;
Get the crucified cross of a holy hell and gone out of
    here.
You too, take that, you vandal. Get a lift from my
    sandal.
You're the last one, might as well get what's left behind.

Well . . . Phew . . . ! Say, I made it, didn't I? Just about
in time.

Menaechmus I

Young man, whoever you are, may the gods always
shine
On your face. If it hadn't been for you I wouldn't have
lasted
Through sunset today.

Messenio

By all that's holy, if you wanted
To reward me, oh Master, you could free me.

Menaechmus I

Me liberate you?
I'm afraid I don't follow, young fellow. Aren't you
making some mistake?

Messenio

Me make a mistake?

Menaechmus I

By our father Jupiter, I swear
I am not your master.

Messenio

Don't talk that way.

Menaechmus I

I'm not lying.
No slave of mine ever helped me as you did today.

Messenio

Well, then, let me go free, even if you say you don't
know me.
Then I won't be yours.

Menaechmus I

But of course! Far as I'm concerned,
Thou art henceforth free—and thou mayest go wherever
thou wantest to.

Messenio

You say that officially?

Menaechmus I

Hercules, yes. In my official capacity,
Insofar as that governs you.

Messenio

                    Thanks very much.
And greetings, dear patron! Now that I'm free to be
    your client
And depend on you on equal terms. [*Turns to audience.*]

> *Gaudete! He's free today!*
> *Good show for Messenio!*
> *Aren't you all glad he's let go?*

[*Audience cheers and applauds—and that is some stage
    direction.*]
[*Still to audience.*]
Well, I guess I'll accept it from you; thanks for the
    congratulations.
You've all given me quite a hand. I feel *man you mitted.*
But, Menaechmus, my patron, I'm just as much at your
    service
As I was when I used to be your slave. I want to stay
    by you.
And when you go home I want to go with you too.

Menaechmus I
[*Aside.*]
God, no! Not another client.

Messenio

                    I'll ankle downtown
To the tavern and bring back the baggage and cash.
    That purse
I hid away and locked in the trunk with the traveler's
    checks.
I'll go get it now and deliver it all back to you.

Menaechmus I
Oh yes, do bring that.

Messenio

                I'll bring it all back intact
Just as you handed it over. You wait here for me.
[*Exit.*

Menaechmus I
There's a bumper crop of miracles manifesting marvels
    by the millions

Around here today: some people saying I'm not who
    I am
And keeping me out from where I belong; then comes
    along
This slave who says he belongs to me, whom I've just
    set free.
Now he says he'll go bring me back a purseful of cash;
And if he does that I'll insist he feel perfectly free
To take leave of me and go where he wants, just in case
When he comes to his senses he begins asking back for
    the dough.
The doctor and my father-in-law, though, claim I'm
    out of my head.
At least, that's what they said. It's all very hard to get
    hold of,
Like a dream you dream you're having or are just being
    told of.
        Oh well, I'll go on in here to visit my mistress,
          even though
She's provoked at me, and do my best to prevail
On her to give back the dress. I can certainly use it
    as bail
To get off the street and into my house, *id est*, my jail.

scene seven

[MENAECHMUS II *and* MESSENIO.

Menaechmus II

You have the nerve to be telling me you reported back
    to me
Since the time I sent you away and told you to meet
    me?

Messenio

Exactly. Only a moment ago I saved you from de-
    struction
At the hands of those four whipsters hoisting you on
    their shoulders
And carting you off, right in front of this house. You
    were letting out
Loud shouts, calling on all the gods and on men,
When I roared in and pulled you loose by sheer brute
    strength

And knocked the block off them all, much to their
surprise.
And for the service I rendered in saving you, you set
me free.
Then I told you I'd go get the baggage and our cash—
and then *you*
Doubled round the corner as fast as you could, to
meet me
And deny the whole thing.

Menaechmus II

I told you you could be free?

Messenio
Positive.

Menaechmus II
I'm more positive still that before I'd see
You turned free man I'd turn into a slave, yes me, man.

scene eight

[MESSENIO, MENAECHMUS I, *and* MENAECHMUS II.

Menaechmus I
[*Comes out of* DÉSIRÉE'S *house.*]
You can swear by your two jaundiced eyes if you want,
that won't
Make it any more true that I took away the dress and
bracelet today,
You whole bunch of blue-eyed, organized man-eaters
for pay.

Messenio
Heavens to . . . let's see . . . What's this I see?

Menaechmus II
So, what
Do you see?

Messenio
You're looking glass, boss.

Menaechmus II
You mean to say what?

Messenio

I say I see your reflection over there. I could swear
It's your face exactly.

Menaechmus II

God, if it isn't like me,
When I stop to consider how I look.

Menaechmus I

Oh boy, there, whoever you are,
You saved my life. Glad to see you.

Messenio

Young man, I wonder
If you'd mind telling me what your name is, by God
in heaven?

Menaechmus I

Heavenly God, no, of course I don't mind. The favor
You did me rates in return my nonreluctant behavior:
After all, you're my savior. I go by the name of
Menaechmus.

Menaechmus II

So do I, for God's sake.

Menaechmus I

I'm Sicilian, from Syracuse.

Menaechmus II

And my native city is the same.

Menaechmus I

What's that you claim?

Menaechmus II

Only what's the truth.

Messenio

I can tell you which is which easily.
I'm his slave [*points to* MENAECHMUS I], but I thought
all along I was his.
And I thought you were him. That's why I talked back
that way.
Please excuse me if I've spoken too stupidly for words
to you.

Menaechmus II

You're raving right now. Think back. Remember how

You got off the ship with me today?

Messenio

A fair enough question.
I'll change my mind. You're my master and I am your
slave.
So long, you. Good afternoon, again, to you. And I
mean you.
I say, this one's Menaechmus.

Menaechmus I

I say that's me.

Menaechmus II

What's the story, you? Menaechmus?

Menaechmus I

Yep. Menaechmus. Son of Moschus.

Menaechmus II

You're my father's son?

Menaechmus I

No, fellow, *my* father's. I'm not
After yours. I don't want to hop on yours and take him
from you.

Messenio

By all the gods, all over heaven, can my mind
Be sure of what it hopes for so desperately? *I've got 'em
untwined:*
These men are the two twins who separately now are
combined
To recall the same father and fatherland they shared
in their likeness.
I'll speak to my master. Ahoy there, Menaechmus.

Menaechmus I and Menaechmus II
[*Together.*]
What is it?

Messenio

No, no, not both. I only want my shipmate.

Menaechmus I

Not me.

Menaechmus II

But me.

Messenio

You're the one I must talk to. Come here.

Menaechmus II

Here I am. What's up?

Messenio

That man's either your absolute brother
Or an absolute fake. I never saw one man look more like
    another.
Water's no more like water, or milk more like milk
Than you two drops of the same identical ilk.
Besides, he cites the same fatherland and father.
Don't you think investigating further might be worth
    the bother?

Menaechmus II

Say, that's very good advice you're giving me.
Thanks very much.
Keep boring in, I implore you, by Hercules' knee.
If you come up with my brother, I fully intend to see
That *thou shalt go free.*

Messenio

I hope I come out right in the end.

Menaechmus II

I hope the same thing for you.

Messenio

[To MENAECHMUS I.]
Now, fellow, what do you say?
Menaechmus, I believe that is what you said you were
    called.

Menaechmus I

Right you are.

Messenio

Now this fellow here has the name of Menaechmus,
Just like you, and you said you were born at Syracuse.
So was he. Now both of you pay close attention to me,
And see if what I work out doesn't prove well worth it.

Menaechmus I

You've already earned the right to whatever you want
From me. You've only to ask and you'll gain it. If
    it's money

You want I'm ready to supply it. Just ask. I won't
deny it.

Messenio

I am hopeful at the moment of setting about to discover
The fact that you two are twins, born for each other
And on the same day to the very same father and
mother.

Menaechmus I

That sounds miraculous. I wish you could keep that
promise.

Messenio

I'll come through all right. Now listen here, each one
of you
To just what I say. And answer my questions in turn.

Menaechmus I

Ask what you will. I'll answer and never keep back
Anything I know.

Messenio

Is your name Menaechmus?

Menaechmus I

I admit it.

Messenio

Is that your name too?

Menaechmus II

So it is.

Messenio

You say that your father
Was Moschus?

Menaechmus I

So I do.

Menaechmus II

Me too.

Messenio

You're from Syracuse?

Menaechmus I

That I am.

Messenio

How about you?

Menaechmus II

Naturally, me too.

Messenio

So far, it all checks perfectly. Now let's forge ahead.
Tell me, how far back do you remember having been
    in your country?

Menaechmus I

Well, I remember the day I went to Tarentum, to
    the fair
And wandered off away from my father among some
    men who took me
And brought me here.

Menaechmus II

Jupiter One and Supreme, that can only mean . . . !

Messenio

What's all the racket? Can't you pipe down? Now,
    how old
Were you when your father took you with him from
    Sicily?

Menaechmus I

Seven. I was just beginning to lose my first teeth,
And I never saw my father again.

Messenio

Here's another question:
How many sons did your father have?

Menaechmus I

Two, to my knowledge.

Messenio

Were you the older, or was the other?

Menaechmus I

Both the same age.

Messenio

That's impossible.

Menaechmus I

I mean, we were twins.

Menaechmus II

                    The gods are on my side.

Messenio

If you keep interrupting, I'll stop.

Menaechmus II

                    No, no. I'll be quiet.

Messenio

Tell me, did you both have the same name?

Menaechmus I

                    Not at all. I had
The name I have now, Menaechmus. They called him
    Sosicles.

Menaechmus II

The lid's off! I just can't keep from hugging him hard.
My own twin brother, *ciao!* It's me: Sosicles!

Menaechmus I

How come you changed your name to Menaechmus?

Menaechmus II

After they told us how you had been taken away
From our father, and carried off by strangers, and
    father died,
Our grandfather gave me your name. He made the
    changes.

Menaechmus I

I bet that's just how it happened. But tell me something.

Menaechmus II

Ask me something.

Menaechmus I

               What was our dear mother's name?

Menaechmus II

Henrietta Battleship.

Menaechmus I

             That's it, all right. Never on a diet.
Oh, *brother*, this is a riot. I just *cain't* keep quiet.
Imagine meeting you here after all these years, I mean
I never thought I'd ever lay eyes on you again, much less

Wring your neck, you old numero *uno,* I mean *duo.*

Menaechmus II

Oh, you big beautiful brute you. *Et ego et tu.* You know
How long I've been hunting for you, and how much
    trouble
I've gone to to locate my double! I'm glad to be
    here, lad.

Messenio

You see, boss, that's why that mercenary much of a
    wench in there
Called you by his name. She thought he was you when
    she hauled
You in to dinner.

Menaechmus I

As a matter of heavenly fact, I did order dinner set up
Behind my wife's back, right here today, and sneaked
    out a dress,
And gave it to Désirée.

Menaechmus II

Wouldn't be this dress, brother,
Would it?

Menaechmus I

That's it, brother. But how did you happen to come
    by it?

Menaechmus II

I just happened to come by and the girlfriend pulled
    me in to dinner
And said I'd given her the dress. I dined very well,
I wined like a lord, I reclined with my refined escort.
Then I took away the dress, and this gold bracelet too.

Menaechmus I

Good for you,
Old boy. Because of me, you've at least enjoyed
Your day in Epidamnus. I'm glad of that. Now, when she
Called you in, she of course, thought sure you were me.

Messenio

Ahem! Need I wait much longer to be free as you
    commanded?

Menaechmus I
Brother, he's asking for only what is his just due.
Just do it
For my sake, won't you?

Menaechmus II
Thou art henceforth free.

Menaechmus I
> *Gaudete! He's free today!*
> *Good show for Messenio!*
> *Aren't you all glad he's let go?*

Messenio
Congratulations are all very fine, but perhaps something
    more *exchangeable*
Like, say, money, will make a free future not only
    assured but *manageable.*

Menaechmus II
Now, brother, everything's finally worked out so well,
Let's both go back to our homeland.

Menaechmus I
> I'll do anything you wish,
Brother. I'll have a big auction here and sell all I own.
Meanwhile, temporarily, here we go home rejoicing.

Menaechmus II
I'm with you.

Messenio
> I've a favor to ask.

Menaechmus I
> Don't hesitate.

Messenio
Appoint me auctioneer.

Menaechmus I
> Sold! To the former slave!

Messenio
Well, shall I announce the sale then?

Menaechmus I
> Sure, for a week from today.

Messenio

[*To audience.*]

Big auction at Menaechmus' house a week from today!
Must sell slaves, furniture, town house, country estate!
Everything's going, everything, for whatever you
    can pay!
He'll even sell the wife to any buyer willing to try her.
We'll make a million dollars and we may even go higher
If you count my commission. All invited! It ought to
    be great!
—But, oh, wait, Spectators! Don't forget the theater's
    laws.
We'll leave you first, on a burst of good loud applause!

Plautus

THE MERCHANT

Adapted by Arthur Wilmurt

Characters   MEN:

Charinus *- young merchant*

Acanthio *- servant of Charinus*

Demipho *- father of "*

Lysimachus *- neighbor*

Eutychus *- son of Lysimachus*

A Servant

WOMEN:

Peristrata *- mother of Charinus*

Lycissa *- maid of Peristrata*

Syra *- maid of Lysimachus*

Dorippa *- wife of Lysimachus*

Pasicompsa *- mistress of Charinus*

*A Cook

*Scullions

*Although written for a man, the cook may be played by
a woman, and the scullions may be either sex or mixed.

THE SCENE: *A Street in Athens.*

The scene is wide and shallow, with two doors in the back, separated by as much space as is feasible. The door on the left is that of Demipho's house, the one on the right leads into Lysimachus's. The port is down the street to the right; the country is up the street to the left. Between the two houses is a wayside shrine dedicated to Apollo.

[CHARINUS *enters from the right, a very dreamy look in his eye.*

Charinus

Alas, I am undone. I am in love.

[*He glances at the audience, then takes it in and looks as if he wishes it weren't there.*]

Each month to me is mad as maddest June.

[*The audience gets another, dirtier look.*]

My poor heart flutters like the gentle—

[*He looks again, frowns, and goes on uncomfortably.*]

—dove.

All night I seek the moon—

[*With just a glance at his public he hurries on.*]

—I swoon at noon.

[*He abandons this doggerel with some relief and comes down to the apron.*]

If you keep staring at me like that I'll get the idea that you want me to talk to you. Well, why not? I've got to talk to somebody. This is how it is: two years ago I made a very interesting acquaintance—[*He loses control.*]

First love! Ah, any love! Thy sweet delights!

Insomnia, a troubled mind, a wildly beating heart!

Madness and covetousness and sleepless nights—

Sorry. Well, on my twenty-first birthday I brought this acquaintance home with me for a little party. I thought my acquaintances were my own business. But I found I was wrong when my father caught me—well . . . im-

proving our acquaintanceship. Then he found out I'd
spent all my money on her and he sent her out of town.
Then he found out I'd spent quite a lot of *his* money
on her and he sent *me* out of town. To Assus, on business—[*And he's off again.*]

> But how could I have ever dreamed of love
> Before that night in Assus when I met—
> Met? What a word! When two stars meet
> In predetermined flight and mingle brilliance—

Well, how would you describe it? I don't know. Anyway
I made this other acquaintance, gave a down payment
on her, and brought her home with me yesterday. Not
quite home, of course, but if I pay off what's still due on
her and tell my father I bought her as a servant for
my mother—Ye Gods, here's Acanthio! I told him not
to leave the ship!

> Oh stars ill-starred! Some evil! I'm undone!

[*He falls against the left side of the proscenium, afraid to
face his fate.* ACANTHIO *totters in hastily from the right.
His knees are sagging and as he passes Lysimachus's
door they fold up; he drops on the step.*

Acanthio

[*Panting and groaning as he cajoles his legs.*] Listen, friends,
rise up. We've got to be nice to the young master,
haven't we? We've got to protect him; help him out
of this crisis he's in, and we're not going to get anywhere bent double like this. [*He tries to get up but
fails, and goes on pleading.*] Friends, we're almost
there. It's going to be easier now, anyway. Down at
the port, I had to let you do all the running while I
pushed the crowds into the gutters and told them off
when they criticized, but now I'll be right in there with
you.

[*He struggles again to get up.*

Charinus

Ye Gods, he's been running. That's never happened
before. Oh, it must be very, very serious.

Acanthio

[*Having managed to rise, he is staggering toward Demipho's door.*] This is the end. I'm washed up, see?
Washed up. It'll take a week in a bath to get the old
joints working again.

Charinus

[*Exaggerating.*] Look at him tear! Come on, Acanthio! I can't stand it!

Acanthio

[*Sinking down on Demipho's doorstep.*] I can't stand it, that's all, I just can't stand this rush rush rush!

Charinus

I can't stand this suspense! What's he want to tell me, and why doesn't he come and tell it?

Acanthio

Come on, friends, one more unbend. [*He tries to unbend his knees.*] Ah, what's the use. How do I even know he's home.

Charinus

[*Stamping his feet in agony.*] Maybe I'd rather not know. Maybe it's too awful. Oh, I *know* it's too awful.

Acanthio

No! We mustn't take that attitude. We must try everything. [*He rises, sizes up the door, and throws himself against it melodramatically. A whole street in Athens quivers.*] Master! Master! [*He beats feebly on the door.*]

Charinus

[*Resigning himself.*] Yes, he really has something to tell me.

Acanthio

[*At the door.*] Charinus! Where's Charinus? Open the door, can't you?

Charinus

[*Going to him, all a-tremble.*] What's the matter, Acanthio?

Acanthio

[*Turning on him.*] Dammit, the service around here is terrible!

Charinus

I hope it's no worse than your news.

Acanthio

I wouldn't say that. [*He realizes whom he's talking to.*] Oh, master, master, you're undone!

Charinus

That's a sweet way to greet a friend.

Acanthio
Who's trying to be sweet? Boy, are you undone!

Charinus
Well, go on, tell me.

Acanthio
I just told you. You're undone. Couldn't I have a little rest before I go into details?

Charinus
Wipe your face and get on with it!

Acanthio
That's gratitude after I bust a lung to get here. Look! [*He dribbles saliva into a red bandana.*] Blood!

Charinus
[*Unimpressed.*] All you need is a little honey and resin; that'll ease the pain.

Acanthio
Why not a little hot tar and hemlock? That'll ease all my pains plenty.

Charinus
Don't try to be funny. I'm just giving you advice for your own good.

Acanthio
What good's good when it gives you a bellyache?

Charinus
Acanthio, you must learn that there is no good without its compensating evil; no pleasure without the cost of pain.

Acanthio
Don't give me your fancy philosophy. Put it with your honey and resin.

Charinus
[*Deciding to try a new tack.*] Look, Acanthio, shake hands.

Acanthio
Why not?
[*They shake hands.*

Charinus
Now, be good to me, won't you?

Acanthio
Look, I'm panting, I'm soaking from rushing the news to him. I'm ruptured and he asks me to be good to him!

Charinus
Acanthio, I'll make you a free man in a month.

Acanthio
Oh, go on. Flattery, that's all. Flattery.

Charinus
Have I ever lied to you?

Acanthio
No, but what's the catch?

Charinus
There's no catch.

Acanthio
I mean, what do you want me to do?

Charinus
Just one little thing.

Acanthio
Well, what is it, what is it, what is it?

Charinus
Do you mind if we do it quietly?

Acanthio
What's the matter? Afraid of waking up the audience?

Charinus
No, no, no. I'd just like it better done quietly.

Acanthio
[*Yelling.*] What do you want me to do?

Charinus
[*Topping him.*] Tell me what the hell your news is!!!

Acanthio
[*Quieting down.*] Oh, it's terrible, terrible. You're undone.

Charinus
You told me that!

Acanthio
All right, all right! I'll shut up.

Charinus

[*With quiet desperation.*] Acanthio, you can do one of three things. You can tell me your news, you can get out of here, or you can be beaten clean out of your paenula.

Acanthio

See? Flattery again.

Charinus

Acanthio, you're a darling. You're just the nicest, kindest, most obedient, loyal, trustworthy, helpful, courteous, kind, cleanly, cheerful servant anybody ever had. Please tell me what's happened.

Acanthio

You think I'm pretty good, eh?

Charinus

I think you're wonderful.

Acanthio

I like you too, whan you're sincere.

Charinus

Tell me, has the ship sunk?

Acanthio

No, it's all right.

Charinus

And the merchandise?

Acanthio

Fine. Just fine.

Charinus

Then for the love of heaven what's wrong?

Acanthio

[*Who has become more interested in catching flies.*] Don't be so damned impatient! Keep quiet a minute! Holy mother of Mercury, if I was bringing you good news there'd be some reason for you to climb all over me like this. What do you want to hear bad news for?

Charinus

[*Strolling away.*] Oh . . . I'm just curious, that's all. Any time you care to tell me . . .

Acanthio
[*Not liking this attitude.*] Well, if you really want to know
—[*He runs after his master.*] You remember your father?

Charinus
My father? Of course I remember him. A fat man.

Acanthio
And you remember your mistress?

Charinus
Of course. [*He puts one and one together and his calm
is shattered.*] What about her?

Acanthio
Well, your father's seen your mistress.

Charinus
My father!

Acanthio
Saw your mistress.

Charinus
Oh dear gods. I am undone.

Acanthio
[*In control again.*] So I was telling you.

Charinus
How could he have seen her?

Acanthio
You know. With his eyes.

Charinus
I mean, how did it happen?

Acanthio
I guess he just happened to have them open.

Charinus
Where was she?

Acanthio
On the poop. He came wandering along the dock and
saw her, and came aboard. I think they had quite a talk.

Charinus
And where were you during this party? Why didn't you
keep her out of sight?

Acanthio

Listen, I had my own baggage to look after, didn't I?
[*Something in his voice and a movement of his hands
suggests that his baggage was well worth it, too.*] First
thing I knew he was up on the poop with her.

Charinus
[*Off again.*]

Oh Father, you've undone me. I'm undone.

Oh, tempests, storms and waterspouts passed
through

To gain the seeming shelter of home shores,

Only to find in waters thought so safe

Rocks, angry waves, reefs, hurricanes—

(My old man?) Dad!

What happened?

Acanthio

Right away he began asking who owned her.

Charinus

What did she tell him?

Acanthio

I was there by that time so I told him.

Charinus

What?

Acanthio

That you'd bought her to be a servant to your mother.

Charinus

Do you think he believed you?

Acanthio

I know damn well he did.

Charinus

How?

Acanthio

Because right away he started making passes.

Charinus

At *her?!*

Acanthio

Not at me!

Charinus
[*Clasping his hands in the obvious place.*]
>Oh then, my heart, dissolve, dissolve, dissolve . . .
>Like salt in water, so it melts away . . .
>I am undone.

Acanthio
[*Lying down somewhere.*] I thought probably you would be.

Charinus
How can I expect a man like my father to believe I'd buy that gorgeous, that exquisite, that ravishing creature to be a servant to a woman like my mother? How can I lie to my parent? It's wrong; it's shameful. Besides, he wouldn't believe me.

Acanthio
You don't have to tell him anything. I tell you he believed *me*.

Charinus
He knows she's my mistress.

Acanthio
He don't know nothing! He goggled at her the way he does all the new maids.

Charinus
[*With a slap on the brow.*] Alas, that—that suffices. Let me die—
[PERISTRATA *strolls out of Demipho's house, followed by her maid* LYCISSA, *who is fanning her or carrying her props, or something equally useful.* ACANTHIO *goes to accept* LYCISSA's *greetings, which are enthusiastic.*

Peristrata
[*Ignoring the antics of the lower classes.*] Charinus, darling boy, how divine that you're back. Was the trip too utterly—

Charinus
Mother, help me! I've brought you a present.

Peristrata
Oh, how nice. Lycissa, go help your young master carry—

Charinus

No, no, she can walk it. But—well there's a final installment to pay on her and—well, I'm broke.

Peristrata

She, you say? But son, another woman present—

Charinus

This one's personal, Mother. Just for you.

Peristrata

But what would I do with a thing like—

Charinus

For your own room. You know how busy Lycissa is— waiting on father and all.

Peristrata

[*Staring at* LYCISSA *coldly.*] I don't *know*, and although I have my suspicions I really don't think—

Charinus

Mother, if I don't make a payment in the flicker of a sundial she'll be snapped up.

Peristrata

Will you let me complete a sentence! I don't think I can afford a gift from you just at this time.

Charinus

You're not broke, too! Mother, you've got to accept this! Think, an import—from Assus—

Peristrata

'Rinus darling, you're so intense about this!

Charinus

[*Pulling back a little.*] Oh no, it's just that—

Peristrata

I know; you always like to have the house full of nice things, don't you. Well, come inside; we'll see if there's anything in the emergency fund under the penates.
[*She turns to go in.*

Charinus

Mother! One more thing: I don't want father to know about this until the deal's closed. You understand.

Peristrata

Dear boy, have you forgotten our routine? We never

tell your father anything.
[*She enters the house.*

Charinus
Acanthio, you'd better shake a leg back to the harbor
and keep an eye on our little gift. And remember: just
an eye.
[*He follows his mother.*

Lycissa
They'll find no emergency fund under this house's
penates; I can tell you that.

Acanthio
The old lady won't be able to buy our boy his candy?

Lycissa
Not after what I get out of the master every Moonday.

Acanthio
Jupiter, he *will* be undone.

Lycissa
Well, I've been saving your cut. Go on, now, shake a
leg.

Acanthio
One more shake and it'll drop off.
[*He trots back toward the port;* LYCISSA *goes into the
house. Almost immediately* DEMIPHO *comes in from the
right.* DEMIPHO *is not the type of man who should skip,
but he is skipping now and clapping his hands softly,
and singing to himself.*

Demipho
Tra-la-la. La, la-la. Tra-leeee, tra-la. [*When he becomes
articulate, he indulges in a sort of extemporaneous
recitative.*]

    Oh, it's happened, it's happened, it's happened
       to me.
    I'm in love at last; it's come to me at last.
    When I was young, before I was married, there
       were all those . . .
    And I thought that was love.
    And when I was married I thought that was love.
    Uh-*uh*.
    And then later there were all those . . .
    No.

But this is love, 'tis love, 'tis love; it's wonderful!

I must tell someone. I must tell someone—

[LYSIMACHUS *comes out of his house followed by a* SERVANT.

Lysimachus

Well, if the old goat's giving my wife so much trouble, we'll have to have its horns trimmed. Go back to the farm and do it yourself.

Demipho

Hail, Lysimachus, hail, all—

Lysimachus

[*Stopping him with a look and calling back his* SERVANT, *who has started off left.*] Wait a minute! Tell my wife not to expect me and to stay where she is. Tell her all my suits are coming up for judgment this week and I'm as busy as a one-armed lion-tamer.

Servant

Anything else?

Lysimachus

No, that ought to hold the precious old harpy.

[*The* SERVANT *departs to the left.*

Demipho

[*Trying again.*] Hail, Lysimachus, hail, all hail.

Lysimachus

[*Without enthusiasm.*] Greetings, Demipho. How are you?

Demipho

Wretched, friend, simply wretched.

Lysimachus

[*Not really caring.*] What's the matter?

Demipho

Lysimachus, do you see in me an old man?

Lysimachus

[*Looking him over.*] Not too old to be dead.

Demipho

Your eyes deceive you. My friend, I am a child.

Lysimachus

You've reached that stage, eh? Well, we all come to it if we live long enough.

Demipho
This is no second childhood, friend. I have found my youth. I am in my first flush.

Lysimachus
[*Deciding he's crazy.*] That's good.

Demipho
It is not, my friend. It's terrible.

Lysimachus
[*Starting to go in.*] All right then, it's not good.

Demipho
[*Clutching at him.*] Lysimachus, will you listen if I really tell you something?

Lysimachus
It would be an interesting change.

Demipho
I started to go to school today.

Lysimachus
[*Finding this no change.*] Good. Keep plugging and in twenty years you'll get a Ph.D.
[*He starts in again.*]

Demipho
What would I want with a Ph.D.? I'm learning life!

Lysimachus
[*Stopped dead at last.*] From a professor??

Demipho
From a dream. Lysimachus, I'm in love!

Lysimachus
[*Reeling a little.*] What? You in love?

Demipho
Isn't it dreadful?

Lysimachus
It's worse than that.

Demipho
I knew you'd sympathize. Ah, friend, it's terrible.

Lysimachus
It's revolting. [DEMIPHO *finds this hardly comforting.*] If you're in love so's my laundry bag.

Demipho

Lysimachus, if you please!

Lysimachus

Are you pulling my leg, Demipho?

Demipho

Cut my throat if I am. Cut me up in little pieces joint
by joint; I wouldn't even notice. [LYSIMACHUS *is edging
away;* DEMIPHO *goes on his knees to him.*] Oh Lysimachus, how can you know the torture of true, true love?

Lysimachus

I guess it's got you all right.

Demipho

And you think it's dreadful of me.

Lysimachus

[*Backing away from the kneeling figure.*] No, no. It's just
a mite embarrassing, that's all.

Demipho

[*Scrambling after him.*] Now you're censuring me.

Lysimachus

[*Trying again to go in.*] Never, friend, never. [DEMIPHO *is
blocking his way.*] Anything else?

Demipho

Lysimachus, please, as an old school chum, please don't
hold it against me.

Lysimachus

[*Abandoning his home.*] Look, I've got to hurry down to
the harbor. Business, you know. I'm very busy.

Demipho

The harbor! Business! Lysimachus, pause! [LYSIMACHUS,
*who has almost made the right exit, pauses but does not
turn. He seems to be waiting for a blow in the back
of the head.*] Lysimachus, would you spurn the cry of a
lover for aid?

Lysimachus

This is what I was afraid of.

Demipho
List, Lysimachus: do me one eentsy-teentsy favor. While you're at the harbor, will you pick up my sweetiekins?

Lysimachus
[*Turning disgustedly.*] Your sweetiekins! All this yearning has been from afar? You haven't even picked her up?

Demipho
No, no, you mistake me—

Lysimachus
You mistake *me*, asking a favor like that. I know when a man's picking up days are over—I think.

Demipho
Lysimachus, what I'm asking is right up your alley. The girl's about to be sold for overdue installments. Now here, take this—[*he seizes* LYSIMACHUS's *fist and fills it with solid gold minae*]—and pay up everything that's due on her.

Lysimachus
She's worth all this?

Demipho
Minae can't equal her worth. Her cost is your only concern.

Lysimachus
Demipho, I'm not sure I like your trusting me with a commission like this one. I mean, it's a kind of a slur on my attractions.

Demipho
[*Poking him in the ribs.*] I see your point, you modern Paris, but I have nowhere else to turn.

Lysimachus
Why aren't you making your own payments?

Demipho
My son intends to buy the beauty for my wife, and then where would I be? I must acquire her, you see, without my family knowing anything about it. Now, you can hide her—

Lysimachus
I get the whole picture, Demipho. What alley is she up?

Demipho

She's on a vessel. You can't miss her; she'll be mooning on the poop.

Lysimachus

Say no more. All I hope is that someday you can do as much for me.

[*He sets out for the harbor with what little alacrity he can muster.*

Demipho

[*Calling after his vanishing figure.*] Now stick to business, Lysimachus. Friendship, remember! [*Now he is alone.*] Ah, what beauteous qualities friendship holds. Only two things are sweeter: business and—[*he blows a kiss into the air*]—better business. [CHARINUS *drifts out of his house and* DEMIPHO *seeks a corner.*] But stay! Here comes my son. He must be restrained from the harbor—and that'll be quite a business.

Charinus

[*No happier than usual.*]

> Ne'er was a man more wretched than I—than *am* I,
> Who, finding dearest love, the which I buy
> In hopes of being happy on the sly,
> Inflamed, then soothed as with a rich supply
> Of unguents, find in my ointment such a fly
> As no man ever knew save only I.
> Oh, father-fly! By you I am undone.
> How can I tell that meddling dotard one
> About this purchase being not for his son
> But for his wife? And if the lie I shun
> He'll take away my darling and my fun.
> Death scores on love like this. I am undone.

Demipho

[*Muttering.*] Still undone? I thought by the time he got back from Assus he'd be pinned up.

Charinus

Ye gods, there's father! Then brighten, face; quicken, tongue! Help me now!

Demipho

[*Stepping forth.*] My son! Home at last, eh? Well, well, well. How are you, my boy?

Charinus
Oh fine, fine. I feel wonderful.

Demipho
You don't look it. You're the color of an old toga.

Charinus
Oh well . . . it was a rough crossing and—you know
how it is.

Demipho
Ah, yes. Not a sailor yet, eh? Why don't you just go
inside and—ah—lie down, or something.

Charinus
I haven't time. There's some business I have to do—
for a friend.

Demipho
Good, good, good. Well, be off about it. I shan't
interfere.

Charinus
That's very good of you. [*He starts to hurry off toward
the harbor.*] That was easy.

Demipho
[*Realizing that it's now or never.*] Here, here. Ah . . . wait
a minute. [CHARINUS *turns.*] Just a few questions about
your trip.

Charinus
I'm in pretty much of a hurry.

Demipho
Yes, yes, just a few little questions. Ah . . . how are
you?

Charinus
I'm all right.

Demipho
Good, fine. No sea sickness or anything?

Charinus
Not here in the street, no.

Demipho
Good, fine. Ah . . . by the way, what's this about your
bringing home a serving maid for your mother?

Cl.arinus
[*No longer thinking it's easy.*] Yes, I brought one.

Demipho
What's she like? Her looks, boy, how are they?

Charinus
Not bad.

Demipho
And her manners?

Charinus
[*Carried away again.*] Manners? Like Diana's. Like—
[*He cannot go on.*

Demipho
[*Carried away perhaps a little farther.*] Exactly what I thought when I saw her.

Charinus
[*Feigning surprise.*] Oh, you've seen her?

Demipho
Ah—yes. Just for a moment, on the poop. She won't do, my boy; I don't like it.

Charinus
Why not?

Demipho
Not the type; not the type at all. Your mother needs a girl who can chop wood, who can grind corn, who can sweep and scrub and weave and spin and stand a lashing. This girl hasn't the figure for it.

Charinus
That's what I like about her.

Demipho
No, no, she won't do at all. Don't give her to your mother. Don't even mention at home that you bought such a thing.

Charinus
[*Seeing a beautiful picture of his future.*] You can't mean it!

Demipho
But I do, I do. Why, she couldn't even attend your

mother in the street. A scandalous figure like that. Why, everybody would be winking and whistling and following her home and singing under our windows. Your mother would look like a madam out showing samples.

Charinus

Maybe you're right. Where should I put her?

Demipho

Leave everything to me. I'll get your mother a good useful girl with a build like a boxer and a face like the Minotaur. As to your girl—

Charinus

[*Quickly.*] I could take her back and say she doesn't suit.

Demipho

No, no, no, people in our position don't ask for refunds. I'd rather take the loss myself; it's more dignified. I'll find a buyer for you and see if we can't make a profit.

Charinus

[*The vision fading.*] Well . . . she's awfully dear, father.

Demipho

Yes, isn't she though! I mean I dare say, I dare say. However, it so happens that an old gentleman—a friend of mine—has asked me to pick him up just that type of thing.

Charinus

The fact is, a man I know is looking for a thing like this, too.

Demipho

My friend will pay twenty minae.

Charinus

Mine will pay twenty-seven.

Demipho

[*Quickly.*] Twenty-eight.

Charinus

[*Before he's through.*] Twenty-nine.

Demipho

Ahem. [*He makes an elaborate pretence of signaling to someone off left.* CHARINUS *takes the opportunity to peek into his own purse.*] My friend is right down the street there. He's signaling me to offer thirty.

Charinus
[*Not believing it.*] My friend will give thirty-five.

Demipho
[*Broods a minute and then indulges in some more fancy sign language.*] Forty.

Charinus
[*Weakly, clutching his purse.*] F-f-f-fifty.

Demipho
[*Deciding to turn to persuasion.*] Look, son, this friend of mine is half mad with love for beautiful girls. He'll pay anything. Heh heh heh. Silly old ape, isn't he?

Charinus
My friend is completely mad with love for this particular girl and he won't let anyone else have her.

Demipho
The old ape's richer than your friend, I imagine. He'll have her if it breaks him.

Charinus
He can't have her!

Demipho
Why not?

Charinus
[*Inspired.*] Because—because she isn't mine to sell. I only have a half interest in her.

Demipho
I think your partner will consent when he hears the terms.

Charinus
Well, he'd have to be consulted and he isn't here.

Demipho
If he doesn't mind selling her to your friend, why should he mind selling her to mine?

Charinus
He wants to be sure she has a good home.

Demipho
Pooh, pooh, pooh. She'll have an excellent home, very exclusive and private. I can promise you that.

Charinus
She wouldn't like that! She's too fond of company.

Demipho
My friend will keep her company just as often as—as he can get away.

Charinus
I can't sell her, I tell you!

Demipho
My boy, your ignorance of business ethics embarrasses me. You can't help selling her. If you turn down an offer, you're robbing your partner of his rightful profits, which is only ethical when he has no redress. Now I'm off to the ship to carry out the deal.

Charinus
I'd better come with you.

Demipho
Certainly not. Go about that business you spoke of.

Charinus
[*Resorting to fury.*] It would be done now if you didn't talk so much!

Demipho
You may blame the delay on a father's love. Just stay away from the harbor.
[*He ducks away to the right.*

Charinus
[*Tearing his hair.*] I'm lost! I am undone!
> Oh, Orpheus,
> Rent all to little pieces by the Furies,
> Surely the fragments of you were as chunks
> Compared to the tid-bits in which I am torn!
> Why do I live thus shredded? I do know
> An apothecary who will sell me poison
> To end this life from which my love is raped.
> I'll go to him directly. I'm undone.
[*He starts out left.*
[EUTYCHUS *comes blithely out of Lysimachus's house.*

Eutychus
Charinus! I'd stay away from that stuff if I were you.

Charinus
[*Stopping.*] Who calls me back?

Eutychus
You remember me.

Charinus
[*Turning.*] Eutychus! Oh, Eutychus, if you knew—

Eutychus
I know; you're undone.

Charinus
How do you know?

Eutychus
You're always undone. Besides, I was behind the door.

Charinus
What did you hear?

Eutychus
Just that your father wants to sell your mistress.

Charinus
Just that! You heard enough.

Eutychus
I must say I don't think it's much.

Charinus
How did you know she's my mistress?

Eutychus
It's always your mistresses that undo you.

Charinus
Eutychus, I'm going to die. What do you think is a good way?

Eutychus
Oh, stop talking drivel.

Charinus
But I must. I have to.

Eutychus
Nobody has to talk drivel.

Charinus
I mean die. What else is there for me to do?

Eutychus
Hasn't it occurred to you to make a fool of your pater?

Charinus
How, Eutychus, how?

Eutychus
Suppose I walk down to the harbor—

Charinus
Oh, fly, Eutychus, fly—

Eutychus
Sorry, I'm not up to that. But I could hike down there and get you the fair lady, for a sum.

Charinus
Oh, Eutychus! Pay her weight in gold!

Eutychus
Where do I get the gold?

Charinus
I'll pray to Achilles to lend me Hector's ransom.

Eutychus
That'll be helpful.

Charinus
Don't ask me to be helpful, Eutychus. I'm dazzled. I'm—

Eutychus
I know; you're undone. Well, I'll see what I can do with pop's credit. Only sooner or later the collector'll be around.

Charinus
Don't worry, Eutychus, just hurry!

Eutychus
Very well, I go. Fare you well.

Charinus
How can I fare me well until you bring me my darling?

Eutychus
Well, at least pull yourself together. Do yourself up.
[*He patters out right.*

Charinus

Be quick. I'll wait right here.

[SYRA *staggers in left, from the country, muttering to herself in a way she has.*

Syra

Corns, bunions, housemaid's knee; that's all I get out of life. Why, master Charinus, when did you get back? Oh, you look sick.

Charinus

Hello, Syra, I am sick. Love—anxiety—I can't talk about it. How is everything in your household? Is Lysimachus well? And your mistress?

Syra

My mistress and I have been poked away in the country for weeks and Lysimachus keeps telling her not to come home, and I'm sure he's up to some hanky-panky. The household's all broken up.

[*She loves this sort of thing.*

Charinus

[*Not a bit interested.*] It's always darkest just before the dawn.

Syra

Well, this dawn's going to come up like thunder, I'm warning you.

Charinus

How so?

Syra

The poor dear madam can't stand it any longer, that's how so. She's on her way back from the country to find out what her husband's been up to, that's how so.

Charinus

I just saw Eutychus; he didn't say anything was wrong.

Syra

Eutychus doesn't know what his father's like. I brought him up a nice boy.

Charinus

He ought to be back in a minute; I'm waiting for him to do an errand.

Syra

He won't know anything. I can't wait for him anyway; I was sent ahead to gather some laurel for the mistress to offer with a prayer for revenge against the master, and I've had to run all the way, and I couldn't find any laurel anywhere—everybody *knows* this isn't the season for laurel—and I told the mistress so, but the poor dear soul is so upset by her husband's goings-on that she wouldn't pay any attention to me. She never pays any attention to poor old me anyway; to her I'm just an old—are you paying attention?

Charinus

What? No, Syra, I can't keep my mind on anything. I've got to be alone.

[*He escapes into Demipho's house.*

Syra

Poor young fellow; that's what comes of going off on boats. Well, I'd better see if I can go any farther; if Lysimachus should come out and find me here it would spoil the poor mistress's surprise. I'll see if I can get to the market before I drop dead.

[*It seems unlikely, but she gets off right.*

[LYSIMACHUS *appears from the left, trailed by* PASICOMPSA. *Oh boy!*

Lysimachus

I don't mind making purchases for my neighbor; I don't even mind bringing them home with me, but when they tag along bellowing through the streets, I want to know why.

Pasicompsa

[*Who is crying prettily.*] Then please, sir, answer me one question?

Lysimachus

Dry your eyes and ask it, dear. Anything you want to know.

Pasicompsa

Why have you bought me?

Lysimachus

[*With a look that makes the answer obvious.*] Why . . . just the usual reasons.

Pasicompsa

I can't milk cows. I can't nurse children. They all hate me.

[*It makes her very unhappy.*

Lysimachus

There, there. Who cares what a lot of children and cows think?

Pasicompsa

I can't cook.

Lysimachus

Nobody expects you to cook. Don't you worry. All I want is a good girl.

Pasicompsa

You want a good girl?

Lysimachus

That's all.

Pasicompsa

Then you've been robbed.

Lysimachus

What? How? Who?

Pasicompsa

Don't blame me. Where I come from, nobody wanted a good girl.

Lysimachus

Oh. Well, of course there are different kinds of good girls. How are you with a distaff?

Pasicompsa

There isn't a girl my age anywhere that can handle a distaff better than I can.

Lysimachus

That's what I call a good girl.

Pasicompsa

I had a lovely teacher.

Lysimachus

Never mind, you needn't tell me. What did you say your name was?

Pasicompsa
Pasicompsa.

Lysimachus
Pasicompsa, how would you like, for your very own, a large, rare old antique?

Pasicompsa
[*Surveying him dubiously.*] Antique?

Lysimachus
Oh no, it's not me, not me. It's . . . heh heh heh.
[*He makes vague gestures toward Demipho's house.*

Pasicompsa
[*Deciding to try anything once.*] Well, I make it a practice never to refuse presents. I don't think it's ladylike.

Lysimachus
Pasicompsa, I have to tell you something. You don't belong to me.

Pasicompsa
[*Weeping again.*] Well, who do I belong to?

Lysimachus
My next-door neighbor. [*This time his gesture to Demipho's house is definite.*] He just asked me to put the deal through.

Pasicompsa
[*Looking the house over and drying her tears.*] Why that's my boyfriend's house!

Lysimachus
[*Startled.*] How do you know?

Pasicompsa
My boyfriend's a very vivid describer. We've been over every inch of his facade many, many times. Oh, this is too sweet.

Lysimachus
Well, good. And I'm sure he'll set you free. He's been off his head with love of you all morning.

Pasicompsa
Oho. He's been off his head with love of me for the past two years.

Lysimachus
    What? You mean he's been deceiving his wife for two
    years?

Pasicompsa
    [*Quite sure of herself.*] Oh, he isn't married. Two years
    ago he swore he loved only me and I swore I loved
    only him. Tee hee hee.
    [*Too ridiculous, really.*

Lysimachus
    He's been lying to you!

Pasicompsa
    Oh, he never would. He's the sweetest boy in the world.

Lysimachus
    Boy? Infant! His front teeth just fell out.

Pasicompsa
    His teeth?

Lysimachus
    Now don't you worry. He's been deceiving you, but I'll
    take care of you. Come inside. Don't be afraid, dear,
    my wife's in the country.
    [*He ushers her into his home.* DEMIPHO *comes in from the
    right, skipping again.*

Demipho
    [*Another experiment in recitative.*]
        Magnificent, superb, I've managed it.
        Beautiful, beautiful, I've gone to the dogs.
        This is the life: to be old and have a mistress
            and enjoy yourself.
        Wine, women and song and a song and a song,
            that's what becomes my age.
        When you're young you can't waste time on love;
        You have to make money.
        But when you reach my age, then it's hey for the
            life of ease, sing hey,
        And living is your business.
        After all, each year you keep alive is sheer velvet
            at my age.
    [LYSIMACHUS *comes out of his house. He has slipped into
    something pretty gaudy in the way of a toga. It is not
    becoming.*

Lysimachus
[*Talking sulkily over his shoulder.*] All right, all right. I'll bring him if I see him.

Demipho
Lysimachus, my pretty ape—

Lysimachus
What do you mean, ape?

Demipho
Never mind, never mind. Is the little lady in there?

Lysimachus
Now, Demipho, you're too old—

Demipho
I'm going in to see her.

Lysimachus
Now?

Demipho
Why not now?

Lysimachus
Well, no reason, only—can't you wait a little while?

Demipho
What for?

Lysimachus
Oh . . . just to think things over.

Demipho
No, old friend. Lovers like myself don't think. We act!

Lysimachus
That's the point. You old ruin, you shouldn't go in there.

Demipho
Ruin indeed. I'f I'm a ruin, you're an unexhumed fossil.

Lysimachus
Look, Demipho, if you go in there you'll be wanting to sit beside her and . . . put your arm around her, and . . . kiss her and all that—

Demipho
And why not, pray?

Lysimachus
Well, it wouldn't be nice.

Demipho
I, not nice?!

Lysimachus
[*Desperately.*] You need a bath! Your clothes are dirty!
Neither of your hairs is brushed! You'd make her queasy.

Demipho
You're right. I'll go and change all that. [*He starts
toward his house.*] You're quite clever after all, Lysimachus, to think of this. And by the way, *you* look
pretty well dressed up.

Lysimachus
[*Feebly choosing an inadequate adjective.*] I always try to
be neat.

Demipho
You aren't in love, by any chance?

Lysimachus
What, an old fossil like me? Heh heh heh.

Demipho
Hah hah hah.

Lysimachus
[*Backing up.*] Heh heh heh.
[PASICOMPSA *comes out of Lysimachus's house.*

Pasicompsa
Whoo-hoo, mister man.

Lysimachus
[*Turning with a wince.*] Yes, yes, what is it?

Pasicompsa
I looked at all your etchings. I think they're divine.

Lysimachus
That's nice. Now look at the statuary.

Pasicompsa
No. Come on in and play.

Demipho
Harrumph.

Pasicompsa
Oh my gods. I know *him.*

Lysimachus
And you think he's the sweetest boy in the world?

Pasicompsa
What, him? Why he's just an old man I met on a poop.

Demipho
Oh, how adorable of you to remember.

Lysimachus
My pet, this will be a shock to you: this is your master.

Pasicompsa
What, that old poop?

Lysimachus
Now you must be brave, child, and don't think it's my fault. I'm very, very fond of you, if I may say so.

Demipho
Lysimachus! It's not up to you to tell her to be brave.

Lysimachus
Well, somebody ought to.

Demipho
Lovely flower, couldn't you guess there on the poop, that I—that I—oh, to be near you—it's almost too much to bear!

Pasicompsa
That's my feeling. Mister, make him go away.

Demipho
Now, precious, I know I don't look my best, but wait 'til I change my clothes and visit my barber and—

Pasicompsa
Barber! All you need is a buffer.

Demipho
Sweetiekins, I'm going to hire the best cook in town to set us up to a wonderful big feast, and we'll make a night of it. Doesn't that appeal to you?

Pasicompsa
No. I'm going to bed early.

Demipho

[*Leering revoltingly.*] Well, I don't mind.

Pasicompsa

Oh, go away, you mangy werewolf.

Lysimachus

[*Coming between them.*] Now, why don't you go in and lie down. I'll come with you.

Demipho

Lysimachus! You'll come with me! What would your wife say.

Lysimachus

My wife's a lot farther away than yours.

Demipho

[*With a glance over his shoulder.*] I—I don't think we'd better loiter here in the street. Come, sweet, we'll go and buy all the expensive presents we can find. Does *that* appeal to you?

Pasicompsa

Well . . . a girl who's just come to town, like me, has to be careful who she's seen with. . . .

Demipho

You couldn't be seen with better people. Why, my whole family came over on the *Argo*.

Pasicompsa

Is that so? Did they bring the golden fleece?

Demipho

Don't you worry about that, my pretty. Come along, we'll find you some little gem of a house, where you can be queen of all you survey.

Pasicompsa

[*Won over.*] Do you mean it?

Demipho

From the depths of my being.

Pasicompsa

Well, come on. And remember, I can survey a lot of territory.

[*She is off so quickly that* DEMIPHO *finds himself trailing behind.*

Lysimachus

[*Going out a poor third.*] I've got just what you'd like!
I've been foreclosing mortgages all spring.

[*They have disappeared off left.* CHARINUS *comes out of Demipho's house.*

Charinus

Eutychus should be back by now, even with a broken
leg.

> Oh, thou who overlookest gods and men,
> Thou who I'm certain lookest over mistresses,
> Make Eutychus successful in his shopping!
> If father got there first, or bid the sky,
> And Eutychus has failed—oh, then I am—

Eutychus is coming, looking terrible! Alas, I am—

[EUTYCHUS *comes in from the right.*

Eutychus

[*Trying to be casual.*] Oh, hello, Charinus.

Charinus

Eutychus, tell me the verdict. Do I live or die?

Eutychus

Well, I don't know.

Charinus

You mean you've brought me immortality?

Eutychus

I haven't brought you a thing.

Charinus

The girl! Where's the girl?

Eutychus

Obviously not with me.

Charinus

Eutychus, you murderer!

Eutychus

Don't be silly. I didn't see her, let alone touch her.

Charinus

It's me you're murdering. You should hang for this.

Eutychus

Oh, you won't die. You may come a bit more undone,
but you won't die.

Charinus

Tell me all, Eutychus. Stab me and stab me. Who bought her?

Eutychus

I don't know. She'd already been knocked down and dragged out when I got there.

Charinus

You mean she's been kidnapped?

Eutychus

Auctioned, you fool!

Charinus

[*Wailing.*] To who?

Eutychus

Did you say "Boo hoo" or were you asking a question?

Charinus

To who? To who?

Eutychus

You mean "To whom."

Charinus

To whom, then. Stop quibbling. To whom?

Eutychus

I don't know. I told you that.

Charinus

You're a fine help, you are.

Eutychus

Just what would you like me to do?

Charinus

Die of grief with me.

Eutychus

Sorry, I'm busy all this week.

Charinus

Then leave me, leave me.

Eutychus

Charinus, the gods know it wasn't my fault.

Charinus

Maybe they do, but they haven't told me.

Eutychus
Well, you'll have to take my word for it.

Charinus
I wouldn't take your word for the weather! Didn't you promise to trick my father?

Eutychus
I promised to try.

Charinus
And what happens? You crawl down there on your hands and knees, apparently, and find her gone, and don't even find out who got her. She may be on her way to Persia by now, for all you know. Oh, I am—

Eutychus
If you say that again, I'll kick you clear over the Parthenon! As a matter of fact, the man who bought her lives right here in Athens.

Charinus
Oh, you did find that out, did you? I don't suppose you asked what he looks like?

Eutychus
I not only asked; I memorized it. Would you like to write it down?

Charinus
Just describe him slowly. I'll remember.

Eutychus
Well, he's bowlegged—[CHARINUS *ticks off the adjectives on his fingers*]—pot-bellied, gray-haired, big-mouthed, watery-eyed, splay-footed, round-shouldered, weak-kneed, skinny-armed, slack-jawed, snaggle-toothed, sloppily dressed, and freckled.

Charinus
[*Who has started on his toes.*] Is that all?

Eutychus
I think they said he had a floating kidney.

Charinus
This is all one person?

Eutychus
So they tell me.

Charinus

For all the good it does me, it could be a syndicate. I'm through.

Eutychus

That's a new way for you to put it.

Charinus

I'm through with Athens. Exile is all I have left.

Eutychus

Exile! I suppose if you go to Corinth you'll forget your girlfriend?

Charinus

I can't stand it here, I tell you.

Eutychus

So you go to Corinth to forget. Presto chango, you do forget. So you fall in love in Corinth. So you go to Lesbos to forget. Presto chango, you fall in love in Lesbos. So you go to Megira to forget. Presto chango, you're off to Crete. Eretria. Cyprus. All points west. And what's the result? We get another scroll on Understanding the Aegean.

Charinus

There'll be no result! Just one more look at my home and my poor old mother and then, farewell, Athens, I'll never see thee more!

[*He rushes into his home.*

Eutychus

Well strike me terra-cotta. If that's the way he feels about it, I'd better find him his girlfriend.

[*He goes off right. At this point* DORIPPA *returns from the country, very definitely.*

Dorippa

Busy, is he? Him and his suits. Trimming my goats indeed. Where's that Syra? [*She spots her off right and calls.* DORIPPA'S *principal asset is her lung power.*] Syra! Hurry, will you?

[SYRA *staggers in with a bundle of greens.*

Syra

How can I with my burden?

Dorippa

[*Pointing at the twigs.*] Those things? They wouldn't burden a flea.

Syra

They would if she was eighty-four years old.

Dorippa

[*Taking the bundle.*] Oh, stop whining and get in the house. Eighty-four indeed. You're no older than I am.

Syra

I never said I was.
[*She flounces into Lysimachus's house.*

Dorippa

[*Placing the twigs on the wayside shrine.*] Apollo, hear my daily prayer. Give my husband an excuse for living and my son as good a wife as I've been.
[*This is too much to ask. The shrine disintegrates with a discouraged whistle.* SYRA *comes back in a rush.*

Syra

Oh, madam! Poor, dear, wronged madam!

Dorippa

What are you howling about?

Syra

A woman's been in there!

Dorippa

A woman? What woman?

Syra

I don't know, but her fancy clothes are all over the place.

Dorippa

Fancy clothes, eh? So that's what he meant by suits.

Syra

She's a bad woman or I've never been one.

Dorippa

[*Banging into the house.*] Just let me see this important business of his!

Syra

[*Close behind her.*] They're not what we wore in *my* day.

[*She shuts the door just as* LYSIMACHUS *comes in from the left.*

Lysimachus

It's bad enough for the old barrel to be in love, but the way he's spending his money! What's he think he's doing, entertaining fifty visiting buyers? Well, I suppose I'll have to wait here for this cook he had me order.

[DORIPPA *backs out of her door and stands yelling into the house.*

Dorippa

A fine husband! When I think of the dowry I brought that old ghoul . . .

Lysimachus

Ye gods, she's back!

[*He starts to creep away.*

Dorippa

[*Turning around.*] Bringing a woman like that into my house. Unpacking her clothes all over my peristyle. [*She sees her vanishing spouse.*] Where are you off to? Got another suit somewhere?

Lysimachus

Why, hello, darling. I didn't know you were back.

Dorippa

I can see that.

Lysimachus

And how is everything in the country?

Dorippa

How is everything here?

Lysimachus

Fine, fine.

Dorippa

Busy, I take it.

Lysimachus

Oh, yes. You know how it is. Always something doing.

Dorippa

For instance.

Lysimachus
Oh . . . suits . . . shopping . . .

Dorippa
Whose woman's been in my house?

Lysimachus
What? Oh, surely you didn't see any woman in there, pet.

Dorippa
I saw her baggage.

Lysimachus
And you want to know whose baggage it is.

Dorippa
I want to know whose woman it is.

Lysimachus
Yes, I thought that's what you said.

Dorippa
Well?

Lysimachus
Why, she's just a—ah—

Dorippa
I know what she is.

Lysimachus
I mean, she's just—well . . .

Dorippa
Go on.

Lysimachus
Yes, of course. She's—she's just—

Dorippa
I'm waiting.

Lysimachus
Be patient, can't you? I'd tell you if you'd let me get a word in.

Dorippa
Get in all the words you need, only get going.

Lysimachus
[*Resorting hopefully to brazenness.*] There's no point in

taking that tone. I have nothing to hide. I'll be glad to tell you who she is.

Dorippa
Proceed.

Lysimachus
Certainly I'll tell you. It's nothing for me to be ashamed of.

Dorippa
[*Shrieking.*] Well, who is she???!!!

Lysimachus
[*Suddenly sighting an exit.*] I don't know!!!
[*Complacently, he thinks this settles everything.*

Dorippa
Then why did you let her in?

Lysimachus
Now you're jumping at conclusions. I never took any girl into the house.

Dorippa
I suppose all that lingerie's a present for me.

Lysimachus
Ah . . . no.

Dorippa
That's the first thing you've said that I believe.

Lysimachus
The fact is, a lady friend of a gentleman friend of mine just came to town and she left the clothes as a deposit on a house she's going to rent from me.

Dorippa
A deposit, eh? And why are they deposited all over my peristyle?

Lysimachus
Naturally, I had to examine them.

Dorippa
Did you have to chase her all over the house to get at them?

Lysimachus
No, no, no. Oh, my pet, surely you don't think that I—?

Dorippa
That you what?

Lysimachus
That there's anything between the girl and me. Why—
hah hah hah.

Dorippa
Oh, of course not. Ha hah hah. [*She becomes grim
again.*] What put that idea into your head?

Lysimachus
Why, I just thought that there was a little something in
your tone . . .

Dorippa
I never suggested it.

Lysimachus
No, of course not. You know I'd never, never—
[*A* COOK *comes in from the left, followed by several*
SCULLIONS *carrying a great many provisions.*

Cook
[*As he comes.*] Hurry, my sweet louts; we're cooking for
an old hawk in love, which means we must cook especially divinely because we'll get most of the food
ourselves. [*He has crossed to an appalled* LYSIMACHUS.]
Sir, I am here, at your service.

Lysimachus
[*Suddenly hard of hearing.*] Hey?

Cook
Of course you remember me.

Lysimachus
Never saw you before in my life.

Cook
Was I not ordered here to cook a dinner?

Lysimachus
Go away.

Cook
Away?

Lysimachus
Away!

Dorippa
What's this, another deposit?

Cook
Aha! This must be the little lady. Madam, you are indeed fortunate to have this gentleman for a lover—

Lysimachus
[*Pointing at his wife.*] Not that!

Cook
Your pardon. [*He proceeds, poking* LYSIMACHUS *in the ribs.*]—For a friend, ahahaha, since this gentleman has had the good taste to hire me to cook for you—

Lysimachus
Ye gods, will you get out?

Cook
—and I cook only for the mistresses of the most glamorous men in town—

Lysimachus
Shut up!

Cook
You're to be congratulated too, sir. She's a good, substantial dish.

Lysimachus
Nobody asked you.

Cook
No offense meant, I assure you. Come, lovely oafs, we shall go in. [*He gets to Lysimachus's door and turns.*] I suppose the viper's still in the country?

Dorippa
[*Stepping up.*] What viper?

Cook
Oh, you don't know the viper?

Dorippa
What viper???!

Cook
His wife.
[*He starts in again.*

Dorippa
Oh, so his wife's a viper, is she!

Cook
[*Airily.*] That's just *his* opinion.

Dorippa
And she's in the country, is she?

Lysimachus
No, she isn't!!!

Cook
Your mistake?

Lysimachus
[*Pointing.*] My wife!

Cook
Oh, indeed? Charmed, madam.

Lysimachus
Now will you stop annoying me?

Cook
You won't be requiring my services?

Lysimachus
No, no, a thousand times no!

Cook
Then I'll take my fee, if you please.

Lysimachus
Fee? What for?

Cook
Of course, you did send for me to cook a dinner for your mistress and promised to pay me well, but if you'd rather I brought suit—

Dorippa
Why not? He loves suits.

Lysimachus
Ask for it tomorrow.

Cook
I'm sorry to embarrass you before your wife, but if you don't choose to keep your bargain—

Lysimachus
Oh, get the hell out of here!

Cook
[*Turning dense.*] You mean you wish we'd go?

Lysimachus
That's what I mean.

Cook
Oh.
[*He stands there, nodding understandingly.*

Lysimachus
Well?

Cook
Well, just give us our pay and away we'll go.
[LYSIMACHUS *groans and gives up his purse.*] Thank you
kindly. Just put the foodstuffs down, boys; they're his.
Come, my little acolytes.
[*He floats away with his train of* SCULLIONS.

Dorippa
[*Striding to her door.*] Syra! [*She turns to her husband.*]
A viper, am I?

Lysimachus
Dear, I can explain evearything. He made it all up.
Some friends of mine—

Dorippa
You and your friends! Syra!
[*Since* SYRA *is already at the door, she gets this full in the
face.*

Syra
Oh, madam, my poor deaf eardrums. You've torn them
to shreds.

Dorippa
[*Pulling out some more stops.*] Can you hear this?

Syra
You don't need to do that!

Dorippa
See if you can keep this house respectable while I go
get my father. [SYRA *goes in again.*] We'll see what he

has to say about a husband who brings strange chemises into my house.

Lysimachus
Sweetheart, I can explain everything—

Dorippa
Call me a viper, you snake in the grass!
[*She kicks him in the stomach and heads for the country.*

Lysimachus
[*Picking himself up.*] Damn that Demipho, wait 'til I get hold of him. Fine treatment for a friend. [*He falls over the baskets of provisions and makes his way to his door.*] Syra, will you take in all this food? We're all going to be hungry along about Thursday. [*The house stands silent.*] Oh well, she cooks it or it stands here and marinates—it'll taste the same in the end.
[*He drags himself gloomily out right.* PASICOMPSA *just misses him as she stalks in from the left.*

Pasicompsa
[*In high dudgeon.*] That old fool! Who does he think he is, making passes at a girl right in the agora? And that house! The pigs can move right back in. [*She mounts Lysimachus's doorstep.*] I'm staying here.
[*And in she goes as if she owned the place. Immediately there is a dreadful scream from* SYRA, *who plunges forth as from a cannon.*

Syra
[*When the scream becomes articulate.*] Oh, madamadam-adamadam! [*She finds herself alone.*] Oh, I tried, I *tried* to keep a respectable house but what can poor little I do with the Youth of Today marching in in phalanxes? It's no fit place for me to live in, that's all, and when the poor dear madam finds out, it'll probably kill her and I'll have to look for another place. Dammit, I have the foulest luck!
[*She starts woefully out left.*
[EUTYCHUS *comes in from the right.*

Eutychus
It's no use; the girl's vanished.—[*He sees the old family servitor.*] Syra! [SYRA *turns a tear-stained face.*] Why what's the matter?

Syra
Haven't you seen the thing your father's brought home?

Eutychus
No, what?

Syra
A mistress, that's what.

Eutychus
What, *Father?*

Syra
That's who.

Eutychus
[*Finding this very amusing.*] Why, what would he do with a mistress?

Syra
[*Giggling a little herself.*] It's not for me to answer questions like that. I'm only your old nurse.

Eutychus
But, Father! I don't believe it.

Syra
Go in and see for yourself.

Eutychus
I've been under-estimating the old boy.
[*He hurries in.*

Syra
[*Calling after him.*] I never did. [*She turns to go again.*] Oh, where is the madam? She should be back by now even if she *is* twice my age.
[*She hobbles off left in search of the madam.*

[CHARINUS *comes out of Demipho's house, dressed for traveling.*

Charinus
Farewell, oh doorsill, lintel, handle, jamb!
Close all against me. Cut me off from home.
Oh, household gods, keep peace within this house
That never more is mine. I'm off. Undone.
Alone. No groom, nor even any horse
Do I require, for Cupid carries me.
Nor shall the wind nor hail nor rock nor sea

Nor heat nor rain nor hunger pangs nor pain
Stay me upon my self-appointed course:
To find my mistress or, if not, my death.
Home, Athens, friends, I hate thee; cast thee out.
[EUTYCHUS *prances out of his house.*

Eutychus
Oh home, oh Athens, oh friends, oh Pasicompsa, really
you're sweet. Wait 'til I tell Charinus—[*He finds*
CHARINUS.] Charinus! Wait!

Charinus
Who calls me back?

Eutychus
Must you always ask me that?

Charinus
You! You sheep with a wolf's whistle, out of my sight.

Eutychus
Now just a minute, Charinus. I have something to
tell you.

Charinus
As usual. But you've undone me for the last time, see?
[ACANTHIO *wanders aimlessly out of Demipho's house.*]
I'm getting out of here. Want to come, Acanthio?

Acanthio
If we don't have to walk.
[*What follows is accompaniment for an elaborate pan-
tomime performed by* CHARINUS *and especially* ACANTHIO
while EUTYCHUS *gets more and more bored and finally
sits down. A little music would not be inappropriate.*

Charinus
No, just step into the chariot here and we'll be off for
Cyprus.
[*There is no chariot, of course, but* CHARINUS *steps in any-
way and* ACANTHIO *hangs on behind.*

Eutychus
Charinus, have you gone insane?

Charinus
[*Driving like mad.*] We've got to find her, Acanthio,
wherever she is.

Eutychus
[*Trying to block the way.*] You're pretty warm right now!

Charinus
That Eutychus is certainly a liar.

Eutychus
So help me, it's true!

Charinus
[*To* ACANTHIO.] My pal!

Acanthio
Our pal.

Eutychus
[*Giving up.*] Undone from top to toe, obviously.
[*He retires to his doorstep.*]

Charinus
Whoa! Here we are. Cyprus.

Acanthio
[*Getting out and tying a weight on the horse.*] Don't look much different from the old country.

Eutychus
Every place is pretty much the same, don't you think, if your girl isn't there?

Charinus
[*Having inspected the neighborhood.*] She isn't here, Acanthio. Let's try Colchis.
[*He and* ACANTHIO *get back in the chariot.*]

Acanthio
Colchis it is.

Eutychus
If you have any luck, drop me a line.

Charinus
[*Covering the miles.*] I've got a friend in Colchis who may know where she is.

Acanthio
[*Spotting a signpost.*] Colchis, a hundred and seventy miles.

Charinus
Zacynthus, his name is.

Acanthio
[*Pointing at a rapidly passing village.*] Look: Colchis!
You'll miss it.

Charinus
Whoa!
[*He draws the horse up short.*]

Eutychus
[*Rising for one more attempt.*] Charinus, if you'll come
home to us, *I'll* tell you where your girl is.

Charinus
Well, if it isn't my old friend Zacynthus.
[*This startles* EUTYCHUS *considerably.*

Acanthio
Hi, Grandpa!

Charinus
[*Getting out of the chariot.*] Tell me, have you seen
Pasicompsa lately?

Eutychus
[*Deciding to play too.*] Yes! She went off to Athens with
some thickhead.

Charinus
You don't say . . .

Eutychus
It's the truth.

Charinus
Athens, eh . . .

Eutychus
Yes, Athens! In there!
[*He points to his father's house.*

Charinus
[*Trying not to be impressed.*] Where's there? I can't see
as far as Athens.

Eutychus
You see where I'm pointing? That's Lysimachus's house.
L, Y, S, imachus. [*Very slowly and distinctly.*] Lysi-
machus is a friend to your father. Your father has bought
Pasicompsa and is hiding her in the home of Lysi-
machus.

[*It sounds as if he were reading it out of a primer, and* CHARINUS *can't help feeling that it could happen.*

Charinus
Is this true?

Eutychus
As true as my name's Eutychus.

Acanthio
[*Not seeing how the situation is changing.*] You're cheating. Your name's Zacynthus.

Eutychus
[*Trying to please everybody.*] I meant Zacynthus.

Charinus
You're lying. Your name isn't Zacynthus.

Eutychus
I give up. [*He turns homeward.*] Stay in Colchis; it's a break for me.

Charinus
[*Seeing him about to go in.*] Eutychus, wait! Is she really in there?

Eutychus
Really and truly, honest to goodness, cross my heart, hope to die, so help me, indeed.

Charinus
Eutychus, if this is true, you can have anything you wish for.

Eutychus
It's true. I wish for fifty drachmae.
[*He holds out his hand, palm up.*

Charinus
[*Pressing it sincerely.*] Don't worry, the gods will fix you up.
[*He scampers toward Lysimachus's door.*

Acanthio
[*Who obviously has a one-track mind.*] Master, wait! You can't run all the way home from Colchis.

Charinus
[*Willing to prolong anticipation.*] Come on, Acanthio, we'll go by boat.

[*They climb aboard and row home,* EUTYCHUS *riding in the stern leading a chantey. Upon arrival, they cry, "Athens!" simultaneously and leap ashore.*]

Charinus
Well, Eutychus! How've you been? How are all your folks? Tell me everything; I've been away.

Eutychus
[*Insincerely*] It's done you a world of good.

Charinus
Aren't you going to ask me in?

Eutychus
For Venus' sake, come in!
[*He goes to his father's door.* CHARINUS *follows in such a rush that, when* EUTYCHUS *stops to open the door, they collide.*]

Eutychus
[*Turning sharply.*] Must you do that?!

Charinus
Well, let me in!
[*He pushes* EUTYCHUS *ahead of him into the house.*]

Acanthio
Boy, what a trip.
[*He totters in after the boys, worn out.*]

[DEMIPHO *and* LYSIMACHUS *come down the street.* DEMIPHO *has dressed himself up to outshine Lysimachus, but it doesn't make him any prettier.*]

Lysimachus
[*As* DEMIPHO *heads for that alluring door.*] I tell you you *can't* go in there! My wife will be back any minute.

Demipho
Tut tut. Don't worry about a thing. We simply have to coax the little one out and take her around to your other house, and then it's every man for himself.

Lysimachus
If Dorippa catches me, it'll be women and children first.

Demipho
My dear friend, I'll fix it with Dorippa as easily as eating a banana. I have a way with wives.

Lysimachus

[*Unconvinced.*] Then you go in first.

[DEMIPHO *does so and* LYSIMACHUS *follows him, quaking. Just too late to catch her husband,* PERISTRATA *bursts from Demipho's house, followed by* LYCISSA.

Peristrata

Oh, but no, Lycissa, this is too, too outrageous.

Lycissa

I'm just repeating what a sailor told me.

Peristrata

Oh, my poor dear son. Every time he falls in love, his father flies to pieces. It was bad enough sending him off to Assus just because of that little incident on his birthday. But to take away the girl he brings back after two dreadful years of banishment—well, really!

Lycissa

They been saying in the pantry that Charinus is mumbling about exile.

Peristrata

Oh, no no no! I could not bear to lose my son; it would be too much. The girl must be found, Lycissa. She must be given back to him. Where would my husband keep her?

Lycissa

He might hide her next door.

Peristrata

With Lysimachus? Quite likely. I'll go see Dorippa.

Lycissa

[*Pertly.*] Why bother? Here she comes.

[DORIPPA *storms in from the right, trailed miserably by* SYRA.

Dorippa

A fine time for the old man to go to the country. Blast the country! Whose idea *was* the country in the first place? [SYRA *is unable to answer this.*] Well, I'll just go in and throw the hussy out with my own hands.

[*She starts in.*

Peristrata
Dorippa darling!

Dorippa
What the hell do *you* want?

Peristrata
Well, really, darling . . .

Dorippa
Oh, Peristrata, I didn't see who it was. So sorry, dear, but I'm not myself today.

Peristrata
Whatever is the matter?

Dorippa
That decayed husband of mine—[*She wails.*] Oh, Peristrata, it's so nice to have an old friend by you at a time like this.
[*She throws herself on Peristrata.*

Peristrata
[*Just bearing it.*] There, there, dear.

Dorippa
Someone who grew up with me. You've always been like a sister to me, Peristrata.

Peristrata
Thank you, dear.

Dorippa
An elder sister.

Peristrata
[*Setting her chum back on her feet.*] Never mind now. Tell me what's happened.

Dorippa
How would you feel if Demipho brought a mistress right into your house?

Peristrata
Oh, pooh. I hope I'm above resenting a little thing like that.

Dorippa
Above it! Well, that's what Lysimachus has done, and *I'm* not above it.

Peristrata
Darling, if you knew what Demipho's done, you'd be comforting me.

Dorippa
What's he done that's worse than flaunting a brazen hussy right in my atrium?

Peristrata
He's ruined my son's life.

Dorippa
Oh pooh, yourself. Lysimachus did that to Eutychus before he was born. But imagine, at his age—

Peristrata
Dorippa, at his age mistresses can mean no more than milk toast. But what Demipho's done to that poor dear boy—oh, it's too unbearably dreadful.

Dorippa
That's what you say, but *my* husband—

Peristrata
[*Bound to win.*] Think of it: here is my son madly in love with this bewitching little slave girl he's brought home from Assus, and my brute of a husband has taken her and put her up for sale.

[ACANTHIO *comes hurrying out of Lysimachus's house, bursting with the latest dirt from the servants' quarters, which he passes on to* LYCISSA *and* SYRA.

Dorippa
Put her up for sale, says who? You believe a story like that?

Peristrata
Darling, Demipho's not interested in the girl. I know him, dear; those days are over.

Dorippa
I'll bet he's younger than my husband.

Peristrata
Well, sweetheart, who isn't? But he didn't even bring her home; he left her with a friend. That's how interested he is.

Dorippa
[*Smelling a rat.*] He left her with a friend?

Peristrata
I thought it might be Lysimachus.

Lycissa
[*In a poorly suppressed rage.*] Beg pardon, madam!

Peristrata
What is it?

Lycissa
Acanthio says the master isn't selling the girl. He's bought her!

Peristrata
Bought her! For what?

Lycissa
[*Bursting into tears.*] Oh, madam, I saw this coming on. He told me he was going to redecorate his room.

Peristrata
Redecorate indeed! I'll decorate him!
[*She starts for home.* SYRA *breaks out in her finest wail.*

Syra
Oh, my poor dear two madams! [PERISTRATA *and* DORIPPA *turn to stare.*] The hanky-panky's in there! [*She points to Lysimachus's house.*] *Two* households all broken up!

Peristrata
[*With icy dignity.*] Poor, dear Syra, the breakage starts now!
[*She lunges into Lysimachus's house to start it.*

Dorippa
Syra, is my—[*She strangles and points to her door.* SYRA *nods, sobbing.* DORIPPA *pushes her aside and confronts* LYCISSA.] Lycissa, is my—[*She still cannot get the word out, but* LYCISSA *gives one succinct nod and* DORIPPA *thrusts her past her to* ACANTHIO.] Is my—[*Knowing exactly what she means,* ACANTHIO *nods vigorously.* DORIPPA *grimly rolls up her sleeves.*] My, my, MY!!!
[*She is in her house in no time, leaving the echo of a roar.*

Acanthio
[*Hoarsely.*] My my my . . .

Lycissa
Well, that'll fix that one. I guess I can have my old

job back if I want it. [*A terrific racket shakes
Lysimachus's house.*] I guess I don't want it!

[*She grabs* ACANTHIO's *hand and they run off together
with* SYRA *trailing after them, cackling happily at last.*
DEMIPHO *crashes out of Lysimachus's house, followed
by* PERISTRATA, *wielding one of Lysimachus's new
sausages.*

Demipho

[*Halfway between a scream and a whimper.*] My dear, I
hadn't the faintest notion Charinus cared for her. I
understood she was a mere maid.

Peristrata

Really! Just your type!

[LYSIMACHUS *is chased out of the house by* DORIPPA, *who
is batting his head rhythmically with a saucepan.*

Demipho

Lysimachus! Tell my wife—

[*The* COOK *and his* SCULLIONS *come in, unconcernedly pick
their way through the melee, pick up the baskets of
food, and go, the* COOK *depriving* PERISTRATA *of her
sausage on his way out.*

Lysimachus

You tell mine! You have a way with wives!

[CHARINUS *and* PASICOMPSA, *arm in arm, are ushered out of
the house by* EUTYCHUS.

Dorippa

[*Driving* LYSIMACHUS *out left.*] We're not stopping 'til we
get to the country.

[*They are gone.*

Demipho

[*Waving to* CHARINUS *from his doorway.*] Good luck, my
boy! Morituri salutamus!

[*He is kicked through the door by* PERISTRATA, *who follows
him in. The door shuts behind them.*

Pasicompsa

[*Casting a backward glance at* EUTYCHUS] Come on to my
house.

[CHARINUS *thinks she is talking to him; he happily leads
her away.* EUTYCHUS *starts to follow, but stops, snaps
his fingers carelessly, and surveys the empty street.*

Eutychus

That'll teach the old boys not to cut in on the younger generation. It's a pretty sight when they begin shedding their tunics and their teeth at the same time. If you agree with me, you know what you can do. [*He pats his hands together.*] If you don't—

[*He makes a flip gesture at you and goes home.*

Terence

PHORMIO

Translated by Lionel Casson

Characters   *Davus, a servant (slave)*

Geta, servant (slave) of Demipho

Antipho, a young man about town, son of Demipho, in love with Phanium

Phaedria, a young man about town, son of Chremes and cousin of Antipho

Demipho, an elderly, well-to-do Athenian

Phormio, a young, penniless adventurer who lives by his wits, friend of Antipho and Phaedria

Hegio

Cratinus   } *elderly Athenians, advisers to Demipho*

Crito

Dorio, a slave dealer

Chremes, Demipho's brother, an elderly Athenian married to a rich wife

Sophrona, Phanium's old nurse

Nausistrata, Chremes' wife

[Phanium, a beautiful young girl living in straitened circumstances.]

SCENE. *A street in Athens. Three houses front on it:* DORIO'S, DEMIPHO'S, *and* CHREMES'. *The exit on stage left leads downtown, that on stage right to the waterfront.*

Prologue

[*The* PROLOGUE *addresses the audience. Unlike Menander and Plautus, who use the prologue to introduce the play itself, Terence utilizes the opportunity to reply to his critics, in particular an older contemporary named Lucius Lanuvinus, whom for some reason he avoids naming directly. The play proper he introduces through the dialogue of the opening scene.*]

Prologue

That Senior Member of the playwrights' circle hasn't suc-
ceeded in driving your author from the field and forcing
him to retire, so now he's resorting to abuse to keep
him from writing. He goes around saying that, in
everything your author has turned out so far, the
dialogue has been flat and the writing undistinguished.
[*Adopting a sarcastic tone as he proceeds to cite one of
the Senior Member's signally unsuccessful touches of
inspiration.*] Granted, your author's pen has never
produced a scene in which a love-mad hero watches a
doe fleeing before the hounds and does nothing when
it breaks into tears and begs him for help. Well, if the
Senior Member only realized that, back in the days
when his last play was a hit, this was more because of
what the leading man did for it than the author, he'd
be a lot less inclined to throw brickbats than he is.

Some of you may be thinking, "Oh, well, if the
Senior Member hadn't cast the first stone, this young
fellow, without anyone to trade insults with, wouldn't
have anything to say in his prologues." The answer to
that is that, although the way to success is open to
anyone who makes a career of writing drama, the old
fellow was doing all he could to throw your author out
of the profession and into starvation, and your author
just wanted to answer him back, not hit him back. If he
were interested in trading compliments, he'd hear

plenty of nice things about himself; just let him realize he's getting back simply what he's been handing out. Well, I'm done with talking about him—although he's not done with doing harm.

Now, what I really have to tell you is this—and please listen. I have a new play for you. In Greek it's called *He Who Goes to Court,* but your author has titled his Latin version PHORMIO, since a scrounger by that name has the leading role and triggers most of the action— as you'll see if you'll do the author the favor of hearing it through. Please be good enough to listen in silence, and pay attention. I don't want to have happen what happened once before when, because of a disturbance, our company had to leave the stage—a stage we've returned to only because of the efforts of our leading man and the aid of your generosity and good will.

Act One

[DAVUS, *a fellow slave of* GETA, *enters stage left, wearing the traditional red wig of slaves in Roman comedy and carrying a small purse. Actually,* DAVUS *is introduced simply to facilitate the exposition of the play; once the scene is over, he leaves the stage for good.*

Davus

[*To the audience.*] My best friend Geta came to me yesterday. He's had a little money out on loan to me for the longest while and there's still a bit of a balance outstanding, a few cents. He asked me to pay it up in full. Well, I'm paying it up in full and [*jingling the purse*] here's the money. I hear that his master's son got married; I guess he's collecting his pennies to buy the bride a gift. It's a crime the way the have-nots always have to be handing out to the haves. The poor devil scraped together a little nest egg, penny by penny, from his monthly allowance by denying himself everything his heart ever desired—and she's going to take it

from him in one swoop without a thought for all the
trouble it took him to get it. And, when she has a
baby, Geta will be nicked for another gift, and then
another on the child's birthday, and another when it
gets confirmed. The mother's going to carry off everything he has; the child will be a steady excuse for gift
collecting. [*The door of Demipho's house opens, and*
GETA *emerges.*] Ah, here's Geta, I think.

[GETA *is Demipho's personal slave, a young, able, resource-*
ful chap, whom DEMIPHO *has enough confidence in to*
leave in charge of the household when he goes away on
business trips. GETA *is a tough-minded character who*
generally has no difficulty in facing up to emergencies;
at this moment, however, his whole demeanor reveals
that something is very much on his mind.

Geta

[*Talking through the open door to a servant inside.*] If
some redhead comes looking for me—

Davus

[*Interrupting.*] Wait, he's right here.

Geta

[*Turning and seeing* DAVUS.] Oh, Davus. I've been trying
to find you.

Davus

[*Handing him the purse.*] Here it is. No counterfeits, and
the exact amount I owed.

Geta

[*Taking it.*] Thanks very much. Much obliged to you for
not forgetting about this.

Davus

The way people are these days, it's got to the point
where you've got to make a point of being grateful
when someone pays you back what he owes you.
[*Noticing that* GETA *is too preoccupied to acknowledge*
this sally.] What are you so unhappy about?

Geta

[*Startled out of his preoccupation by the question.*] I? You
have no idea of the fix I'm in, and the worries I've got.

Davus

What's the matter?

Geta

[*Lowering his voice and looking around guardedly*.] I'll tell you—provided you know how to keep a secret.

Davus

Use your head, will you? A man you found could be trusted with your money and you're afraid to trust him with a few words? There's no profit in absconding with words, you know.

Geta

All right then, listen.

Davus

I'm all ears.

Geta

Do you know Chremes, my master's older brother?

Davus

Of course.

Geta

And Phaedria his son?

Davus

As well as I know you.

Geta

Well, it so happened that both the old men went abroad at the same time, Chremes to Lemnos, and my master to Turkey. An old business associate got him out there by flooding him with letters promising him everything but the royal mint.

Davus

And he was interested? A man with all his money?

Geta

Never mind. That's the kind he is.

Davus

[*Bitterly*.] *I* should have been a millionaire!

Geta

When the two old men went away, they left me as a

sort of guardian for their sons.

Davus
That's a tough assignment they handed you, Geta.

Geta
Don't I know it! I've been through the mill. When I think it over, I'm convinced I got the job because my guardian angel was sore at me. In the beginning I tried to make the boys toe the line. All I need tell you is that, so long as I did my duty by the old man, I kept losing the skin off my back.

Davus
I figured as much. There's no sense in fighting when you can't win.

Geta
So I began to yes them and do whatever they wanted.

Davus
You learned to play the game.

Geta
At first I had no trouble with Antipho—that's my master's boy—but right off that Phaedria picked up some chorus girl and fell madly in love with her. She belonged to the world's slimiest slave dealer, and we didn't have a dime to pay for her; the old men had seen to that. The only thing the poor fellow could do was feast his eyes, tag along after her, and escort her back and forth when she went for her dancing lessons. Antipho and I had nothing else to do so we used to go along to help him out. There was a barbershop right opposite the dancing school, and we used to hang out there until she was ready to go home. One day while we're sitting around in there, in comes a young fellow, all upset. We're curious. We ask him what's the matter. "Until this minute," says he, "I had no idea what a miserable burden poverty could really be. Just now, right near here, I passed a poor young girl mourning her mother's death. There she stood before the corpse, and there wasn't a friendly face, not a neighbor or relative, to stand by her during the funeral, except for one old woman. It was pitiful. And the girl was a beauty." All I need tell you is that it affected all of us. Right off Antipho said, "What do you say we pay her a

visit?" Then someone else said, "Good idea. Let's go. Would you show us the way?" We leave, we walk over there, we see her. She *was* beautiful. And, what's more, there wasn't a thing to help out her natural good looks: there she was, hair hanging down, unkempt, crying, feet bare, clothes dirty—all the things that would have buried any beauty except that rare kind that comes from within. Phaedria, of course, was in love with his chorus girl, so he could only say, "Not bad," but Antipho—

Davus

[*Interrupting.*] I know: he fell in love at first sight.

Geta

Ah, but how! Listen to what happened. The very next day he goes up to the old woman. He begs her to arrange a rendezvous for him. But she refuses: tells him he's not behaving as he should; that this is a respectable girl, of respectable parents, an Athenian citizen as a matter of fact; that if he's willing to marry her he's perfectly free to do so legally but, as far as anything else goes, the answer is No. Well, Antipho didn't know what to do: he wanted to marry her, but he was afraid to while his father was away.

Davus

Why? Wouldn't his father have agreed to the match when he got back?

Geta

That man let his son marry some nobody without a dowry? Not a chance!

Davus

What finally happened?

Geta

What happened? There's a certain scrounger, Phormio's his name, and when it comes to sheer, unmitigated gall, this fellow—[*overwhelmed by the mere thought of* PHORMIO] god, do I wish he was in hell right now!

Davus

What did he do?

Geta

I'll tell you what he did. He thought up a scheme.

"There's a law," he tells Antipho, "that female orphans have to marry their next of kin. The same law states that the next of kin must assume the obligation of such a marriage. Now, I'll pretend I used to be a friend of your girl's father. Then I'll claim that you're the next of kin and sue you to make you marry her. We'll go to court. I'll work up all the details: who her father was, who her mother was, how she's related to you—whatever will make a good story and hold water. And, since your not going to deny any of it, I can't lose. Your father comes back, he sues me—so what? By that time we've got the girl."

Davus

He's got so much nerve it's funny.

Geta

He talks the boy into it, they set everything up, go to court, the court orders the marriage—and he marries her.

Davus

What's that you say?

Geta

You heard me.

Davus

My god, Geta, what's going to happen to *you?*

Geta

God knows. [*Theatrically.*] One thing I do know: whatever Fate may bring, I'll bear the blow bravely.

Davus

That's what I like to hear. That's acting like a man!

Geta

[*Resolutely, chin up.*] There's only one person I can count on—myself.

Davus

Bravo!

Geta

I suppose I could get someone to plead my case for me, someone who'll say, "Demipho, please, let him off just this once. But if he tries anything like it hereafter, I won't lift a finger for him." Which is the same as saying, "As soon as I leave, you can slit his throat."

Davus

How about the boy who walks the girls home from school, the one who's after that chorus girl? How's he doing?

Geta

[*With a* comme ci comme ça *gesture of the hand.*] Not getting very far.

Davus

Doesn't have much spot cash to offer for her, eh?

Geta

Spot cash? All he's got to offer is spot hope.

Davus

Has his father come back yet?

Geta

Not yet.

Davus

What about Demipho? When do you expect him?

Geta

I'm not sure. But I just heard that a letter from him is down at the dock. I'm going now to pick it up.

Davus

Well, I've got to be getting along now; anything I can do for you?

Geta

Take care of yourself. Goodbye. [DAVUS *exits, stage left.* GETA *goes to the door of Demipho's house, opens it, and calls inside.*] Boy! Hey, someone came out here! [*A* SERVANT *appears, and* GETA *hands him the purse he had gotten from* DAVUS.] Here, give this to my wife.
[*Exits, stage right.*

Act Two

[*The door of Chremes' house opens, and the two cousins,* ANTIPHO *and* PHAEDRIA, *come out.*

Both are good-looking young fellows in their late teens. Their clothes and bearing make immediately apparent that they come from well-to-do families, that they have at their ready disposal whatever money can provide. But it is equally apparent that the things money cannot provide are unequally divided between them. From ANTIPHO'S *way of talking, his guardedness, studied unobtrusiveness, and shifting glance, one can tell he's a worrier and a weakling; in* PHAEDRIA'S *jaunty air, open face, and direct manner, one can read the direct opposite—a bold, devil-may-care youngster, afraid of nobody and nothing.*

As they come through the door ANTIPHO'S *nervous wringing of his hands and similar symptoms reveal a state of jitters even more highly charged than that which is usual with him.*

Antipho

Things have gotten to the point, Phaedria, where every time I think of his coming home, I start getting scared of him—my own father, the very person who cares the most for me! [*Lapses into gloomy silence for a moment.*] And if I just hadn't acted so thoughtlessly, I could be looking forward to seeing him again as a son should.

Phaedria

What are you talking about?

Antipho

What a question! You know as well as I do what we had the nerve to do! If only Phormio hadn't gotten the bright idea to talk me into it! If only he hadn't pushed me, when I was so vulnerable, right into what started all my troubles! I wouldn't have gotten the girl. Oh, sure, I'd have had a few bad days at the time, but not this daily gnawing at my heart—

Phaedria

[*Interrupting impatiently.*] I know, I know.

Antipho

[*Disregarding the interruption.*]—while I'm waiting around for him to come back and take her away from me.

Phaedria

Other people complain because they can't find love, and you're unhappy because you've got too much! [*Vehemently.*] You're swimming in love, Antipho! My god, your life is what every man searches and hopes for. So help me, if I had the chance to enjoy my love affair even only as long as you have so far, I'm ready right now to offer my life as part of the deal. [*Bitterly.*] Figure out for yourself which of us is better off: here you are with everything and here I am with nothing. To say nothing of the fact that you've got just what you wanted, not a slave who has to be bought, but a respectable girl, a wife, someone you're not ashamed to be seen with. You'd be in heaven if it weren't for just one thing: you don't have the sense to be satisfied with what you've got. If you had to deal with that pimp that I have to, you'd see what I mean. Well, that's the way most of us are, never happy with what we have.

Antipho

It's the other way around, Phaedria; right now I think you're the one who's lucky. You're still in a position to make up your mind all over again about what you want to do—keep the girl, love her, or let her go. A poor devil like me is on the spot: I can't let her go and I'm not going to be able to keep her. [*Hears something and and looks toward the wings.*] What's that? Is that Geta running this way? [*Peering hard.*] It's Geta, all right. Oh, lord, he's got something to tell me and I'm scared to hear it.

[GETA *bursts in, stage right—he has run all the way from the waterfront—and stops abruptly at the side of the stage, away from the two boys.*

Geta

[*To himself, not noticing* ANTIPHO *and* PHAEDRIA.] What a load of trouble I've got on my neck now! And so sudden! And me not ready for any of it! Geta, if you don't find a way out of this fast, your name is mud. [*Thinks a moment, then desperately*.] I can't think of a way to bypass it or, once I'm in it, to get out of it. And we can't keep things under cover any longer—not what we had the nerve to do!

Antipho

[*Not able to hear* GETA *but alarmed at his manner, to* PHAEDRIA.] What in the world's he so upset about?

Geta

[*To himself.*] Demipho's back. That means I've got just about sixty seconds flat to come up with an idea.

Antipho

[*Still more alarmed, to* PHAEDRIA.] What's the matter with him?

Geta

[*To himself.*] When he hears what's happened he's going to hit the ceiling, and what in the world can I do to stop it? Explain things? He'll burn up. Keep my mouth shut? That'll just needle him. Try to clear myself? Sheer waste of energy. It's bad, it's real bad. It's not only myself I'm scared about; there's Antipho too. That's what's driving me out of my mind: poor devil, I'm worried sick about him. He's the one who's holding me back now. If it weren't for him, I could look after myself. If the old man took it out on me, I'd get even with him—I'd pick up some of the valuables around here and pack off, on the double.

Antipho

[*Catching* GETA'S *last words and now puzzled as well as alarmed, to* PHAEDRIA.] What's this talk about robbing and running?

Geta

[*To himself.*] But where's Antipho, anyway? I don't even know where to look for him.

Phaedria

[*Finally catching what* GETA *said, to* ANTIPHO.] He's talking about you.

Antipho
[*His jitters getting steadily worse.*] From that messenger
   [*gesturing toward* GETA] I expect nothing but trouble,
   lots of it.
[*Turns to run.*

Phaedria
[*Grabbing him.*] Are you out of your mind?

Geta
[*Turning and making for Demipho's door.*] I'll try him at
   the house; he's generally there.

Phaedria
[*To* ANTIPHO.] Let's call him over here.

Antipho
[*Raising his voice, to* GETA.] Stay where you are!

Geta
[*Stopping in his tracks and without turning around.*] Wow!
   You sound as if you mean it, whoever you are.

Antipho
   Geta!

Geta
[*Turning and finally seeing* ANTIPHO.] Just the man I'm
   looking for!

Antipho
   Now, please say what you have to say and cut it short, if
   you can.

Geta
   Right.

Antipho
[*Nervously.*] Come on, out with it!

Geta
   Just now, down at the dock—

Antipho
[*Going white and sagging at the knees.*] You saw him!

Geta
   You guessed it.

Antipho
   I'm sunk!

Phaedria
[*Not quite following the cryptic interchange.*] What?

Antipho
[*To himself.*] What'll I do?

Phaedria
[*To* GETA.] What's this you say?

Geta
[*To* PHAEDRIA.] I just saw his father. Your uncle.

Antipho
[*Holding his head in his hands, moaning.*] I'm lost. This is the end. There's no way out. And so sudden! [*Drawing himself up like a tragic figure and looking toward the house, where his wife is.*] Phanium! If my fate has reached the point where I have to give you up—life for me won't be worth living!

Geta
[*Sharply.*] And since that's the situation, Antipho, now you've really got to be on your toes. [*Comes up to him and claps him on the shoulder.*] Faint heart ne'er won fair lady.

Antipho
[*Wildly.*] I can't think straight!

Geta
I tell you, Antipho, now's the time you need your straightest thinking. If your father gets the idea you're scared, he's going to think you're guilty of something.

Phaedria
[*To* ANTIPHO.] That's the truth.

Antipho
[*Desperately.*] I can't change what I am!

Geta
What would you do if you had to face up to something even harder?

Antipho
[*Miserably.*] Something harder? I can't even do anything about this!

Geta

[*Finally giving up the effort to inject some spirit into him.*]
We're getting nowhere, Phaedria. Let's go. What's the
use of wasting our energy on him? I'm getting out of
here.

Phaedria
Me too.

Antipho
[*In a funk.*] No! Please! Look—what if I pretend? [*Making
a pathetic attempt to assume a resolute expression.*]
How's this?

Geta
[*Turning on his heel in disgust.*] Don't talk nonsense.

Antipho
[*Making another attempt.*] Here, look at my face. How
about this?

Geta
[*Taking a look and wincing.*] God, no!

Antipho
[*Trying still another expression.*] What about this one?

Geta
[*Takes a quick look, turns away, then does a double-take
in surprise.*] You've almost got it!

Antipho
[*Trying an improvement.*] How's this?

Geta
That'll do—keep it just that way. Now, you've got to
give him back word for word, tit for tat. He's going to
work himself into a rage, but just don't let him shout
you down.

Antipho
[*Busy thinking over what he's let himself in for and only
half listening.*] Uh huh.

Geta
Remember: you didn't want to get into this, you were
forced into it.

Phaedria
The law was against you. The court made you do it.

Geta

Got it? [*Hearing something, looks off into the wings.*] Who's that old man there at the end of the street? [*Peering hard.*] It's Demipho!

Antipho

[*In a choking voice, panic-stricken.*] I can't go through with it!
[*Turns and makes a dash for the house.*

Geta

Hey! Antipho! What are you doing? Where are you going? Come on back, I tell you!

Antipho

[*As he goes through the door, whimpering.*] I know what I'm like. I know I did wrong. My wife, my life—I'm leaving everything in your hands!
[*The door closes behind him.* PHAEDRIA *and* GETA *look at each other in silence for a moment.*

Phaedria

[*Blankly.*] Well, Geta, what happens now?

Geta

Unless I'm very much mistaken, you're going to hear the riot act and I'm going to get hung up and horsewhipped. [*Thoughtfully.*] You know the advice we just gave Antipho? Well, we ought to take it ourselves.

Phaedria

Forget about this "ought" business. Just tell me what you want me to do.

Geta

Remember, when you went into this affair, what all of you kept saying when you were figuring how to keep yourselves clear of blame? That Phormio had a foolproof case against Antipho, easy to prove, sure to win, absolutely airtight?

Phaedria

I remember.

Geta

All right. That's just the kind of talk we need now. Even better and smarter, if we can do it.

Phaedria

I'll give it everything I've got.

Geta

You take the front line. I'll be the rear guard and [*falling in line behind* PHAEDRIA's *broad back*] take up a concealed position in case the enemy breaks through.

Phaedria

Forward march!
[*They march off to the side of the stage.*
[PHAEDRIA *and* GETA *station themselves in an unobtrusive spot where they can't easily be observed but can overhear whatever is said on stage.* DEMIPHO *now enters, stage right. He is a hale, solid old fellow with a direct, no-nonsense manner. Clearly he's a man accustomed to giving orders and being obeyed without cavil, just the sort of father who would turn a son into a weakling like* ANTIPHO. *His first words reveal that he already has a pretty fair idea of what has gone on during his absence —and doesn't like any of it.*

Demipho

[*To himself.*] So Antipho got married without my approval, did he? Didn't think twice about my rights in the matter. My rights? Wasn't even bothered that I'd get angry with him! What a way to act! The nerve of him! A fine guardian that Geta!

Geta

[*Aside.*] Finally he got around to me.

Demipho

[*To himself.*] I wonder what they're going to tell me— what excuse they'll think up.

Geta

[*Aside.*] Don't worry, I'll think one up.

Demipho

[*To himself.*] I suppose he'll tell me [*imitating* ANTIPHO *in an access of contrition*], "I didn't want to do it but the court made me." All right, he's got a point there.

Geta

[*Aside.*] That's what I like to hear.

Demipho

[*To himself, ironically.*] And I suppose the court also

made him keep his mouth shut and hand the case over to the other party when he knew the true facts all the time.

Phaedria
[*Sotto voce, to* GETA.] Hey, he's got something there!

Geta
[*Sotto voce, to* PHAEDRIA.] Leave it to me. I'll figure something out.

Demipho
[*To himself*.] I simply don't know what to do. I never expected anything like this to happen. It's incredible! It's got me so angry I can't collect my thoughts. [*Paces up and down agitatedly for a moment, then continues more calmly*.] Things like this make you realize that it's just when everything is going fine that you'd better start worrying about how to handle trouble when it comes—what to do if you get into an accident or go bankrupt or have to leave home. When you come back from a trip you've always got to keep in mind that your son may be in jail, your wife dead, or your daughter sick. If you remember that these things can happen, and to anybody, then you'll be ready for anything. So, then, whatever turns out better than you expect, you can count as absolutely pure profit.

Geta
[*Sotto voce, to* PHAEDRIA.] Phaedria, I'm way ahead of him. I *did* worry about all the trouble I was in for when he got back from his trip: the ball and chain, the horsewhip, the rock pile, and hard labor on the farm. I *was* ready for all these. And whatever turns out better than I expect, I *am* going to count as absolutely pure profit. [*Giving* PHAEDRIA *a push*.] What are you waiting for? Go on up to him and start things off by giving him a big hello.

Demipho
[*Noticing* PHAEDRIA, *to himself*.] Ah, here's my nephew Phaedria coming to see me.

Phaedria
[*With a great air of being overjoyed at the meeting*.] Well, Uncle! How are you!

Demipho

[*Curtly.*] Fine. Where's Antipho?

Phaedria

[*Bypassing the question.*] What a pleasure to see you—

Demipho

[*Interrupting.*] Sure, sure. Now answer my question.

Phaedria

He's around. He's just fine. [*Rubbing his hands and beaming.*] Well, did you find everything just the way you want?

Demipho

[*Grimly.*] I wish I had!

Phaedria

[*Putting on a convincing act of being surprised.*] Why, what's the matter?

Demipho

What's the matter? That's quite a fine little marriage you fixed up here while I was away.

Phaedria

[*Shifting from surprise to amused incredulity.*] Are you mad at him about *that?*

Geta

[*Delighted with the performance, aside.*] The boy's a professional!

Demipho

And why shouldn't I be? I'd like to have him right here in front of me this minute. I'd show him how that kind and gentle parent of his had to turn himself into a tyrant through nobody's fault but his.

Phaedria

Now, Uncle, he didn't do anything to get mad about.

Demipho

[*Wearily, addressing the world in general.*] Look at that! Always the same story. They're all alike. You know one of them, you know them all.

Phaedria

That's not true!

Demipho

[*Still addressing the world in general.*] If one of them gets into trouble, the other's right there to cover up for him, and vice versa. It's a mutual assistance pact.

Geta

[*Aside.*] He doesn't know it but that's a perfect description. That's just what they do.

Demipho

Phaedria, if what I say wasn't true you wouldn't be taking his side right now.

Phaedria

[*As if speaking from deep conviction.*] Uncle, if Antipho has really done something wrong, something that's going to make him less careful about his own good and his reputation than he should be, I wouldn't be on his side; let him get what's coming to him. But if someone who knows every crooked move in the book happened to hale a pair of green youngsters into court and put one over on them, is that our fault? How about the judges? They're always ready to hurt a rich man out of spite and help a poor one out of pity.

Geta

[*Shaking his head in admiration, aside.*] If I hadn't been at the trial, I'd believe every word he says.

Demipho

And is there a judge who's going to know your rights in the case if you do what he did and don't open your mouth to answer?

Phaedria

[*Glibly.*] He simply reacted the way any decent young fellow would have. When he got before the court he just couldn't speak his piece. He was so scared and ashamed, he was tongue-tied.

Geta

[*Aside.*] Good work, Phaedria! But what am I waiting for? I'd better speak up right away. [*Coming forward.*] Well, Demipho, greetings! It's a pleasure to see you back!

Demipho

[*Balefully.*] Greetings to you, my keeper of the hearth, my vigilant overseer, my son's trusty guardian in my absence!

Geta

[*Playing the injured innocent to the hilt.*] I've just been listening to these accusations you're making against us. None of us deserves it, and least of all myself. Just what did you want me to do under the circumstances? Slaves don't plead cases in court, you know; they can't even testify.

Demipho

[*Taken a little aback.*] Granted, granted. And I'll concede that he's just a boy and didn't know what was going to happen and got frightened; and, all right, you're just a slave. But I don't care how close a relative she was, he didn't have to go and marry her. You should have given her a dowry as the law says, and let her find someone else to marry. Didn't he have sense enough not to bring a penniless bride into the house?

Geta

[*Promptly.*] He had the sense, all right. It's the money he didn't have.

Demipho

He could have gotten it somewhere—

Geta

[*Interrupting.*] Somewhere? Easy enough to say!

Demipho

Then he should have borrowed it if there was no other way.

Geta

[*Snorting.*] Hah! That's a good one. And just who'd give credit to a minor like him as long as you're alive?

Demipho

[*Exploding with exasperation as each of his suggestions is neatly parried.*] Well, it's just not going to be. It can't be! I'm not going to let him stay married to that girl one day longer. This calls for stern measures. I want you to let me see that fellow or let me know where he lives.

Geta

You mean Phormio?

Demipho
[*Sneering.*] That defender of women's rights.

Geta
I'll go get him.

Demipho
Where's Antipho now?

Geta
He's out.

Demipho
Phaedria! Go find him and bring him here!

Phaedria
[*With alacrity.*] I'll go right now.
[*Exits, stage right.*

Geta
[*Aside.*] To his girlfriend, he means.
[*Exits, stage left.*

Demipho
[*To himself.*] First I'll go into the house to pay my respects there. Then I'll go downtown and round up a few friends to stand by me in this business. I want to be ready for that Phormio when he comes.
[*Goes into his house.*

Act Three

[*Enter* GETA *and* PHORMIO, *stage left, deep in conversation.* PHORMIO *is a gaunt young fellow dressed sprucely and smartly in clothes that have long since seen their best days. Officially he is a* parasitus, *that is, someone who keeps his belly filled and himself entertained by scrounging. But you can see at a glance that he is no run-of-the-mine specimen. There's an engaging openness of manner about him, an alertness, a definite flair, that stamps him as someone special—in dress and looks and attitude toward life an Alfred Jingle wearing a seedy mantle instead of seedy jacket and trousers. As a matter of fact, in Phormio's case, scrounging is merely the lowest level of his activity. He has raised the technique of living by his wits to a fine art; he is a virtuoso at it. And, like any true artist, he uses his talents not merely for the baser object of getting enough to live on but creatively, for the sheer pleasure of exercising a unique gift. It was* PHORMIO *the parasite who had, no doubt, cadged many a meal and night's entertainment from* ANTIPHO—*but it was* PHORMIO *the artist who had paid him back by working out the magnificent scheme of the phony trial.*

Phormio

So you say that Antipho was so scared of seeing his father that he cleared out?

Geta

Exactly.

Phormio

And left Phanium all alone?

Geta

Right.

Phormio

And the old man's in a state?

Geta

Hopping mad.

Phormio

[*Thoughtfully, to himself.*] Phormio, there's only one broad back to bear this burden—yours. You made this mess; you've got to clean it up, all of it. Phormio, strip for action!

Geta

Yes, Phormio, please!

[PHORMIO *proceeds to go into a trancelike state of deep thought and, oblivious of everything about him, conducts in dumb show an imaginary harangue with* DEMPHO.

Phormio

[*Struck by an idea disturbing enough to make him talk out loud.*] Suppose he asks me . . .
[*Goes off again into dumb show.*]

Geta

You're our only hope.

Phormio

[*Disregarding* GETA *completely in his concentration.*] Ah hah—what if he answers . . .

[*Again goes off into dumb show.*]

Geta

You got us into it.

Phormio

[*Abruptly coming out of his imaginary confrontation with* DEMIPHO.] I think I've got it.

Geta

You've got to help us.

Phormio

[*Not hearing* GETA, *and beaming with self-satisfaction.*] Bring on the old man. I've got my whole strategy worked out.

Geta

What are you going to do?

Phormio

If I clear Antipho, keep him married, and draw all the old man's fire on myself, you'll be satisfied, right?

Geta

[*Overwhelmed by the magnanimity of the offer.*] Phormio! You're a real friend. And a brave man. But I get worried that a brave fellow like you will wind up walking right through a prison gate.

Phormio

[*With the candor that comes from an objective appraisal of one's capabilities.*] Oh, no. I've been over the ground. I know how to watch my step. Have you any idea how many people I've fleeced out of their last penny—I mean counting out-of-towners as well as locals? The better I get at it, the more I do it. Well, you never heard of anyone suing me for damages, did you?

Geta

Why don't they?

Phormio

[*Confidentially.*] A person doesn't go fishing for sharks. They're dangerous. He goes after what can't hurt him.

There he stands to gain; going after sharks just means a lot of work with nothing to show for it. And another thing. People know I don't have a dime. It's the fellows who have something they can be skinned out of some way or other who have to watch out. I know what you're going to say: What if one of my dupes demands his dues and sues, and wins me to take home as a slave until I settle up? Oh, no, he doesn't want to bring a man with an appetite like mine into his house. And, if you ask me, he's using his head. Why should he pay me back for a bad turn I did him by doing me a good one three times a day?

Geta

Well, Antipho will never be able to pay you back for what you're doing for him.

Phormio

On the contrary, I'll always be in *his* debt. [*Earnestly.*] The one person you can never pay back is the fellow who picks up the check. [*Gazing raptly in the distance, like a lover remembering some treasured moment.*] You go to his club, have a swim, then a massage—and all on the cuff. There you are, nothing on your mind, and there he is, eating his heart out with worry at the expense. You're waited on hand and foot—and he has to go around barking at everybody. You have a fine time, get served your drink before he does, get a place at table before he does, sit down to a drive-you-crazy dinner—

Geta

What do you mean a "drive-you-crazy" dinner?

Phormio

Where the menu's so long it drives you crazy to make up your mind. Now, when you figure how very pleasant all this is and how much it all costs, what are you going to call the fellow who makes it possible? [*Emphatically.*] An angel, that's what he is, an angel from heaven for us down here.

Geta

[*Happening to glance toward the wings.*] The old man's coming! Watch your step. It's that first volley that's the hardest. Stand up under that and from then on *you* can call the shots.

[*Enter* DEMIPHO, *stage left. He is deep in conversation with three cronies he has rounded up to stand by him and advise him. The three—*HEGIO, CRATINUS, *and* CRITO *—are staid old fellows, pillars of society, sensible, serious, solid citizens.*

Demipho
[*To his advisory council.*] That's what he did to me. Did you ever hear of anything more outrageous in your whole life? You've got to stand by me.

Geta
[*Sotto voce, to* PHORMIO.] He's sore, all right.

Phormio
[*Sotto voce, to* GETA.] You haven't seen anything yet. Watch this—I'm going to get a rise out of him. [*Taking Geta's arm, he walks to the center of the stage. At the same time he raises his voice to make sure that* DEMIPHO *hears every word.*] God almighty, you mean to tell me Demipho has the nerve to say that Phanium isn't related to him? He actually said she wasn't his relative?

Geta
[*Picking up the cue and raising his voice, too.*] That's what he said.

Demipho
[*Pointing to* PHORMIO, *to the council.*] Look! I think that's the fellow I was telling you about. Follow me!
[*The four draw near.*

Phormio
He doesn't know who Stilpho was?

Geta
That's what he said.

Phormio
[*Switching from incredulity to righteous indignation.*] It's because the poor girl's been left without a penny. That's the reason for this never having heard of her father and this abandoning her. [*Shaking his head sorrowfully.*] What greed will do to people!

Geta

[*Assuming the role of Demipho's defender.*] If you're going to make nasty insinuations about my master, you're going to hear some nasty things about yourself!

Demipho

[*To the council.*] Of all the unmitigated nerve! He's actually come here to accuse *me!*

Phormio

Now, there's no sense in my getting angry with a youngster like Antipho for not knowing her father. After all, the man was much older. Besides, he was so poor he always had to work and hardly ever got into the city. My own father gave him a piece of land to farm. [*Reminiscently.*] Back in those days the old fellow used to tell me time and again how this cousin of his would have nothing to do with him. What a grand old man! Never met anyone finer in my life.

Geta

[*Trying his hand at scorn.*] Take a look at yourself alongside this man you're telling me about—

[*Indicates by a gesture that the difference is too great for words.*

Phormio

You can go to the devil! Believe me, if I didn't think so highly of him I wouldn't have started a serious fight like this with your people. But I have an obligation to his daughter, and that master of yours has shut the door in her face. And he calls himself a gentleman!

Geta

[*Switching from scorn back to indignation.*] Listen, you foul-mouth, are you going to keep on saying nasty things about my master behind his back?

Phormio

Certainly. He deserves it.

Geta

Oh, he does, does he?

[*Pretends to take a swing at* phormio.

Demipho

[*Loudly.*] Geta!

Geta
[*Pretending not to hear—and creating some synthetic words to go with his synthetic feelings.*] Swindlerizer! Shysterizer!

Demipho
[*Shouting.*] GETA!

Phormio
[*Sotto voce.*] Answer him!

Geta
Who wants me? [*Turning and quickly assuming a look of astonishment.*] Oh!

Demipho
Stop this!

Geta
But he's been saying terrible things about you behind your back all day! Things he ought to be saying about himself.

Demipho
That's enough out of you! [*Turning to* PHORMIO *and speaking with frigid politeness.*] Now, young man, first of all there's something I'd like to find out from you if you'll be so good as to answer me. Will you kindly make clear to me just who is this man you say was your friend and just how he claimed I was related to him?

Phormio
[*Assuming the expression of a man who's too smart to be trapped.*] Fishing for information, eh? As if you don't know who he was!

Demipho
I know him?

Phormio
That's what I said.

Demipho
[*Still managing to be polite.*] I tell you I don't. Since you say I do, you'd better refresh my memory.

Phormio
What's this? You didn't know your own cousin?

Demipho

[*Losing his carefully maintained composure.*] You'll be the death of me! [*Controlling himself again.*] Tell me the man's name.

Phormio

[*Suddenly losing his aplomb.*] His name? Er—be glad to. [*Starts signaling surreptitiously to* GETA.

Demipho

Come on, speak up.

Phormio

[*Aside.*] My god, everything's ruined! I forgot the name!

Demipho

Eh? What did you say?

Phormio

[*Sotto voce, to* GETA.] Geta! Do you remember that name she mentioned? Whisper it in my ear! [*Aloud, to* DEMIPHO.] Oh, no—I'm not going to tell you. As if you don't know it! You're just trying to test me.

Demipho

What do you mean, trying to test you?

Geta

[*In a stage whisper.*] Stilpho!

Phormio

[*Abruptly recovering his aplomb.*] All right, I'll tell you. What do I care? It's Stilpho.

Demipho

[*Genuinely puzzled.*] Who?

Phormio

Stilpho. You knew him, all right.

Demipho

[*Emphatically.*] I did not. And I never had a relative by that name.

Phormio

Oh, is that so? [*Gesturing toward the advisory council, whose three members have been blankly following the interchange.*] Aren't you ashamed of yourself? In front of these good people? [*Shakes his head dolefully.*] Now, if he had left an estate of three hundred thousand—

Demipho
[*Interrupting.*] Oh, damn you!

Phormio
[*Continuing unruffled.*] —you'd have been the first one to reel off from memory the family tree from the founding father down.

Demipho
[*Grimly.*] That's right. And if I had been there when the will was probated, I'd have stated exactly how his daughter was related to me. And that's just what you're going to do right now. Come on; how is she related to me?

Geta
[*To* DEMIPHO.] Good work! [*Sotto voce, to* PHORMIO.] Hey! Watch out!

Phormio
[*Truculently.*] You'll find a clear and complete statement where it belongs—in the court records. And if I falsified any facts there, how come your son didn't enter a denial?

Demipho
[*Exploding with exasperation.*] Don't mention that son of mine to me! He's so stupid, it defies description!

Phormio
And if you're so smart, why don't you go to court and have the case tried all over again? After all, Your Highness sits on the throne here alone; only you have the right to have the same case tried twice.

Demipho
[*Throwing up his hands in despair.*] It's an absolute outrage, but rather than go to court or listen to you any longer, let's make believe she is my relative. The law says I've got to provide a dowry; here's twenty-five hundred, take it, and get her out of here!

Phormio
Ha ha ha! Pretty slick!

Demipho
[*Surprised.*] What's the matter? What's wrong with my proposition? Can't I even get what's common justice?

Phormio

[*Switching abruptly from the canny operator to the man of stern morality.*] I ask you, just what do you think the law wants? To have her paid off and sent packing like some whore you're tired of? Or to have her married to her next of kin for the rest of her days so that a respectable woman like her will never be forced into a life of shame because of poverty? But that's what *you* don't want.

Demipho

[*Sourly.*] All right, all right, to marry her to the next of kin. But just how and why do you figure that we—

Phormio

[*Interrupting.*] Now, now, you know what they say: a case decided is a case ended.

Demipho

[*Snarling.*] Ended, is it? No, sir! I'm not going to quit until I settle this business!

Phormio

[*Patronizingly.*] You're being very silly, you know.

Demipho

Never mind!

Phormio

[*As if suddenly struck by a new idea.*] When you come right down to it, Demipho, you have nothing to do with me in this business at all. It's your son who lost the suit, not you. [*Archly.*] You're a little too old by now for marriage, you know.

Demipho

[*Grimly.*] You can take it for granted he'll say exactly what I've been saying—or I'll turn him out of the house along with that wife of his.

Geta

[*Aside.*] He's sore, all right.

Phormio

Better turn yourself out.

Demipho

[*Baffled, seeing his last hope go glimmering.*] So that's it,

damn you! Ready to cross me up whatever I do, aren't
you?

Phormio

[*Sotto voce, to* GETA.] He's afraid of us even though he's
doing all he can to cover it up.

Geta

[*Sotto voce, to* PHORMIO.] The first round goes to you.

Phormio

[*In his best let-bygones-be-bygones manner.*] You can't
get out of it, so why don't you put up with it? You'll
be acting like the man you really are, and we can be
friends.

Demipho

[*Exploding.*] Me be your friend? I don't want to see you
or hear that voice of yours ever again!

Phormio

[*As before.*] You know, if you make up with her, you'll
have someone to make you happy in your old age. Remember, you're getting along.

Demipho

[*Snarling.*] You take her. Let her make you happy.

Phormio

[*As before.*] Now, now, watch that temper!

Demipho

Now, listen here. Enough of this talk. If you don't get
that woman out of here, and right away, I'll throw her
out. That's all I've got to say to you, Phormio.

Phormio

And if you don't treat her exactly as a respectable girl
should be, I'll slap on you the biggest suit you ever
heard of. That's all I've got to say to *you*, Demipho.
[*Sotto voce, to* GETA.] Psst. If you need me for anything, I'll be at my house.

Geta

[*Sotto voce, to* PHORMIO.] Right.
[PHORMIO *exits, stage left.*

Demipho

[*To himself.*] The trouble and worry that boy let me in

for when he got himself—and me—mixed up in this marriage! Why doesn't he come to see me and let me at least find out what he has to say for himself in all this? [*Turning to* GETA.] Go and see if he's come home yet.

Geta

Right.
[*Goes into the house.*

Demipho

[*To the advisory council.*] Well, you see how things stand. What should I do? Hegio, what's your opinion?

Hegio

[*After a moment of deep thought.*] My opinion is that Cratinus should tell us his, if it's all right with you.

Demipho

Cratinus, what's your opinion?

Cratinus

[*Sparring for time.*] You want my opinion?

Demipho

Yes.

Cratinus

[*With great deliberation.*] I'd like to see you do what's best for your interests. Now, this is the way I see it. What your son did took place while you were away. Therefore it's only right and fair to have the slate wiped clean—and you won't have any trouble doing this. That's my opinion.

Demipho

Tell us your opinion now, Hegio.

Hegio

[*With a deferential gesture in* CRATINUS' *direction.*] I think Cratinus here has given some very thoughtful advice. But you know the human equation: number of men equals number of opinions; each person has his own way of thinking. Now, as I see it, you can't revoke something the law has decided, and it's unethical to try.

Demipho

What's your opinion, Crito?

Crito

[*After a moment of deep lucubration.*] I think the situation needs more thought. [*Profoundly.*] It's a very serious matter.

Hegio

Well, we've got to be going; anything more we can do for you?

Demipho

Thank you very much for your help. [*The council files out, stage left. To himself.*] I'm more up in the air than before.

[GETA *emerges from the house.*

Geta

They say he's not back yet.

Demipho

[*With an air of finality.*] I have to wait for my brother. I'll put it to him and I'll follow whatever he has to say— and I'll go down to the dock right now to find out when he's expected.

[*Exits, stage right.*

Geta

[*To himself.*] And I'll go and find Antipho to tell him what's happened here. [*Starts walking off, stage left, and then stops.*] There he is! Couldn't have come at a better time.

Antipho

[*Muttering to himself as he walks slowly on stage, buried in thought.*] What a heel I am! I deserve to be called every name in the book. To run off like that and leave the girl who means everything to me for others to pro- tect! What could I have been thinking of? That others would look after my own interests better than I? But all the other considerations don't matter—it was I who brought her into my house, and it was up to me not to run out on her and leave her in a position to be harmed just because she had put her trust in me. Poor girl, I'm the only hope she has; I'm everything to her.

Geta

[*Breaking in on the soliloquy, tartly.*] As a matter of fact we've got our own complaints to make against you for running out on us the way you did.

Antipho

[*Uneasily.*] I went looking for you.

Geta

[*Disregarding the palpably false excuse and continuing his thought.*] But, even so, we didn't let you down.

Antipho

[*Screwing up his courage at this.*] Tell me, how do things stand? What's going to happen to me? Does my father smell anything fishy?

Geta

Nothing yet.

Antipho

You mean there's hope?

Geta

I don't know.

Antipho

[*His courage becoming unscrewed.*] Oh.

Geta

But Phaedria was in there fighting for you every minute.

Antipho

[*Warmly.*] I knew he would.

Geta

And Phormio too. He worked his head off for you, just as he's always done.

Antipho

What did he do?

Geta

The old man was hopping mad but he talked him down. Did a perfect job.

Antipho

Bravo, Phormio!

Geta

[*Pointedly.*] And I did what I could, too.

Antipho

[*Happily.*] Geta, you're true friends, every one of you.

Geta

Well, that's how the first round went. Right now things

are quiet. Your father's waiting for your uncle to get back.

Antipho
[*The happiness draining out of him.*] Why him?

Geta
He said he was going to consult him and do whatever he advised.

Antipho
Oh, Geta, I can't tell you how scared I am now at the thought of my uncle's coming back! Don't you see? This is a matter of life or death for me, and, if you're right, everything's going to depend on what he decides.

Geta
[*Happening to look at Dorio's house.*] There's Phaedria.

Antipho
Where?

Geta
[*Pointing to the door of Dorio's house, and sniggering.*] There, coming out of the—er—playground.
[*Two figures emerge from Dorio's house, the owner himself with* PHAEDRIA *tagging at his heels.*
DORIO *is a slave dealer, a heardheaded businessman who owns a string of handsome girls carefully trained in all that is necessary to make a successful courtesan.* DORIO *either rents them out or sells them when he can find someone willing to pay the price—and the price was generally fairly stiff, since the girls were hand-picked to start and had received an expensive education. Because of the nature of their occupation, dealers such as* DORIO *faced the same sort of problems that money-lenders do—and suffered the same sort of reputation.*

Phaedria
[*Pleading.*] Dorio! Please! Listen to me!

Dorio
[*Walking away.*] No.

Phaedria
[*Grabbing his arm.*] Just for a minute.

Dorio
Let go of me!

Phaedria

Listen to me. I've got something to tell you.

Dorio

I've heard it a thousand times already. I'm sick and tired of it.

Phaedria

This time it's something you'll be glad to hear.

Dorio

[*Swiveling around at this.*] All right, I'm listening. Let's have it.

Phaedria

I want you to do me a favor. Give me just three days more. Please! [DORIO *about faces and starts walking again.*] Hey, where are you going?

Dorio

[*Disgusted with himself.*] I should have known you wouldn't have anything new to tell me.

Antipho

[*Sotto voce, to* GETA.] I'm scared of that pimp! [*Catching a contemptuous glance from* GETA.] I mean that he's going to get himself in trouble.

Geta

[*Sotto voce to* ANTIPHO, *ironically.*] Just what I'm afraid of, too.

Phaedria

Don't you trust me?

Dorio

About as much as a crooked fortune-teller.

Phaedria

But I give you my word.

Dorio

Your word? Hot air!

Phaedria

Just do me this one favor. It'll pay off for you, really pay off. You'll say so yourself.

Dorio

Don't give me that line.

Phaedria

Believe me, you'll be glad you did it. It's the truth, I swear it.

Dorio

Wake up, will you!

Phaedria

Give it a try. Just three days.

Dorio

[*Wearily.*] The same old song and dance.

Phaedria

[*Working himself up.*] Dorio, you'll be more to me than my best friend. More than my own father, my own—

Dorio

[*Interrupting.*] You're wasting your breath.

Phaedria

[*Desperately.*] What's the matter with you? Don't you have a heart? Here I am begging you, and you just can't feel pity for a fellow.

Dorio

[*Mimicking him.*] What's the matter with *you*? Don't you have a brain? Here you are handing me a line and I'm supposed to hand you one of my girls free of charge!

Antipho

[*Sotto voce, to* GETA.] Poor Phaedria!

Phaedria

[*To himself.*] He knows the score. I give up.

Geta

[*Sotto voce, to* ANTIPHO.] Acting just the way you'd expect, both of them.

Phaedria

[*Bitterly, to himself.*] And this had to happen now, just when Antipho's having troubles of his own!

Antipho

[*Coming forward with* GETA.] Phaedria, what's going on here?

Phaedria

[*Bitterly.*] Antipho, you don't know how lucky you are!

Antipho
Who? Me?

Phaedria
The girl you love is safe in your own home. You've been spared the experience of coming up against trouble like this.
[*Gesturing toward* DORIO.

Antipho
Safe in my own home? Oh, no! I'm like the fellow in the story—I've got a tiger by the tail: I can't hang on and I can't let go.

Dorio
[*To* ANTIPHO, *gesturing toward* PHAEDRIA *and dropping for the moment his harsh tone.*] My situation exactly with this fellow here.

Antipho
[*To* DORIO.] Well, well, our pimp's getting soft. [*To* PHAEDRIA.] What's he done?

Phaedria
Done? Just about the most inhuman thing a human being could. He's sold my girl!

Antipho
Sold her?

Geta
Sold her?

Phaedria
Sold her.

Dorio
[*Sarcastically.*] Oh, sure, an absolute outrage—selling a girl I bought with my own money.

Phaedria
I've been begging him to break the agreement with the buyer and give me just three days more to collect the money my friends promised me, but he won't do it. [*To* DORIO.] If I don't get it to you by then, you don't have to wait another minute.

Dorio
You bore me.

Antipho

Dorio, he's only asking for three days. Come on, give in. Do him the favor and he'll pay you back for it twice over.

Dorio

I want action, not words.

Antipho

[*Working himself up.*] Are you going to let that girl leave the city? They love each other—how can you sit back and see them be separated?

Dorio

[*Grimly.*] Neither you nor I—

Phaedria

[*Interrupting.*] I hope to god you get what's coming to you!

Dorio

[*To* PHAEDRIA.] Now, look here. Against my better judgment I've put up with your promises for months now. And all I've gotten is tears and no cash. Well, now I've found just the opposite, someone with cash and no tears. He goes to the head of the line.

Antipho

[*Who, during* DORIO's *speech, has been in deep thought, to* PHAEDRIA.] By god, if I remember correctly, you agreed on a date with him for paying the money, didn't you?

Phaedria

We did.

Dorio

[*Unruffled.*] That's right. I'm not denying it.

Antipho

Well, is it past yet?

Dorio

[*Blandly.*] No. But today's offer beat the deadline.

Antipho

[*Hotly.*] You welsher! Aren't you ashamed of yourself?

Dorio

[*Scornfully.*] When it means a profit? I should say not!

Geta

You stinker!

Phaedria

Dorio! Is that any way to act?

Dorio

[*Genially.*] That's the way I am. If you don't like it, take your business somewhere else.

Antipho

What do you mean by cheating this poor fellow that way!

Dorio

[*Losing a bit of his calm.*] Oh, no, Antipho. He's the one who's doing the cheating. He knew what I was like; I thought *he* was different. *He* lied to me; I treated him just the way I always treat everybody. But we'll forget about all that. Here's what I'm going to do. The colonel who wants to buy her said he'd bring the money to-morrow morning. You bring the money first, Phaedria, and I'll use my system with you—first come, first served. So long.

[*Turns and goes into his house.*

Phaedria

[*To himself, gazing after* DORIO *helpleessly.*]

What am I going to do? Where's a poor devil like me, without a dime to his name, going to get that kind of money overnight? And I could have raised it, my friends promised it to me, if I could only have talked him into giving me three days more.

[*Stands distraught, oblivious for the moment to everything about him.*

Antipho

[*To* GETA.] Geta! Are we going to stand by and let him suffer this way? After all, you told me how he stood up for me a little while ago. What do you say we try to return the favor? He could use it now.

Geta

I agree. That's the right thing to do.

Antipho

Then do something. You're the only one who can save him.

Geta
What am I supposed to do?

Antipho
Find the money.

Geta
[*Sarcastically.*] I'm willing. You just show me where.

Antipho
[*Deliberately.*] My father's back home, you know.

Geta
[*Puzzled.*] I know. What about it?

Antipho
[*Hesitating to put what he has in mind into words.*] Well
. . . a word to the wise is sufficient.

Geta
[*Incredulously.*] Get it from *him?*

Antipho
From him.

Geta
[*Exploding.*] God in heaven, what a thing to suggest!
Great, oh, great. Leave me alone, will you! I deserve a
medal if I just get out of *your* marriage with a whole
skin. I don't need any orders now from you to go get
myself drawn and quartered because of him.
[*Gesturing toward* PHAEDRIA.
[GETA's *explosion rouses* PHAEDRIA *and, catching the drift
of the conversation, he starts to listen avidly.*]

Antipho
[*Despondently, to* PHAEDRIA.] He's right.

Phaedria
[*Flaring up.*] What's the matter, Geta? I'm a member of
this family, too, you know.

Geta
I know, I know. But isn't it enough for you that the
old man is mad at everyone of us right now? Do you
have to stick the needle in deeper and throw away
every chance of ever talking him around?

Phaedria
[*Dramatically.*] To think that someone else will take her

from my sight and lead her off to an unknown land!
[*Striking a heroic pose and groaning.*] Oh, Antipho!
Look at me, speak to me, now while you still can, while
I'm still before you!

Antipho

Why? What are you talking about? What are you going
to do?

Phaedria

[*As before.*] I don't care where in the world he carries her
off to, my mind is made up: I'll follow her or die in the
attempt!

Geta

[*Ironically.*] God be with you whatever you do—but just
take it easy, will you?

Antipho

[*To* GETA.] Look, can't you do something for him?

Geta

Something? What, for instance?

Antipho

Think, Geta, think! We don't want to let him do
anything we'll be sorry for later.

Geta

All right, I'll think. [*Paces up and down in deep thought.
Finally, after several false starts, speaks.*] I think we can
save him. But I'm afraid it means more trouble.

Antipho

Don't be afraid. We'll be right there with you to take
whatever comes, good or bad.

Geta

[*To* PHAEDRIA.] Tell me, how much money do you need?

Phaedria

Only fifteen thousand.

Geta

[*Gulping.*] Whew! That's an expensive girl you have there,
Phaedria. Fifteen thousand!

Phaedria

[*Indignantly.*] For a girl like her? It's dirt cheap!

Geta

All right, all right. I'll dig it up for you.

Phaedria

Geta! You're terrific!

Geta

[*Looking around warily.*] Now let's get you out of here.

Phaedria

[*Not hearing the last remark in his excitement.*] I need it right away.

Geta

You'll have it right away. But you've got to let me have Phormio. I need him to help me.

Antipho

He's available. Don't be afraid to load anything you want on him. He'll handle it. He's the one man who knows how to be a friend in need.

Geta

Let's go get him right now.

Antipho

You don't need me now for anything, do you?

Geta

No. Go in the house and cheer up that wife of yours. The poor thing must be scared to death in there. [ANTIPHO, *who had forgotten all about* PHANIUM *in the excitement, stands for a moment conscience-stricken.*] Well, what are you waiting for?

Antipho

[*Galvanized into action.*] Nothing I'd rather do! [*Rushes into the house.*

Phaedria

How are you going to pull this off, anyway?

Geta

[*Taking him by the arm and leading him off, stage left*] Right now let's get you out of here. I'll tell you on the way.

[*They leave.*

Act Four

[DEMIPHO *and* CHREMES *enter, stage right, deep in conversation. There is much the same difference between the two brothers as there is between their sons, although in this case the personalities are reversed.* CHREMES, *like his nephew* ANTIPHO, *is the cautious sort, always harried by worries and misgivings. That he has very little money of his own and lives off the property and income of a rich wife, and that* NAUSISTRATA, *the lady in question, is a most formidable woman, accounts for this in part. But another part, and by far the larger, has a much less prosaic reason behind it.* CHREMES *is a bigamist: he has a second wife and a grown daughter on Lemnos. The very thought of* NAUSISTRATA'S *finding out about his double life is enough to give him the shakes.*

Demipho

Well, Chremes, the only reason you went to Lemnos was to get your daughter and bring her back. Isn't she with you?

Chremes

No.

Demipho

Why not?

Chremes

From what I could gather, when her mother saw that I was staying away longer than usual, she figured the girl was getting too old to put up with this sort of treatment, so she packed up, bag and baggage, and came here to find me.

Demipho

What kept you there so long once you found they had left?

Chremes

[*With an emphasis that is suspicious in view of the innocence of the question.*] God, was I sick! I couldn't get away.

Demipho

How come? Did you catch something?

Chremes

[*Evasively.*] How come? I'm old. That's a sickness right there. [*Changing the subject.*] Now, I've heard from the captain of their ship that they arrived safely.

Demipho

Have you heard what happened to my son while I was away?

Chremes

Yes! [*With even more of a worried air than usual.*] And that's just the thing that's got me in a quandary. [*Throwing a glance at the house to make sure there's no sign of his wife, and dropping his voice.*] You see, if I arrange a match for that daughter of mine with someone outside the family, I've got to tell him the whole story of where she came from, and so on. With your son there was no problem; I knew I could trust you as well as my own self. If some outsider really wants the match, he'll keep his mouth shut all right—but only so long as we're on good terms. There's always the chance he'll fall out with me, and then he's going to know more than he should—and I'm scared my wife would get wind of what's been going on. Once that happens, there's nothing left for me but to cut loose and clear out. After all, the only thing in the house I own is my own skin.

Demipho

I know, I know, and this business has got me worried too. I gave you my word my boy would marry her and I'm not going to give up trying until I make good on it.

[*At this moment* GETA, *returning from his conference with* PHORMIO, *enters, stage left. He doesn't at first notice the two oldsters on stage, and they, deep in their conversation, don't notice him.*

Geta

[*To himself.*] That Phormio! What brains! Never saw anything like it! I go to see him to tell him we need money and start to explain how we can get it. Halfway through he cuts me short because he's caught on. Said he was glad to do it, was proud of me, was ready for the old man, and thanked heaven he had a chance to show he was as good a friend of Phaedria's as Antipho's. I told him to wait downtown; I'd bring the old man to him. [*Suddenly notices* DEMIPHO.] Hey, there he is! Who's that back of him? Wow! Chremes has come back. [*Getting a grip on himself.*] Dumbbell! What did you get so scared about? Because you've got two to take over the ropes instead of one? Use your head—two chances are better than one. [*Gesturing toward* DEMIPHO.] Go after the one you started with; if he comes across, fine. If not, tackle this new arrival.

[*At this moment* ANTIPHO *emerges from the door of his house.*

Antipho

[*To himself, as he comes out.*] I wonder how soon Geta's going to get back. [*Looks up and his jaw drops as he sees the two oldsters.*] My uncle! And my father with him! Now that he's back, what's he going to make my father do? Now I'm really scared!

[*Sneaks over to a corner where he can hear without being observed.*

Geta

[*To himself.*] Here goes. [*Walks up to the two old men and puts on his best greetings-to-a-long-lost-friend manner.*] Well, well, Chremes!

Chremes

Hello, Geta.

Geta

It's a pleasure to see you back.

Chremes

Thanks.

Geta

How are things? A man always finds lots of changes when he comes back from a trip, doesn't he?

Chremes

[*Pointedly.*] He certainly does.

Geta

That's right. Have you heard the news about Antipho?

Chremes

The whole story.

Geta

[*To* DEMIPHO.] Did you tell him? [*To* CHREMES.] A down-right outrage, Chremes, the way that boy was taken in!

Chremes

[*Nodding vigorously.*] I was just going over it with Demipho here.

Geta

[*Earnestly.*] As a matter of fact, I've been going over it too, in my own mind. From every angle. And, you know, I think I've found the solution.

Chremes

[*Eagerly.*] What, Geta?

Demipho

[*Suspiciously.*] What kind of solution?

Geta

[*Directing his remarks principally at* DEMIPHO.] When I left you a little while ago, I just happened to run into Phormio.

Chremes

Phormio? Who's he?

Geta

The fellow that the girl—

Chremes

[*Interrupting with a nod.*] I got you.

Geta

It looked to me like a good chance to sound him out. So I take him off to one side and I say to him: "Phormio, how about a little cooperation so that we can settle things between us in a friendly way without any friction? Now, my master's a gentleman; he likes to steer clear of courtrooms. I tell you this because all his friends have advised him, to a man, to throw the girl out. It's the god's honest truth."

Antipho

[*Aside.*] What's he trying to pull now? Just where is he going to wind up anyway?

Geta

[*Continuing his imaginary discourse with* PHORMIO.] "I know you're going to tell me that if he throws her out you're going to hale him into court and make him pay through the nose. Well, he's already gone into that. Boy, you're going to sweat plenty once you start up with that man—he's a trained trial lawyer! But, let's just suppose he does lose the case: *he's* got the money to pay the fine and stay out of jail; but if you lose . . ." [*Expressive gesture to indicate that such an event would be disastrous for the penniless* PHORMIO.] When I figured I had softened him up with this sort of talk, I say to him: "Look, nobody can hear us now. Here's the proposition: my master gives up his case, the girl clears out, and you stop bothering us. All right, name your price."

Antipho

[*In a frenzy, aside.*] Has he gone stark raving mad?

Geta

[*Continuing the imaginary dialogue.*] "You give us a figure that comes anywhere near being fair and square and, believe me, with an honest man like my master, we'll settle things in three shakes."

Demipho

[*Visibly repressing an urge to take* GETA *by the throat.*] And just who told you you could say that?

Chremes

[*Sotto voce, to* DEMIPHO.] Let him alone! It's the best possible way to wind up where we want to.

Antipho

[*Aside.*] I'm sunk!

Demipho

[*To* GETA.] Go on, what did he say then?

Geta

At first he went wild.

Chremes

How much did he ask for, anyway?

Geta

How much? Too much! The first figure that came into his head.

Chremes

What was it?

Geta

Well, if you'll give him thirty thousand—

Demipho

[*Exploding.*] I'll give him hell, that's what I'll give him! What a nerve!

Geta

Exactly what I told him. I said to him, "How much do you think he'd have given an only daughter of his own? A fat lot he's saving by not having one! Not when you turn up with a girl who's out to hold him up for a dowry!" Well, to cut it short and skip all his ravings, this is what he wound up telling me: "This girl was my friend's daughter, it was my duty to marry her, and I wanted to right from the very first. After all, I had in mind all along what the poor girl, without any dowry, would have to put up with if she married a rich husband and had to spend her life slaving for him. But I'll be frank with you. I need a wife who'll bring me a little something I could use to pay off some debts. Matter of fact, I'm engaged to a girl right now who can. But, even so, if Demipho's willing to give me what I stand to get from my fiancée, there isn't anyone I'd rather marry than that girl."

Antipho

[*Aside.*] I don't know what to think! Why's he doing this? Is he just plain stupid or just plain rotten? Is he blind or does he know what he's doing?

Demipho

[*Suspiciously.*] Supposing he's up to his ears in debt?

Geta

He mentioned a farm with a mortgage on it for five thousand.

Demipho

All right, all right. Let him marry her. I'll pay it.

Geta

And a house for another five.

Demipho

[*Shouting.*] Whoa there! That's too much!

Chremes

[*Throwing a worried glance at his house to make sure the noise hasn't brought out his wife.*] Pipe down! I'll pay that five.

Geta

And he'd have to buy his wife a maid. And a few more pieces of furniture. And the cost of the wedding. Another five, say, for all this.

Demipho

[*At the top of his lungs.*] I don't care if he brings a hundred suits against me, I'm not giving him a dime. Let that godforsaken good-for-nothing have another laugh on me?

Chremes

[*Throwing another anguished look toward the house.*] Please! Take it easy! I'll pay it. All you've got to do is get that boy of yours to marry . . . [*checks himself from mentioning further details, with a worried glance at the house*] the one we want him to marry.

Antipho

[*Aside.*] Geta! You and your schemes! You've ruined me, that's what you've done!

Chremes

[*Sotto voce, to* DEMIPHO.] We're getting rid of her because of me; it's only fair I take the loss.

Geta

And he also said: "I want to know as soon as possible if they're going to give me the girl, because I've got to know just where I stand. I'll have to break off with my present fiancée and that means giving up the dowry her parents agreed to pay me."

Chremes

[*Panicked at the very thought of losing* PHORMIO *as the solution to his problems.*] Tell him to tell them it's all off. Tell him he'll get the money right away. Tell him the marriage is all set.

Demipho
[*Between his teeth.*] And I hope it kills him!

Chremes
Luckily I happen to have some cash on me, the rents I collected for my wife from her property on Lemnos. I'll take it out of that. I'll tell my wife you needed it.
[*The two go into Chremes' house.*]

Antipho
[*Coming out of his corner.*] Geta!

Geta
[*Turning around and seeing him for the first time.*] You here?

Antipho
And just what was all that about?

Geta
I was getting the old men to cough up the money.

Antipho
[*Threateningly.*] Is that all?

Geta
[*Deliberately misunderstanding the question.*] God almighty, what do you want from me? That's all you told me to do!

Antipho
Listen, you double-crosser, answer my question!

Geta
What are you driving at?

Antipho
[*Wildly.*] What am I driving at? Are you so blind you can't see what you've done? Set the stage for my suicide, that's what! Damn you, I hope you rot in hell! [*To the world at large.*] Hey, everybody! If you've got a job you really want well done, here's your man! [*To* GETA.] Why did you have to mention my wife and open up that wound again? I can't think of anything more senseless. Now you've filled my father full of hope that he can kick her out. Look at what's going to happen. As soon as Phormio gets the dowry, he's going to have to take her and marry her. What do we do then?

Geta

[*Quietly.*] He's not going to marry her.

Antipho

[*Sarcastically.*] Oh, sure. And then, when they ask for their money back, I suppose he'll be ready to rot in jail just for me and Phaedria?

Geta

[*Still keeping calm.*] Antipho, there isn't anything you can't spoil by stressing only what's bad about it. You're mentioning only the bad side of the picture and leaving out the good. Let's turn it the other way around. You say that once Phormio gets the money, he's got to marry the girl. Agreed. But he's got to arrange the wedding, send out the invitations, see to the clergyman —all this is going to take a little time. In the meanwhile, Phaedria'll collect the money his friends promised him and Phormio can use that to pay the old men back.

Antipho

On what grounds pay them back? What's he going to tell them?

Geta

[*Impatient at* ANTIPHO's *sticking at what, for him, is a mere detail.*] Tell them? [*Launching into an imitation of* PHORMIO *in the imaginary act of reeling off excuses.*] "After I left you, I can't tell you how much bad luck I ran into! A black cat crossed my path, I dropped a mirror in the house, walked under a ladder, my horoscope was terrible, my fortune-teller said absolutely no—and I knew I shouldn't have started this business until after Friday the thirteenth." Matter of fact, that's the best excuse of all. [*Comfortingly.*] Everything will be all right.

Antipho

Everything better be!

Geta

[*Confidently.*] Everything will. Leave it to me. [*The door of Chremes' house opens.*] Your father's coming out. Run and tell Phaedria we've got the money.

[ANTIPHO *rushes off, stage left.* DEMIPHO *and* CHREMES *emerge from the house.* DEMIPHO *is carrying a well-filled purse.*

Demipho

Take it easy, will you? I'll see to it he doesn't try any tricks. You don't think I'd part with this money without witnesses present? What's more, I'll make it crystal clear to them who's getting it and for what.

Geta

[*Aside.*] Look how careful he is. A lot of good it's going to do him!

Chremes

Right. That's the way you've got to do it. But hurry, before he changes his mind. If that fiancée of his starts putting pressure on him, he may welsh on us.

Geta

[*Aside.*] You hit the nail on the head!

Demipho

[*Turning to* GETA.] I'm ready. Take me to him.

Geta

I've been waiting for you.

Chremes

[*To* DEMIPHO, *struck by a last-minute idea.*] When you're done with him, drop in on my wife. Ask her to go see the girl before she leaves and explain the situation to her: that we're arranging for her to marry Phormio, but there's no reason for any hard feelings—he's from her own circle and will make her a much better husband, and we're giving him every penny of the dowry he asked for; we're not forgetting our obligations to her for one minute.

Demipho

[*Testily.*] What the devil do you care?

Chremes

A lot, Demipho. For a man to do the right thing isn't enough. People have to know about it and say he did right. I want the girl to go into this of her own free will so she won't go around saying we threw her out.

Demipho

But why your wife? I can do it myself.

Chremes

It takes a woman to handle a woman.

Demipho

All right, I'll ask her.

[*He and* GETA *leave, stage left.* CHREMES *watches them go off. He heaves a sigh of relief at the thought that this much of his trouble is apparently taken care of.*

Chremes

[*To himself.*] And now I wonder where I can find that daughter of mine?

[*At this moment the door of Demipho's house opens and* SOPHRONA *comes out.* SOPHRONA *is* PHANIUM'S *nurse, the old woman* ANTIPHO *had first approachced and who had discouraged his dishonorable, and encouraged his honorable, advances. She walks toward the front of the stage, visibly agitated, without noticing* CHREMES *who is standing near the door of his house.*

Sophrona

[*To herself.*] What am I to do? Dear, oh, dear, I don't have a single friend, not a soul to help me or talk things over with. My poor little girl! When I hear how terribly Antipho's father is taking what's happened I'm frightened to death for her. Something dreadful may happen to her and all because she listened to me!

Chremes

[*To himself.*] An old woman coming out of my brother's house? And all upset? Who can she be?

Sophrona

[*To herself.*] I knew all along this marriage would be shaky but, without a penny to our name, there was no other way out. I only told her to do it so that, at least for the time being, she'd have a roof over her head.

Chremes

[*Taking a long look, to himself.*] God almighty! Unless I'm going crazy or my eyes are going bad, that's my daughter's old nurse!

Sophrona

[*To herself.*] And there's not a sign—

Chremes

[*In great agitation, to himself.*] What do I do now?

Sophrona

[*To herself.*] —not a single sign of her father.

Chremes
[*As before.*] Go up to her? Or wait here until I get a better idea of what she's talking about?

Sophrona
[*To herself.*] If I could only find him now, I'd have nothing to worry about.

Chremes
[*To himself.*] It's Sophrona, all right. [*Letting his voice assume a natural pitch as he makes up his mind.*] I'll call her.

Sophrona
[*Frightened at the sound of a voice.*] Who's talking there?

Chremes
[*Aloud.*] Sophrona!

Sophrona
[*Dreading to turn around.*] He knows my name!

Chremes
Look at me!

Sophrona
[*With a start.*] Oh, my god! Is that Stilpho?
[*Walks toward him.*

Chremes
[*Dropping his voice.*] No!

Sophrona
[*Confused and alarmed.*] No?

Chremes
[*Taking her by the arm and leading her away from the door of his house, with an anxious look over his shoulder as he does so.*] Sophrona, please! Get a little further away from that door! This way, here. [*Leads her a safe distance away.*] Now, don't ever call me by that name again!

Sophrona
[*Utterly confused.*] Why? Aren't you the person you always said you were?

Chremes
[*With an anguished look at the door.*] Sh!

Sophrona

What are you so scared of that door for?

Chremes

I've got a wild animal caged up in there—my wife. Now, about that name. It's an alias. I used it with you on Lemnos just to be on the safe side. Otherwise, if you people were careless and let the story leak out, there was always a chance it could get to my wife.

Sophrona

My god! So that's why we poor women could never find you here!

Chremes

Tell me, what have you got to do with the family that lives here? [*Gesturing toward Demipho's house.*] In that house you just came out of? [*Suddenly remembering something more important.*] And where are the others?

Sophrona

[*Bursting into tears.*] Oh, dear!

Chremes

What's the matter? Aren't they alive?

Sophrona

Your daughter is. But her poor mother just pined away.

Chremes

[*Not exactly laid prostrate by the news.*] What a pity!

Sophrona

There I was, left all by myself, an old woman without a penny and not knowing a soul. I did what I could. I arranged for your daughter to marry the boy who lives here.

Chremes

[*Not believing his ears.*] Antipho?

Sophrona

Yes. That's the one.

Chremes

[*Roaring.*] What! Has he got two wives?

Sophrona

[*Puzzled.*] He? Heavens, no. Only one, your daughter.

Chremes
[*Puzzled himself now.*] What about that other one who's supposed to be a cousin?

Sophrona
[*Catching on.*] That's your daughter.

Chremes
[*Incredulously.*] What's that you say?

Sophrona
We made that story up. The boy was in love wtih her, and that way he was able to marry her without a dowry.
[CHREMES *stands stunned for a moment as this sinks in. When he starts to talk, it is half to himself.*]

Chremes
God in heaven! So many times things you wouldn't even dare hope for, happen by pure luck! I come home and run into my daughter married just the way I wanted, to just the man I wanted. Here we were, my brother and I, beating our brains out to arrange just this, and the boy did it all by himself without any worry on our part—but plenty on his!

Sophrona
There's something you've got to take care of right away. Antipho's father's come back and they say he's simply furious at what's happened.

Chremes
It's nothing to worry about. [*Wagging his finger in her face.*] Now, in the name of all that's holy, nobody's ever to find out that she's my daughter, understand?

Sophrona
[*Stoutly.*] Nobody will from me.

Chremes
[*Moving toward the door of Demipho's house.*] Follow me. I'll tell you the rest inside.

Act Five

[DEMIPHO, *followed by* GETA, *enters, stage left. He has just left* PHORMIO—*and the experience of handing the money over has been searing.*

Demipho
[*To himself.*] It's our own fault it pays people to be crooks. We're so intent on getting a reputation for being good and kind, we're pushovers. [*Clenching his fist as he thinks of the ordeal he has just been through.*] Talk about adding insult to injury! Wasn't it enough I had to swallow the injury he did to me? Did I have to throw money in the bargain to give him a living until he could spring his next swindle?

Geta
Right. Absolutely right.

Demipho
Turn right into wrong these days and you get a prize for it!

Geta
True, absolutely true.

Demipho
So it shows that the way we handled this affair was idiotic, absolutely idiotic.

Geta
[*With affected casualness, watching* DEMIPHO *narrowly.*] I only hope this plan of ours goes through and he marries her.

Demipho
[*Starting.*] You mean there's any question about it?

Geta
[*Pursing his lips and giving other indications of a con-*

siderable state of dubiety.] Fellow like that? I wouldn't
swear to it that he's not going to change his mind.

Demipho

[*Turning on him.*] What! Change his mind?

Geta

[*Backing down in the face of the reaction he's stirred up.*]
I don't say I know. I only say it could be.

Demipho

[*Somewhat reassured.*] I'll get going on my brother's idea
and have his wife come here and talk to the girl. Geta,
go inside and tell her Nausistrata's coming to see her.
[*Enters Chremes' house to fetch* NAUSISTRATA.

Geta

[*To himself.*] Phaedria's got his money, no word of a
bawling out for Antipho and me, and I've fixed it up so
Phanium doesn't have to leave for the time being. Now
what? What's going to happen next? Geta, my boy,
you're stuck in the same rut; only now you're in deeper.
You didn't get out of your trouble, you just delayed the
day of reckoning. The cat-o'-nine-tails is going to have
kittens, if you don't watch out! Well, I'll go inside now
and explain to Phanium that she doesn't have to worry
about Phormio or anything he tells her.
[*Goes into Demipho's house.*

[*The door of Chremes' house opens, and* DEMIPHO *and*
NAUSISTRATA *come out.* NAUSISTRATA *is all we have
been lead to expect: an imposing woman, with a no-
nonsense air about her, who could, if need be, run a
business as efficiently as she does her household—and
husband. She is, in a way, a female counterpart of*
DEMIPHO *and, as a matter of fact, he is clearly a favorite
of hers.* NAUSISTRATA *is, however, no old battle-ax; be-
neath her businesslike exterior, she is actually quite
warmhearted and good-natured.*

Demipho

You see, Nausistrata, I want you to talk her around.
She's got to do it anyway, but make her want to. You're
good at that sort of thing.

Nausistrata

I'll do it.

Demipho

You'll be doing me as much of a favor in this way as you did a little while ago with that loan.

Nausistrata

Glad to do it. I really don't do as much for you as I ought—and it's all the fault of that husband of mine!

Demipho

What about him?

Nausistrata

My dear man, the way he mismanages the hard-earned fortune my father left me! My father used to get sixty thousand a year from that property, regularly. How one man can be so much better than another!

Demipho

Sixty thousand? You don't say!

Nausistrata

And at a time when things didn't pay as well as today. Yes, sir, sixty thousand.

Demipho

Whew!

Nausistrata

What do you think of *that?*

Demipho

It certainly goes to show!

Nausistrata

I wish I had been born a man! I'd show him—

Demipho

[*Interrupting a little impatiently.*] I'm sure of it.

Nausistrata

[*Disregarding him and continuing her thought.*] —how to—

Demipho

[*Interrupting again.*] Now, Nausistrata, you've got to conserve your energy to deal with the girl. She's a youngster; we don't want her to wear you down.

Nausistrata

I'll do exactly what you want. [*Goes toward Demipho's house but stops when she sees the door opening.*] There's Chremes! He's coming out of your house.

[CHREMES *bursts out, in his excitement rushing right past his wife without seeing her.*

Chremes
Demipho! Did you pay him the money?

Demipho
[*With satisfaction.*] Took care of it right away.

Chremes
[*Taken aback.*] I wish you hadn't. [*Suddenly noticing* NAUSISTRATA, *to himself.*] Wow! My wife! I almost said too much!

Demipho
[*Testily.*] And just why do you wish I hadn't?

Chremes
[*Making frantic signals to* DEMIPHO *to drop the subject.*] It's all right, it's all right.

Demipho
What about you? Have you spoken to the girl and told her why we're sending Nausistrata?

Chremes
[*As before.*] I took care of it.

Demipho
Well, what does she say?

Chremes
We can't send her away.

Demipho
And why can't we?

Chremes
[*Hesitating as he searches for an excuse.*] Because they're in love with each other.

Demipho
[*Exasperated.*] What do we care?

Chremes
A lot. Besides, I found out she's a relative of ours.

Demipho
What! Are you crazy?

Chremes

It's the truth. I mean it. I remembered; it all came back to me.

Demipho

Are you in your right mind?

Nausistrata

Now, Demipho, I don't want you mistreating any relatives!

Demipho

[*Disgusted, to* NAUSISTRATA.] She's no relative.

Chremes

Don't say that. Her father went by a different name. That's what threw you off.

Demipho

[*Getting more and more confused at both the conversation and* CHREMES' *signals.*] She didn't know her own father?

Chremes

[*Disgusted at* DEMIPHO's *lack of comprehension.*] She knew him.

Demipho

Then why did she give the wrong name?

Chremes

[*Giving up trying to flag* DEMIPHO *with signals, pointedly.*] Why can't you leave this to me? Can't you understand?

Demipho

Well, if you're going to talk utter nonsense—

Chremes

[*Sotto voce.*] You're ruining me!

Nausistrata

[*Bewildered.*] What's going on here, anyway?

Demipho

I swear I don't know!

Chremes

[*Throwing caution to the winds.*] All right, you want to know? So help me heaven if you and I aren't the closest relatives that girl's got!

Demipho
[*Losing his patience and temper simultaneously.*] God in
heaven! Let's go see *her*. I want all of us to get to the
bottom of this together.

Chremes
[*Groaning.*] Oh, Lord!

Demipho
[*Sotto voce.*] What's the matter?

Chremes
[*Sotto voce.*] You! Can't you trust me?

Demipho
[*Sotto voce.*] Am I supposed to believe this? [CHREMES
nods frantically.] Should I stop asking questions? [*More
frantic nods.*] All right, I will. But what about that
[*noticing out of the corner of his eye that* NAUSISTRATA
is straining her ears] —er, daughter of "our friend"?
What's going to happen to her?

Chremes
[*Sotto voce.*] It's all right!

Demipho
[*Sotto voce.*] Then should we get rid of her?
[*Nodding in* NAUSISTRATA's *direction.*

Chremes
[*Sotto voce.*] Why not?

Demipho
[*Aloud.*] Then we'll let the girl stay?

Chremes
Yes.

Demipho
In that case, Nausistrata, we won't be needing you.

Nausistrata
I'm glad she's staying. I think it will be much better for
all of us than what you were trying to do. She seemed
like such a nice girl when I saw her.
[*Enters her house.*

Demipho
Now what's this all about?

Chremes
[*Sotto voce.*] Has she shut the door yet?

Demipho
Now she has.

Chremes
[*Whooping.*] Heavenly days! Lady Luck's looking after us!
I found out that my daughter is married to your son!

Demipho
[*Not believing his ears.*] What! Now how could that—

Chremes
[*Looking around warily.*] I can't tell you here. It's not safe
enough.

Demipho
Go inside then.

Chremes
[*As he follows* DEMIPHO *into the latter's house.*] Now, re-
member! I don't even want our own sons to find out
about this!
[*Enter* ANTIPHO, *stage left, back from having reported to*
PHAEDRIA *the success of their plan to raise the money.
At this moment his morale is at low ebb.*]

Antipho
[*To himself.*] No matter how things stand with me, I'm
delighted Phaedria got what he wanted. [*Shaking his
head ruefully.*] That's the smart way: train your mind
to go after only what can be fixed up without fuss if
things go against you. In his case, the minute he got
his money he got his release from worry. But I'm in a
mess that just doesn't leave any way out: to keep my
secret means mental torture, and if I divulge it I'm disgraced. I'm only going back home now because I still
have hopes of holding on to her. But where can I find
Geta? I want to ask him when he thinks would be the
right moment to tackle my father.
[*Enter* PHORMIO, *stage left. He doesn't notice* ANTIPHO,
who is standing near the door of his house.]

Phormio
[*To himself.*] I took the money and paid the pimp. He set
the girl free, but I carted her off and made sure

Phaedria got her all for himself. There's only one thing left on the agenda: to get the old men to give me some time off so's I can throw a wild party. I'm taking a vacation the next few days.

Antipho
There's Phormio. Hi! What's new?

Phormio
About what?

Antipho
About what Phaedria's going to do now. Did he tell you how he plans to drink up his well of love?

Phormio
He's going to take his turn at playing your role.

Antipho
What's that?

Phormio
Keeping away from his father. And he wants you to take your turn at his role. Wants you to plead his cause for him because he'll be away at a party at my house. I'm telling the old men I'm going to run down to the market at Sunium to buy that maid Geta gave them a story about. Otherwise, when they don't see me around here, they'll think I'm off somewhere throwing their money away. Hey, your door's opening.

Antipho
[*Hastily going off to the side.*] See who's coming.

Phormio
It's Geta.

[GETA *bursts out of the door carrying his coat. He's in a transport of joy, and, in his excitement, doesn't see either* ANTIPHO *or* PHORMIO.

Geta
[*To himself.*] Oh, luck, Lady Luck! The favors you've loaded on Antipho today, all by yourself! And so sudden!

Antipho
[*Sotto voce, to* PHORMIO.] What in the world does he mean?

Geta

[*To himself.*] And all his friends can unload their worries now. But what am I wasting time for? Why don't I get into this coat and get going, find him, and tell him what's happened?

Antipho

[*Sotto voce, to* PHORMIO.] What's he talking about? Do you make any sense out of it?

Phormio

[*Sotto voce, to* ANTIPHO.] No. Do you?

Antipho

[*As before.*] None at all.

Phormio

[*As before.*] Same here.

Geta

[*To himself.*] I'll go to Dorio's house; that's where they are. [*Starts off at a gallop.*

Antipho

Hey, Geta!

Geta

[*Not recognizing the voice and thinking it's someone calling him back just for a joke, to himself.*] There you are! The same old joke—call you back the minute you get under way!

Antipho

Geta!

Geta

[*Disregarding the command and moving off, to himself.*] Still at it, by god! Go on, pester me; it's going to get you nowhere.

Antipho

Are you going to stop or aren't you?

Geta

[*Without turning around.*] Go hang yourself!

Antipho

You little stinker, that's just what's going to happen to you if you don't stop this minute!

Geta

[*To himself.*] Wants to wallop me—must be one of the family. [*Turning around.*] Here's the very man I was going after, in the flesh! Come here! Quick!

Antipho

What's up?

Geta

Hail, mortal most favored of all mortals alive! Antipho, you're heaven's favorite son. It's beyond debate.

Antipho

I wouldn't mind. And I wouldn't mind being told just why I should believe it.

Geta

Will you be satisfied if I drench you with joy?

Antipho

[*Angrily.*] Cut it out!

Phormio

[*Stepping forward to join them.*] Just skip the promises and let's have the facts.

Geta

[*Surprised.*] You here too, Phormio?

Phormio

Yes, I'm here. Now stop wasting time.

Geta

[*The words tumbling out in his excitement.*] Listen to this! [*To* PHORMIO.] After we gave you the money downtown just now, we came right home. [*To* ANTIPHO.] Then Demipho sent me to see your wife.

Antipho

[*Suspiciously.*] What for?

Geta

Let's skip it; it has nothing to do with the case. I start to go into her room when her slave boy runs up to me, grabs my coat from behind, and hauls me back. I look around and ask him why he's holding me back; he tells me no one's allowed to go in to her. "Sophrona," says he, "took Chremes in there just now and he's in there now with them." When I heard this, I got on tiptoe, very quietly went up to the doorway, stood there, held my

breath, and stuck my ear against the door. Then I
listened as hard as I could, like this [*demonstrates*], to
catch what they were saying.

Phormio

Good work, Geta.

Geta

And I heard something that was absolutely sensational.
By god, I almost cheered out loud.

Antipho

What was it?

Geta

[*Keeping up the suspense as long as he possibly can.*] What
do you think?

Antipho

I give up.

Geta

It's a miracle. I found out that your uncle is—Phanium's
father!

Antipho

[*Totally unable to believe it.*] What? What's that you say?

Geta

He used to live with her mother in Lemnos. It was a
secret.

Phormio

[*Not convinced.*] You're dreaming! You mean the girl
didn't know her own father?

Geta

Believe me, Phormio, there's some explanation for it.
You think I was able, standing outside that door, to
catch everything that went on between them inside?

Antipho

[*Who had been deep in thought the past moment.*] By god,
I remember hearing some story like that myself!

Geta

Wait, I'll give you even more proof. Pretty soon your
uncle comes out of the house. Then, a little while later,
he goes back inside again with your father. Both of them
now say you're going to be allowed to keep the girl.

Finally they sent me off to find you and bring you back.

Antipho
Hey! Let's go! What are you waiting for!

Geta
Right behind you!

Antipho
[*On the run.*] Phormio! Goodbye!

Phormio
Goodbye, Antipho! So help me, it's wonderful news!
Congratulations! [*Standing, smiling at the departing
figures, to himself.*] What a stroke of luck for those boys!
And right out of the blue! [*The smile opens to a broad
grin as inspiration seizes him.*] This is the perfect time
to blackmail the old men and relieve Phaedria of his
financial worries. Then he won't have to go begging
from his friends. That money—I made them give it to
me, and I'll make them give it to him. I found out how
from what I found out now. This calls for a new pose
and a new look. [*Tries out a posture or two, presumably
typical of forthright men of integrity and dignity.*] I'll
hide in this little back street. Then I'll show myself as
soon as they come out. I won't be going on that trip to
Sunium I gave them a story about.
[*Moves over far to stage left.*
[DEMIPHO *and* CHREMES *come out of the former's house.
They are both euphoric.*

Demipho
Chremes, the good lord deserves all my thanks, now
that things have turned out so well. But what we've
got to do, and right now, is see Phormio and get back
our fifteen thousand before he blows it all.

Phormio
[*Leaving his hiding place and walking toward Demipho's
door, loudly to himself.*] I'll see if Demipho's home. I
want to—

Demipho
[*Interrupting.*] Phormio! We were just going to see *you*.

Phormio
[*Affecting pleased surprise.*] Maybe about the very same
thing, eh?

Demipho
[*Grimly.*] You're absolutely right.

Phormio
[*Innocently.*] That's what I thought. But what did you want to come to my house for?

Demipho
[*Testily.*] Don't be funny!

Phormio
[*Affecting incredulity.*] Were you afraid I wouldn't come through once I got my hands on the money? [*Becoming the injured innocent.*] Now, listen here: I don't care how poor I am, there's one thing I always keep sacred, and that's my word.

Demipho
[*To* CHREMES.] There! Didn't I tell you he was a gentleman?

Chremes
Absolutely.

Phormio
That's just what I was coming to tell you, Demipho: I'm all ready. Set the wedding date whenever you want. Once I saw how you two had your hearts set on it, I thought it was only fair to put everything else off.

Demipho
[*Taken off balance, but thinking fast.*] Well, Chremes here has talked me into not having you marry her. "What are people going to say if you do a thing like that?" he says. "Back when you could have done it decently, you didn't; it would be a scandal to separate them and throw her out now." Just about the same objections you were throwing in my face a little while ago.

Phormio
[*Shifting into high dudgeon.*] You fellows are playing pretty fast and loose with me!

Demipho
How so?

Phormio
What a question! I can't even marry my ex-fiancée now. How do you think I'd look going back to her

after throwing her over the way I did?

Chremes

[*Prompting* DEMIPHO, *sotto voce*.] Say to him, "Besides, I see now that Antipho doesn't want to let her go."

Demipho

[*To* PHORMIO, *quickly, like a schoolboy reciting a lesson*.] Besides, I see now that my son doesn't want to let the girl go. [*In his usual manner*.] So, if you don't mind, Phormio, we'll go downtown now and have that money turned back to me.

Phormio

But I've already turned it over to my creditors.

Demipho

[*Ominously*.] What do we do now?

Phormio

[*Playing his role to the hilt*.] If you want me to go through with the marriage to that girl you promised me, I'm ready. But if you want her to stay there with you, Demipho, then the dowry stays here with me. After all, it was only to help out your family and its reputation that I broke off my engagement. My fiancée's dowry was just as big, and it's not fair for me to be cheated out of it just because of you.

Demipho

You can go to hell, you and your big talk! You think we don't know the kind you are and what you've been carrying on?

Phormio

Now, don't make me lose my temper!

Demipho

So you'd marry her if we let you, eh?

Phormio

Try it.

Demipho

So my son could live with her at your house, eh? That was the plan, wasn't it?

Phormio

[*Ominously*.] Would you mind telling me just what you're talking about?

Demipho
[*Realizing he's gone a bit too far.*] Never mind. Just you hand over the money.

Phormio
Oh, no. Just you hand over my wife.

Demipho
[*Grabbing him by the arm.*] You're going straight to the courthouse.

Phormio
[*Breaking loose.*] The courthouse, eh? All right, if you two are going to keep on annoying—

Demipho
[*Interrupting truculently.*] Just what are you going to do about it?

Phormio
Do about it? Maybe you think I only look after women without dowries. I'm an old hand at taking care of the ones with money, too.

Chremes
What's that to us?

Phormio
[*Carelessly.*] Oh, nothing. [*Turning and looking straight at Chremes.*] Just that I happen to know a certain lady with money around here whose husband had another wife—

Chremes
[*Startled.*] Hah?

Demipho
[*To* CHREMES.] What's the matter?

Phormio
[*Calmly continuing.*] —in Lemnos—

Chremes
[*Aside.*] That's the end of me!

Phormio
—and a daughter. And he's brought the child up behind this certain lady's back.

Chremes
[*Aside.*] You can start digging my grave!

Phormio

And this is just what I'm going to tell her right now.
The whole story.
[*Makes as if to head for Chremes' house.*

Chremes

No! Please! Don't!

Phormio

Oh, so it was you, eh?

Demipho

[*Gnashing his teeth.*] He's making fools of us!

Chremes

[*Desperately.*] We give up. You just go on your way.

Phormio

[*Snorting.*] That's a good one!

Chremes

What do you want, anyway? Keep the money. It's a
gift.

Phormio

[*To* CHREMES, *whose face is full of shocked surprise that*
PHORMIO *isn't grabbing at the chance and running.*] I
heard you. [*Swiftly he resumes his air of high dudgeon;
though he has gotten what he was after, he is enjoying
the situation too much to quit.*] What the devil do you
mean by playing around with me, changing your minds
like a pair of stupid kids? [*Imitating them.*] "I won't, I
will," then, all over again, "I will, I won't"; "Take it,
give it back." You say something, you take it back; you
make a deal, the next minute you break it.

Chremes

[*To* DEMIPHO.] How did he find out about it? Who told
him?

Demipho

[*To* CHREMES.] I don't know! One thing I do know,
though: I didn't tell a soul.

Chremes

[*To* DEMIPHO.] It's a miracle, so help me.

Phormio

[*Aside.*] I've got him on pins and needles.

Demipho

[*To* CHREMES.] Listen here. Are we going to let him stand
there with that grin on his face and do us out of all
that money? God almighty, I'd rather die! Try to be a
man; let's see a little spunk in you! Look, the story's
already leaked out and you can't keep it from your wife
now. She's going to hear it from others, so let's tell it
to her ourselves. It'll have a much better effect. Then
we can get even with this godforsaken good-for-nothing
any way we want.

Phormio

[*Aside.*] Oh, oh, I'm stuck unless I watch out. They're
coming at me with no holds barred!

Chremes

[*In despair, to* DEMIPHO.] I'm afraid nothing will have a
better effect on her!

Demipho

Don't worry, Chremes. I'll get you back in her good
graces. I'm banking on the fact that the mother of this
child of yours has passed away.

Phormio

So that's what you're going to do, eh? Pretty smart
tactics. By god, Demipho, you've been needling me and
it's not going to do that brother of yours any good. [*To*
CHREMES.] What do you mean? After playing around to
your heart's content on Lemnos, not giving a second
thought to that lovely wife of yours, even coming up
with a new way to insult her, you're going to go up to
her now and set everything straight by saying you're
sorry, eh? Why, when I get done talking to her she'll be
so burned up you're not going to put out the fire even if
you squeeze out tears to throw on it.

Demipho

Oh, god damn him! To think that any man alive could
have such gall! This crook ought to be run out of town
to the nearest desert island for the public good.

Chremes

[*Helplessly.*] I'm at the point where I simply don't know
what to do about him.

Demipho
[*Savagely.*] I do. Let's go to court.

Phormio
[*Brightly.*] Court? Right this way, if you please.
[*Starts walking toward the door of Chremes' house.*

Chremes
[*Frantically.*] Follow him! Hold him until I get the servants out here!

Demipho
[*Grabbing* PHORMIO *and struggling to hold him back.*] I can't do it alone. Help me!

Phormio
[*Trying to pull himself free.*] I'm suing you for assault and battery, Demipho!

Demipho
Tell it to the judge!

Phormio
[*To* CHREMES *as he joins in.*] You too, Chremes!

Chremes
[*Hauling away with* DEMIPHO.] Get him out of here!

Phormio
So that's the idea, eh? That means I've got to use my lungs. [*Yelling.*] Nausistrata! Come on out!

Chremes
Shut his mouth! [*Tries to do so without success.*] Damn him! He's strong!

Phormio
Nausistrata!

Demipho
So you're not going to shut up?

Phormio
Me shut up?

Demipho
[*To Chremes.*] Punch him in the belly if he won't come!

Phormio
Poke my eye out while you're at it. But you'll pay for it.

Both of you. Through the nose.

[*The door of Chremes' house opens and* NAUSISTRATA *appears.*

Nausistrata

[*Coming through the door.*] Who's calling me? [*Starting at the sight of the struggle.*] Chremes! Please! What's this ruckus all about?

[*At the sound of her voice, the struggle ends abruptly.* PHORMIO *stands his ground coolly,* DEMIPHO *remains alongside him still breathing fire—and* CHREMES *attempts to make himself as inconspicuous as possible.*

Phormio

[*To* CHREMES.] Hey, what's the matter? Lost your tongue?

Nausistrata

[*To* CHREMES.] Who is this person? [*Waits a moment for a reply.*] Why don't you answer me?

Phormio

[*To* NAUSISTRATA.] Answer you? How can he? He doesn't know he's alive.

Chremes

[*To* NAUSISTRATA.] Don't believe a word he says!

Phormio

[*To* NAUSISTRATA.] Go and touch him; I'll stake my life he's stone cold.

Chremes

[*To* NAUSISTRATA.] It's nothing, nothing at all.

Nausistrata

[*To* CHREMES.] What's going on, then? What's this man talking about?

Phormio

[*To* NAUSISTRATA.] You'll find out right away. Just listen.

Chremes

[*To* NAUSISTRATA.] Are you going to believe him?

Nausistrata

[*To* CHREMES.] My dear man, how can I believe him when he hasn't said anything?

Phormio

[*To* NAUSISTRATA.] The poor devil's so scared he's out of

his mind.

Nausistrata
[*To* CHREMES.] It must be something special to make you sound so scared.

Chremes
Me? Scared?

Phormio
All right, then, since you're not scared and what I have to say is just nothing at all, you tell her yourself.

Demipho
[*To* PHORMIO.] Damn you, he doesn't have to talk for you!

Phormio
[*To* DEMIPHO.] See here, you, you've done enough for your brother.

Nausistrata
Chremes, my dear, aren't you going to tell me—

Chremes
But—

Nausistrata
What do you mean "but"?

Chremes
[*Miserably.*] There's nothing to tell.

Phormio
Nothing for you to tell. But something for her to hear.
[*To* NAUSISTRATA, *slowly and deliberately.*] In Lemnos—

Demipho
[*Finally losing his nerve and deciding to affect ignorance.*]
What? What's that you say?

Chremes
[*Frantically to* PHORMIO.] Shut up, will you!

Phormio
[*Continuing unperturbed.*] —behind your back—

Chremes
Lord help me!

Phormio
—he got married.

Nausistrata

[*Reeling back in shock.*] Oh, no! Oh, god forbid!

Phormio

That's what he did.

Nausistrata

[*Bursting into tears.*] Oh, my god, my god! Oh, this will be the death of me!

Phormio

And he had a daughter. And you were fast asleep all the time.

Chremes

[*Sotto voce, to* DEMIPHO.] What are we going to do?

Nausistrata

God in heaven! Oh, what a miserable, criminal thing to do!

Phormio

That's the story.

Nausistrata

Did you ever hear anything worse in your life? Oh, those husbands! They're only old and feeble when it comes to their wives. Demipho, I appeal to you, since I can't stand talking to *him*. Tell me, is this what all those trips to Lemnos and those long stays there were all about? Is this the reason for the "bad business conditions" that cut down my rents from there?

Demipho

Now, Nausistrata, I don't deny he deserves to be blamed in all this, but there are extenuating circumstances—

Phormio

[*Aside.*] We will now hear the funeral oration.

Demipho

You see, he didn't do it because he didn't care for you or because he wanted to hurt you. About fifteen years ago he got drunk, violated some poor woman, and out of it came this daughter. But he never touched the woman again. She was the stumbling block in the whole business, and now she's dead, she's passed on, she's passed away. And that's why I ask you, please, just as you've always been, be reasonable now.

Nausistrata
Why should I be reasonable? There's nothing I want more than to be over and done with all this. But what's a poor woman like me to expect? That he'll behave better because he's getting older? He was no youngster back then—if getting old has anything to do with a man's morals. Do you think *my* good looks have improved with age, Demipho? What reason can you give me to expect, or at least hope, that this won't happen again?

[DEMIPHO *stands embarrassed and silent before these unanswerable objections.*

Phormio
[*Imitating an undertaker.*] The funeral procession for our dear departed Chremes is about to begin. [*To the world at large.*] That's the way I do things. Come on, whoever wants, take a swing at Phormio. I'll pay you back the same way I did this poor devil. [*Waits a second to see if anyone will take up his challenge. Then, to himself.*] Oh, let's give him his return to grace. I've had enough out of him to satisfy me. And she's got something on him now that she can din into his ears every day as long as he lives.

Nausistrata
[*To* DEMIPHO, *ironically.*] I suppose I deserved this. Demipho, I don't have to give you a list of all the things I did for this man.

Demipho
[*Hastily.*] I know them as well as you do.

Nausistrata
Do you think I deserved what he did to me?

Demipho
You most certainly did not. But look, what's done can't be undone by recriminations. Forgive him: he's on his knees, he confesses, he apologizes. What more do you want?

Phormio

[*Aside.*] Before she starts issuing pardons, I'd better look out for Phaedria and myself. [*Aloud.*] Nausistrata, before you give him any hasty answers, listen to me.

Nausistrata

What is it?

Phormio

I swindled your husband out of fifteen thousand. I gave the money to your son. He gave it to a slave dealer for his mistress.

Chremes

[*Suddenly snapping out of his slough of despond.*] What? What's that you say?

Nausistrata

[*Rounding on him.*] And what seems so terrible to you about that? If you can have two wives, a youngster like Phaedria can certainly have one mistress. You have absolutely no sense of shame. How do you think *you'd* look scolding *him?* Come on, answer me!

Demipho

[*Soothingly.*] He'll do just as you want.

Nausistrata

I'll tell you what I'm going to do. I'm not giving any pardons or making any promises or answering any questions until I've seen my son. I'll let him decide everything. I'll do whatever he says.

Phormio

You're a sensible woman, Nausistrata.

Nausistrata

[*To* CHREMES.] Are you satisfied?

Chremes

[*Hastily.*] Yes! Oh, yes! I never thought I'd get off so easy.

Nausistrata

[*To* PHORMIO, *taking him affectionately by the arm.*] Tell me, what's your name?

Phormio

Mine? Phormio. And, on my honor, ma'am, a friend of your whole family and the best friend of your son, Phaedria.

Nausistrata
Phormio? Well, on my honor, sir, from now on if there's anything you want me to do or say for you, I'll be very glad to help out, as much as I can.

Phormio
That's very kind of you.

Nausistrata
[*Glaring over her shoulder at her husband.*] Lord knows you deserve it.

Phormio
Nausistrata, do you want to start off by doing something right today that will make me very happy—and eat your husband's heart out?

Nausistrata
I'd love to.

Phormio
Invite me to dinner.

Nausistrata
You're invited.

Phormio
Let's go inside.

Nausistrata
Let's. [*She takes his arm again and the two start to walk toward the house. Suddenly she stops.*] But where's Phaedria, our chief justice?

Phormio
I'll have him here in a minute.
[*A* SUPERNUMERARY *steps forward to the front of the stage.*

Supernumerary
The play is over. May we please have your applause.

Terence

THE BROTHERS

Translated by Warren H. Held

Characters   *Micio, an old Athenian*

Demea, an old man and brother of Micio

Sannio, a procurer

Aeschinus, a youth, son of Demea

Syrus, a slave to Micio

Ctesipho, a youth, son of Demea

Sostrata, an Athenian matron

Canthara, an old servant

Geta, a slave to Sostrata

Hegio, an old Athenian

Pamphila, an Athenian maid

Dromo, a boy slave to Micio

Parmeno, a slave to Aeschinus

Bacchis, a courtesan

Since Demea has two sons, to his brother Micio he gives
Aeschinus for adoption, but he retains Ctesipho. When
Ctesipho is overcome with the charm of a girl cithara[1]
player, his brother Aeschinus hides the affair from their
stern and strict father; he has the guilt for the wooing
placed on himself; at length he snatches the cithara
player from the procurer. Aeschinus himself has violated
a poor Attic girl and has given her his pledge to marry
her. Demea scolds and is perplexed. Soon, however, as
the truth comes out, Aeschinus marries the seduced girl;
Ctesipho keeps the cithara player.

Prologue

After the poet realized that his works were to be noticed
by critics and that his opponents would do everything
possible to ruin the play which we are about to put on,
he decided to state his own case and let you be the
judges as to whether his work is praiseworthy or de-
testable. The *Synapothnescontes*[2] is a comedy by Dip-
hilus; Plautus has adapted this story as *The Dying
Friends*. In the beginning of the Greek version, there is
a young fellow who snatches a wench away from a
procurer. Plautus left this part intact. Terence has
borrowed this plot in *The Brothers* and has used it word
for word. We will act it out as a new play: you judge
whether you think this is plagiarism or making use of
what someone else, through negligence, has over-
looked. For that which those malevolent fellows charge,
that some experts help him and that they continually
write together with him: that which they believe to be
a violent accusation, he considers to be his strongest
point, that he can make those men happy with whom

you and all Romans are happy, and of whose accomplishments in war, in times of peace, and in your own affairs each of you in your need has made use without disdain. From this point on, do not expect me to tell you the development of the play. The old gentlemen who come first will tell you a part of it, and the rest will become apparent through the action. Make your impartial judgment so that the poet's zeal for writing may increase.

Act One

[SCENE: *An Athenian street on which stands the homes of* MICIO *and* SOSTRATA. MICIO *enters from his home, calls to someone inside, receives no answer and speaks to the audience. The time is early morning.*

Micio

Storax! [8] Aeschinus didn't come back from the dinner last night, nor did any of the slaves who went for him. Indeed, they say truly: if you are away somewhere and if you dally there, it is better that those things have happened of which your wife accuses you and which she believes in her anger than those which loving parents imagine. If you dally, your wife thinks either that you are making love to someone, or that someone is making love to you, or that you are hitting the bottle and enjoying yourself, and that you are having a good time alone while she languishes. What awful things I am thinking because my son hasn't come home! Now I am worried about such things as whether he may have caught a sniffle, or whether he has fallen somewhere, or whether he has fractured something. Good gosh! That any fellow should become so taken with something that he permits it to become more important to him than he is to himself! And this fellow is not even my son, but my brother's. My brother has had different interests from those I have had from my youth. I have sought leisure and this easy urban life, and I have never married, a circumstance men consider fortunate. He has wanted the opposite of all these things. He has led a life in the country; he was frugal and austere; he took a wife and had two sons. I have adopted for myself the older one of these; I have brought him up from childhood, I have kept him around me, and I have loved him as I would have were he my own. My happiness is in him; he alone is dear to me. I purposely behave in such a way that he will love me, too: I give him things, I close my eyes to his faults, and I do not consider it necessary to interfere in all of his affairs. Furthermore, I have made my boy used to telling me those little confidences which youth has and which other boys keep in secret from their fathers. For anyone who is used to lying to his father or to leading him astray will do these things to others all the more. I think it is better to keep the loyalty of sons through decency and generosity than through fear. My brother disagrees with me, and dislikes my method. He comes to me often, shouting, "What are you doing, Micio? Why are you spoiling the boy for us? Why is he chasing girls? Why is he drinking? Why do you give him the money for these things? You please him too much with clothing. You are foolish in all this." He is much too harsh beyond what is fair and right; and, in my opinion, he is very wrong to think that authority which is created by force is more important and more durable than that which is formed through friendship. I figure it this way, and I believe it is this way. One who does what he is supposed to do because he has been wrongly made to, will be afraid only as long as he thinks he may be found out. If he expects not to be found out, he will return again to his natural way of life. But that youth whom you bind to you with kindness behaves naturally, he wants to return the kindness, and whether he is with you or not, he will be the same. This is a father's function: to accustom his son to be good because he wants to, rather than because he is afraid of someone. This is how a father and a master differ. Anyone who is unable to do this should confess that he does not know how to raise children; but here is the man himself whom I was discussing, isn't it? Certainly it is. I don't know why I see him troubled. I

think he will quarrel now, as he usually does. [*To*
DEMEA.] I am happy to see you so healthy, Demea.
[DEMEA *enters, having come down the street.*

Demea

Well, this is convenient. I was just looking for you.

Micio

Why are you so sad?

Demea

Are you asking me why I should be sad? Where is
Aeschinus, our son?

Micio

[*To the audience.*] I said it would be like this, didn't I?
[*To* DEMEA.] What did he do?

Demea

What did he do? Nothing shames him, he fears no one,
and he thinks that no law restrains him. I won't even
discuss what stunts he's pulled before; what a mess he's
made now!

Micio

Well, what is it?

Demea

He has broken down a door and made his way into
someone's home; he has thrashed the whole family
almost to death and even the master himself; he has
carried off some woman he loves. Everyone is exclaim-
ing that it was done most disgracefully. Micio, how
many people have told me this on my way here! It is on
the lips of everyone. Indeed now, if he has to have an
example, doesn't he see that his brother is working hard
and that he is living a moderate and sober life in the
country? He does not do this at all. When I speak
these things to him, Micio, I am speaking them to
you; you are permitting him to be corrupted.

Micio

No one is ever more unjust than a stupid fellow who
believes that nothing is right unless he does it himself.

Demea

Why do you say that?

Micio

Because you, Demea, are judging these things badly. It's no terrible disgrace, believe me, for a youth to go whoring or to drink; that it isn't—not even to break down doors. If neither of us did these things, we were too poor to do them. Now, do you think you should be praised for what you could not do then because of poverty? That is not right, for if we had been able to do it, we would have done it. And you, if you were a real man, would allow that son of yours to do it while his youth permits rather than that he should do it anyhow when he is much older and when, after a long wait, he has planted you outdoors.

Demea

By Jupiter! Mister, you drive me crazy! It is not a terrible disgrace for a youth to do these things?

Micio

Oh, listen! I don't want to hear any more of this affair. You have given your son to me for adoption; he has been made my son. If he commits any sin, Demea, he sins against me; I bear the brunt of it. If he gives banquets, drinks, or perfumes himself, it comes out of my pocket. If he keeps a girl, he can have money from me as long as it suits me; when it doesn't suit me, her door will probably be closed to him. If he has broken down doors, they will be fixed; if he has torn a garment, it will be mended; thank the gods, these things can be paid for, and up to now they have not been burdensome. Furthermore, either stop complaining or find an arbitrator to settle our differences. I shall prove that you are more wrong than I in this matter.

Demea

Oh, my! Learn how to be a father from those men who know the right way to do it.

Micio

You are his natural father, but I give him advice.

Demea

What kind of advice do you give him?

Micio

I'll go away if you persist in this talk.

Demea

Why do you act like this?

Micio

How often must I hear this same thing?

Demea

I worry about it.

Micio

And I worry about it, too. Really, Demea, let us each tend to his own share: you to the one boy, I likewise to the other; for if you take care of both of them, you are practically demanding back the boy whom you have given to me.

Demea

Oh, Micio!

Micio

It looks that way to me.

Demea

Very well. If it makes you happy, let him throw away your money, let him get lost, let him go to hell—it is of no consequence to me. But if you say one word after this—

Micio

Are you becoming angry again, Demea?

Demea

Don't you believe what I say? Am I asking back the son I gave? It is difficult; I am not a stranger; if I stood in the way . . . well, I won't. You want me to look after my one son; I am looking after him, and I thank the gods that he is everything I wish. That son of yours will realize sometime . . . I don't wish to say anything more unpleasant about him.

[*Exit* DEMEA.

Micio

These things he says are neither all wrong nor are they all true, yet I am not a little troubled by them; I don't want to show him that I regret it. For he is the kind of person who, whether I try to appease him or whether I strongly oppose him and frighten him, scarcely takes it as a favor. Truly, if I should increase or even help his anger along, I would really be as insane as he. Still, Aeschinus is not doing me any favor in this affair. To what local strumpet has he not made love, or to whom has he not given some gift? Finally, just recently (I think he was tired of all of them) he said that he wanted to get married. I hoped that his hot-blooded youth had cooled off now, and I was happy. Just look, now he has started again. Yet, whatever it is, I want to know of it and to confront the fellow if he is in the forum.*

[*Exit* MICIO *in the direction of the forum.*

Act Two

[AESCHINUS *with a courtesan,* SANNIO *and* PARMENO *enter with other slaves. A little time has passed since the end of Act I.* AESCHINUS *has forcibly taken the courtesan from Sannio's establishment and is bringing her home.*

Sannio

I beg you, fellow citizens, aid a wretched and innocent man. Help one who cannot help himself.

Aeschinus

[*Speaking to the courtesan.*] Relax, rest easy here now. Why are you looking around you? There is no risk. He'll never touch you while I'm with you.

Sannio

I'll take her even if all of you are against me.

Aeschinus

[*Still to the courtesan.*] Even though he is a rascal, he won't venture a beating again today.

Sannio

Hear me, Aeschinus, so you don't say that you were unaware of my practices. I sell slave girls.

Aeschinus

I know.

Sannio

Nowhere has any man been found who is more honest
than I am. I shall not be a bit considerate when you
excuse yourself later that you regret this injury which
you have done me. Believe me, I will ask for that which
is legally due me; and it won't be with just talk that
you reimburse me for the wrong you have done me.
I know what your apology will be—"I wish it hadn't
happened; I'll swear that you ought not to have suffered
this wrong"—after I have received this disgraceful
treatment.

Aeschinus

[*To* PARMENO.] Run briskly on ahead of us and open the
door.

Sannio

Do I make no impression on you with my words?

Aeschinus

[*To the courtesan, ignoring* SANNIO.] Go on inside now.

Sannio

Then I'll stop you.

Aeschinus

Go over there, Parmeno. You are too far over that
way; stand against him here. Right, I want you that
way. Now see that you keep watching me so that there
is no delay in pasting your fist on his jaw when I give
you the signal.

Sannio

I just wish he'd try it.
[SANNIO *grabs the courtesan.*

Aeschinus

Hey, look out! [PARMENO *socks* SANNIO *on the jaw.*]
Hands off the girl!

Sannio

What a crime!

Aeschinus

If you don't look out, he'll sock you again.
[PARMENO *socks him a second time.*

Sannio

Oh, my!

Aeschinus

I didn't signal; but it's really a mistake to the good. Now go!

[*All except* AESCHINUS *and* SANNIO *go into Micio's house.*

Sannio

What is all this? Have you possession of a kingdom here, Aeschinus?

Aeschinus

If I had one, you would have been decorated properly.

Sannio

What about your business with me?

Aeschinus

Not a thing!

Sannio

What? Do you realize who I am?

Aeschinus

I couldn't care less.

Sannio

Have I touched anything of yours?

Aeschinus

If you had touched anything, you'd really be badly off.

Sannio

Then why is it any more right for you to have my slave girl for whom I paid good money? Speak up!

Aeschinus

There had better not be a clamor here in front of my own house, for if you continue to be a pest, they'll put you inside and whip you until you're almost dead.

Sannio

Whip a freedman?[5]

Aeschinus

That's the way it will be.

Sannio

You scoundrel! Don't they say that here a freedman is the same as everyone else?

Aeschinus

Now, slave-dealer, if you have raved enough, listen if

you please.

Sannio

Have I been raving at you now, or you raving at me?

Aeschinus

Skip that and come back to the issue.

Sannio

What issue? Where shall I come back?

Aeschinus

Do you want me to speak, now, about the matter which appertains to you?

Sannio

I'd like that as long as the proposal is fair.

Aeschinus

Hah! A slave-dealer who doesn't want me to talk unfairly!

Sannio

I admit I am a slave-dealer, the downfall of youths; a perjuror; a rogue; but, nevertheless, you have never been wronged by me.

Aeschinus

Well, by Hercules, that's one thing you haven't done.

Sannio

I beg you, Aeschinus, go back to the matter which you began.

Aeschinus

You paid twenty minas [6] for her (*I hope you got a rotten deal!*): I'll pay you the same amount of money.

Sannio

What? If I don't want to sell her to you, are you going to force me?

Aeschinus

Not in the least. . . .

Sannio

Oh, I feared that you might.

Aeschinus

. . . Neither do I think that she can be sold: she is free; for I legally claim her as freeborn. Now, choose which you want, to take the money or to prepare your case for court?⁷ Think it over, slave-dealer, until I come back.

[AESCHINUS *follows after the slaves.*

Sannio

[*To the audience.*] Holy Jupiter! I'm not at all surprised that some people go crazy from an injustice. He forced me out of my home, he struck me, he led my slave girl away when I didn't want it, and he rained more than five hundred punches on my ears, wretched fellow that I am. For these crimes he demands to have her for himself at a wholesale price. But since he's really such a deserving fellow, I'll agree; he has a case. So, I'll give in now, as long as he pays the money; but this is foolishness I'm talking. When I claim that I paid a certain amount, he will produce witnesses on the spot that I sold her. The money will be just a dream; he'll say, "Soon, come back tomorrow." I can bear that, too, provided he pays, although it is wrong. But I realize what is going on; when you enter my business, the pranks of young men must be tolerated and kept quiet. Nobody will pay me: I plan these things uselessly.

[SYRUS *enters from the home of Micio.*

Syrus

[*To* AESCHINUS *in the house.*] You've said enough. I'll talk to the fellow myself; I'll arrange it that he will be eager to accept your price and to say that he even got a bargain. [*Turns to* SANNIO.] Sannio, what is this I hear that you have had some fight or other with my master?

Sannio

I have never seen a more unfair fight than the one we had today. I was pommeled, and he struck me until both of us were worn out.

Syrus

You were to blame.

Sannio

What was I supposed to do?

Syrus

You should have let the young man have his way.

Sannio

Was I able to do more? Didn't I even let him punch me on the jaw?

Syrus

Really now, don't you know what I'm saying? Once in a while it is to our best advantage to consider money to be of little consequence. Hah, if now you had somewhat conceded the issue and had yielded to the young man, you wouldn't be afraid that you wouldn't gain something thereby, you most stupid of all human beings.

Sannio

I don't spend my money on idle fancies.

Syrus

You'll never get rich; go away, Sannio. You don't know the way you allure me.

Sannio

I think your method is better; actually, I have never been so astute that I would not rather take what I can in cold cash.

Syrus

Well, I can read your mind: as if twenty minas meant anything at all to you compared to humoring this young man! Furthermore, they tell me that you are ready to go to Cypress . . .

Sannio

[*Surprised.*] What is that?

Syrus

. . . and that you have purchased plenty of goods to export there, and that you have leased a ship. I know that you can't make up your mind. When you come back here again, though, you can complete this business.

Sannio

I'm not budging an inch! Damn it all! [*To the audience.*] This was their intention at the start.

Syrus

[*To the audience.*] He's concerned. I've given the fellow something to worry about.

Sannio
[*Still to the audience*.] What a swindle! Look at the way he attacks me at a very inopportune moment! Many of the women slaves, and also the other wares which I am exporting to Cypress, have been bought. If I don't arrive there for the auction, I'll suffer a very serious loss. Now if I hold off on this matter and then resume it when I come back again from there, I won't get anywhere at all with this affair; it will have been forgotten. The court will ask: "Why do you come now?" "Why have you allowed it?" "Where were you all this time?" Thus it is to my advantage to suffer the loss rather than to stay here any length of time now or to press for it later.

Syrus
Have you figured out now what profit you think will be coming to you after your trip?

Sannio
Is this conduct worthy of him? That Aeschinus should attempt such a thing as to demand that this slave girl be taken away from me by force!

Syrus
[*To the audience*.] He's beginning to crack. [*To Sannio*.] I will make this one suggestion: see if it is satisfactory. Rather than that you, Sannio, should take any risk in saving or losing the whole amount, settle at half the price. He will get ten minas together somehow or other.

Sannio
Oh, me! Now am I going to lose half the investment as well as all of the dividends? Isn't he ashamed of anything? He has shaken loose all of my teeth; furthermore, my whole head is swollen from his punches, and on top of that he wants to cheat me, too! I won't go.

Syrus
As you wish. Do you want anything else before I leave?

Sannio
All right, by Hercules! I ask this, Syrus: however these things have been done, rather than that I should take this case to court, give me at least as much as I paid for the girl originally, Syrus. I know that hitherto you

have not had any use for my friendship, but from now on you will say that I am considerate and charming.

Syrus

I'll try; but there I see Ctesipho. He is happy to have his girl.

Sannio

And the favor I asked of you?

Syrus

Wait a little while.

[CTESIPHO *enters, paying no notice to* SYRUS *and* SANNIO.

Ctesipho

[*Talking to himself.*] It is pleasant to receive a favor from anyone when you need it, but it is especially nice to receive a favor from one who is morally obligated to grant it. Oh brother, why should I sing your praises now? I am reasonably certain that anything I may say to your credit would never be enough to describe your true virtue. And so I believe that I have this particular advantage over other people, that no man has a brother possessing more princely qualities than I have.

Syrus

Ctesipho, sir.

Ctesipho

Hello, Syrus. Where is Aeschinus?

Syrus

He is waiting for you there in the house.

Ctesipho

Ah!

Syrus

What is it?

Ctesipho

What is it? Syrus, his efforts have just saved my life. He's a noble chap who thinks of his own affairs secondarily after my welfare. He transfers to himself the reproaches against me, my disgrace, my trouble, and my errors. He can not go beyond this. But what is that commotion by the door?

Syrus
Stay a moment; he is coming through the doorway.
[AESCHINUS *enters from his home.*

Aeschinus
Where is that rascal who would steal from even the gods?

Sannio
[*To the audience.*] He's looking for me. Does he have his purse? Damn me! I don't see a thing.

Aeschinus
Well, this is fortunate; I was just looking for you, Ctesipho. How are you making out? The whole affair is taken care of, so stop your sadness.

Ctesipho
By Hercules, I shall certainly stop it, since I have such a brother as you. Oh, my Aeschinus! My dear brother! I am afraid to make any more compliments to you in your presence lest you believe they are meant in flattery rather than in gratitude.

Aeschinus
Come now, you blockhead; as if we don't know each other by this time, Ctesipho. I regret that we learned it almost too late and that the situation developed almost to the extent that, if the whole population had wanted to help you, it could have done nothing.

Ctesipho
I was being modest.

Aeschinus
Oh, that is not modesty, it is stupidity. And you were ready to flee from your home for such a trifle! Disgusting! I beg the gods to keep us from the likes of that.

Ctesipho
I made a mistake.

Aeschinus
[*Turns to* SYRUS.] What, then, has Sannio to tell us?

Syrus
Oh, he's gentle now.

Aeschinus
I shall go to the forum to pay him off; you go inside to her, Ctesipho.

Sannio

Syrus, I need your help.

Syrus

Let's go, for Sannio here is about to leave for Cyprus.

Sannio

I'm not leaving as soon as you want me to. I have even time to wait here.

Syrus

He will pay you; don't worry.

Sannio

But he should pay me the whole sum.

Syrus

He will pay you all of it; just keep quiet and tag along.

Sannio

I am tagging along.

[AESCHINUS *leaves in the direction of the forum.* SANNIO *follows after.*

Ctesipho

Hey, Syrus.

Syrus

What is it?

Ctesipho

By Hercules, I beg you, pay off that dirty scoundrel as soon as possible so he won't get to my father in some way if he should be riled any more; then I would be undone for good.

Syrus

He won't do it, don't worry. Meanwhile, you go on inside and enjoy her, and tell them to set the tables for us and prepare some food. When our business is done, I shall come back home with some victuals.

Ctesipho

Please do so. When this matter is favorably settled, let us celebrate the rest of the day.

[CTESIPHO *enters his house as* SYRUS *goes toward the forum.*

Act Three

[SOSTRATA *and* CANTHARA *enter from Sostrata's house.*

Sostrata

I ask you, nurse, what should be done now?

Canthara

What should be done, you ask? By golly, I hope it will be all right.

Sostrata

My dear Pamphila, her pains are just now starting.

Canthara

You worry now as if you were never present at a birth or as if you had never had a child yourself.

Sostrata

How unfortunate I am! I have nobody: we are by ourselves; not even Geta is here, nor anyone else whom I can send for a midwife, nor someone who can summon Aeschinus.

Canthara

Goodness! He will certainly show up soon, for never a day passes when he does not come.

Sostrata

He is the only cure for my troubles.

Canthara

Considering the circumstances, the affair could hardly have come out better than it did, mistress. Since a seduction has occurred, it is most fortunate that she was seduced by the kind of fellow who has such a noble character and nature, and who comes from so important a family.

Sostrata

Yes, it is certainly as you say. I pray that the gods watch over him for us.

[GETA *enters. He has seen* AESCHINUS *abduct the courtesan.*

Geta

[*Unaware of the presence of* CANTHARA *and* SOSTRATA.]
Now things are in such a sorry state that if every
Anthenian bestowed his best advice and sought to
correct this injustice which has been inflicted on me,
on my mistress and on Pamphila, he couldn't assist us
in the least. Wretched man that I am! Suddenly so
many things beset us, and we cannot rid ourselves of
them: violence, destitution, unfairness, desolation, disgrace. What times these are! There are terrible crimes,
people are irreligious, and this fellow is really wicked!

Sostrata

[*On the other side of the stage, speaks to* CANTHARA.]
Dear me, now why is it that I see Geta worried and
hurrying so?

Geta

Neither faith, nor a promise, nor compassion has restrained him or deterred him—not even the fact that
the poor girl whom he had disgracefully seduced was
going to have a baby.

Sostrata

I do not understand his words very well.

Canthara

Let's move closer, I beg you.
[*The women move within hearing of* GETA'S *words.*

Geta

[*Still not noticing the women.*] Oh, dear me! I am scarcely
master of myself, I'm burning so with anger. There is
nothing I would rather have than that this entire family
should cross my path so that I could take out all this
anger on them while my grief is yet fresh. If I could
take vengeance on them in my own way, I think it
would be worth to me any amount of punishment. I
would first snuff out the life of the old fellow himself
who created that villain; and then what delightful ways
I would use to slice up that instigator Syrus! I would
hoist him in the air by his middle and smash his head
on the ground so that his brains would be strewn over
the road. As for that Aeschinus, I would gouge out
his eyes and then send him flying. I would jump on the

others, I would pound them, I would drag them, I would send them sprawling! But shouldn't I hurry to tell the mistress of this bad turn of events?

Sostrata
Let's summon him back. Oh, Geta!

Geta
See here, whoever you are, let me alone.

Sostrata
I am Sostrata.

Geta
Where is she? [*Looks behind him.*] You're the very one I am looking for; you're the one I seek. Very fortunately you have crossed my path, mistress.

Sostrata
What's the matter? Why are you trembling?

Geta
Oh, my!

Canthara
What's your hurry, dear Geta? Catch your wind.

Geta
We are totally . . .

Sostrata
We are totally what?

Geta
. . . undone. We're finished.

Sostrata
Speak, I beg you! What is it?

Geta
Now . . .

Sostrata
What do you mean "now," Geta?

Geta
. . . Aeschinus . . .

Sostrata
What about Aeschinus?

Geta

. . . has estranged himself from our family.

Sostrata

Oh, confound it! How?

Geta

He's taken up loving another woman.

Sostrata

Alas, poor me!

Geta

He doesn't carry on secretly, either; he himself seized her publicly from a procurer.

Sostrata

Are you sure of it?

Geta

I'm sure. I watched him with my own eyes.

Sostrata

Oh, dear me. What should we believe now? Or in whom should we put our faith? To think that this is our Aeschinus, the strength of our lives, on whom all our hopes and resources have depended! He was the one who swore that he would never live one day without her, and who said that he would put their baby in his father's lap and beg that he allow them to be married.

Geta

Mistress, stop crying and plan ahead what has to be done under the circumstances. Shall we suffer this indignity, or shall we tell it to somebody else?

Canthara

Come, come, my good man, have you lost your head? Does this appear to you to be a matter for the public ear?

Geta

It certainly doesn't make me happy either. First, his very deed proves that he has a different attitude toward us. Now, if we should announce this affair openly, I'm convinced that he will deny it; your reputation and your daughter's future will be jeopardized. On the other hand, if he fully acknowledges what he did, inasmuch as he loves someone else, it is impractical for Pamphila to marry him. For this reason, you should keep silent however you look at it.

Sostrata

Ah, I shall not even dream of doing that.

Geta

What are you going to do?

Sostrata

I'll tell everybody.

Canthara

Well, take care how you handle the matter, my Sostrata.

Sostrata

The situation cannot become any worse than it is now. In the first place, she is without any dowry; furthermore her chastity, which is like a second dowry, is gone. I can't marry her off as a virgin. This consolation is left us: if he denies the affair, I have the ring which he lost as proof. In the last place, since I know that I am completely blameless, as she has taken neither money nor any other present and as we have not behaved immorally, I shall seek legal action, Geta.

Geta

All right, I admit that your plan is better.

Sostrata

Go as fast as you are able and report the whole affair, as it happened, to Hegio;[8] for Hegio was our Simulus' most faithful friend and respected our family very highly.

Geta

By Hercules, nobody else looks after us.

Sostrata

Hurry, my dear Canthara; run to get a midwife so that when we need her, she'll be in the house.

[GETA *runs to the forum,* CANTHARA *goes in the opposite direction, and* SOSTRATA *goes into the house. Then* DEMEA *walks in from the forum and knocks on Micio's door. There is no answer.*

Demea

Darn it all! I've been told that my son Ctesipho went along with Aeschinus in an abduction. I'll really be put

out if Aeschinus is able to lead my son, who is actually
worthwhile, into wickedness. Where shall I seek him? I
believe he was led off to some tavern or other. That
immoral fellow has persuaded him; I'm positive of it.
But look, I see Syrus coming. Now I'll learn from him
where my son is. Still, by Hercules, he's one of that
crowd, too. If he realizes that I am looking for my boy,
the wretch will never tell me. I shall not show him that
I wish to find Ctesipho.

[SYRUS *comes in with bundles of food, shifts the bundles
and prepares to open the door.* DEMEA *stands off to the
side.*

Syrus

[*To himself.* We related the whole affair to the old man
in the sequence in which it occurred. No one has ever
appeared happier to me.

Demea

[*To the audience.*] By Jupiter, the stupidity of the fellow!

Syrus

He praised his boy and thanked me, who had given him
that advice.

Demea

I'm fit to be tied!

Syrus

He counted out the money on the spot. He gave half a
mina extra to defray other expenses. The money was
spent as he had intended.

Demea

Well, you can trust this fellow if you want something
taken care of properly.

Syrus

[*Suddenly aware that Demea is standing nearby and listening.*] Oh, Demea, I could hardly see you. How are
things?
[*He hands the bundles to someone inside.*

Demea

How should they be? I am overcome with your behavior.

Syrus

By Hercules, it is odd; even crazy, to speak frankly. [*To*

the slaves inside.] Clean the other fish, Dromo, but let that great big conger eel play a little in the water; we'll bone him when I get back; I don't want it done sooner.

Demea

What immoral doings!

Syrus

They certainly don't please me either; I often protest. [*To the slaves again.*] Stephanio, see that these pickled fish are well soaked.

Demea

Ye gods! Is he doing it because he enjoys it, or because he believes it will make him more worthy of praise if he depraves his boy? Oh, mercy me! I seem to see that time already when he will run off to join the army somewhere.

Syrus

Yes, Demea, that is real wisdom, not only to see that which stands in front of you, but also to look ahead at those things which stand in the future.

Demea

Really now, is that cithara singer still in your house?

Syrus

She's inside.

Demea

Well, is he going to keep her in his home?

Syrus

I think so; he's out of his head.

Demea

He's really doing these things!

Syrus

Because of his father's foolish leniency and immoral disposition.

Demea

I am very much ashamed and disgusted with my brother.

Syrus

I am not saying this just because you're here, Demea, but your natures are much too far apart. As for you,

you're the very epitome of wisdom, and he of foolishness. You wouldn't have permitted your boy to do these things, would you?

Demea

I have permitted him? Wouldn't I have sensed it for six whole months before he began anything?

Syrus

Are you describing your parental watchfulness to me?

Demea

I pray that my watchfulness will continue to be as keen as it is now.

Syrus

As each man wants his son to be, so the son appears to the father.

Demea

What about him? Did you see him today?

Syrus

Do you mean your son? [*To the audience.*] I'll chase this fellow out in the country. [*To* DEMEA.] He's been busy out on your farm all this time, I believe.

Demea

Are you certain that is where he is?

Syrus

Oh, it was I myself who brought him out.

Demea

That's great. I was worried that he might be lingering around here.

Syrus

And he was extremely angry.

Demea

Over what?

Syrus

In the forum he got into a fight with his brother over that cithara singer.

Demea

You don't say!

Syrus
Yes, he said what he thought; by chance, while we were counting out the money, he suddenly interrupted us and started shouting, "Oh Aeschinus, what atrocities you are committing! What indignities you heap on our family!"

Demea
Oh, I cry with happiness.

Syrus
He also said, "You're not wasting just this money but your life as well."

Demea
I wish him good health. He's like his old man.

Syrus
Indeed.

Demea
Syrus, he is filled with those adages.

Syrus
[*Ironically and to the audience.*] And how! [*To* DEMEA.] He had in his home a father from whom he could learn them.

Demea
It was intentional: I forget nothing; I acquaint him with everything; I even tell him to observe the vices of others as he would a mirror, and to mold his own life from them. "Do this," I tell him.

Syrus
Quite sensible.

Demea
"Don't do that."

Syrus
Wonderful!

Demea
"This is worthy of praise."

Syrus
That's the thing!

Demea

"This is given to vice."

Syrus

Tops!

Demea

And besides . . .

Syrus

There really isn't time for me to listen now. I've found some fish I like, and I have to watch that they don't spoil; for that is just as outrageous a thing for me as it is for you, Demea, not to do those things which you just now mentioned; and wherever I can, I offer my slave companions this wisdom in a like manner: [9] "This is over salty"; "this is overdone"; "this is not washed enough"; "that's fine—remember next time how you did it." I intentionally tell them what I can from my own experience; I even tell them to observe their plates as they would a mirror and advise them what should be done. I know that these things we do are foolish, but what can you do? You must treat each man according to his worth. Do you want anything else?

Demea

Only that you be given better brains.

Syrus

Will you go out to the farm?

Demea

Certainly.

Syrus

What else can you do here where nobody would listen if you did advise him well?
[SYRUS *enters the house.*

Demea

I shall indeed go there, since my boy (the reason I came here) went to the farm: I worry over him alone; he is close to me. Because my brother wishes it this way, he will have to watch the other boy himself. But whom do I see in the distance there? Isn't it Hegio, who is in our tribe? [10] If I make him out right, it is, by Hercules. Gosh, he's been a friend of mine since I was a boy. Would to heaven we had more citizens of his caliber now! He's a man with the old values of virtue and trust. The state won't have any wrongs done it through him for a long time. How happy I am when I see those few of his kind surviving these days! Oh, it is really still a joy to live. I'll await the man here to say hello and to talk.

[HEGIO *and* GETA *enter but do not see* DEMEA.

Hegio

By the deathless gods, Geta, this affair is disgraceful. What are you telling me?

Geta

Just what happened.

Hegio

To think that such a low deed should have arisen from that family! Oh Aeschinus, you have demonstrated precious few of your father's traits!

Demea

[*To the audience.*] Naturally, he has heard about this cithara singer; he, an outsider, already bemoans the affair, and the boy's father couldn't care less. Oh my, if only he were some place nearby and could hear these things!

Hegio

Unless they make a fair compensation, they will hardly have heard the end of the matter.

Geta

Our complete hope rests on you, Hegio: you are the only one we have, you are our defender and father. As he was dying, the old fellow commended us to your care; if you leave us, we are ruined.

Hegio

Watch what you say. I shall neither leave you nor could I intend to leave you without betraying his friendship.

Demea

I'll go near. [*To* HEGIO.] I give you my heartiest greetings, Hegio.

Hegio

Oh, I was just looking for you; greetings, Demea.

Demea
What for?

Hegio
Your older son Aeschinus, whom you gave to your brother for adoption, is behaving as neither a decent nor an honorable man.

Demea
What's that?

Hegio
You know of Simulus, who was a friend of mine and of my age?

Demea
Why sure.

Hegio
He violated his daughter, still a virgin.

Demea
Good night!

Hegio
Wait, you still haven't heard the worst of it, Demea.

Demea
But can anything be more serious than this?

Hegio
It is more serious; for this first bit might be somehow tolerated in that he was overcome by the night, by his emotions, by drink and by his young age: he is only human. When he realized his deed, he came voluntarily to the girl's mother, weeping, praying, begging, promising and vowing that he would take her into his home as his wife. We forgave him, we kept quiet about the matter, we believed what he said. Because of him, the girl has become pregnant: this month is her tenth. And now, that fine fellow has arranged (*heaven forbid!*) for a cithara singer to live in his house and has forsaken his former love.

Demea
Are you saying these things with any certainty?

Hegio
The girl's mother is right here, and the girl herself in

her pregnant condition; furthermore here's Geta, who is not bad for a slave, nor lazy. He supports them and takes care of the whole house by himself. Take him away, chain him, and investigate the affair.

Geta

By Hercules, just torture me to see if it didn't happen that way, Demea. Even so, Aeschinus will not deny it. Let me confront him.

Demea

[*To himself.*] I am shamed. I have no idea what I should do or what I should answer him.

Pamphila

[*Moans, then speaks from within the house.*] Wretched girl that I am, I am torn with pains. Oh Juno, goddess of birth, help me. I implore you to aid me.

Hegio

Oh, no! She's not having pains already, is she?

Geta

Yes, Hegio.

Hegio

Well, she begs you now, Demea, to effect voluntarily the marriage which she could legally make you effect. I prefer that these things be done in a manner that befits you, but if you have a different opinion about it, Demea, I shall defend her and her dead father with all my strength. He was related to me; we were brought up from little children together; we were always together in the army and at home; we suffered extreme destitution together. That's why I will fight, contest, go to court, even die before I forsake his people. What's your answer?

Demea

I will see my brother, Hegio.

Hegio

But, Demea, be sure you think of this: since you two live very luxuriously and since you are influential, rich, fortunate and high-born, so much the more should you consider these things fairly if you want to be thought honorable by others.

[GETA *and* HEGIO *turn to go.*

Demea

Come back; I will do whatever is proper.

Hegio

It is only right that you do. Geta, bring me to Sostrata inside.

[GETA *takes* HEGIO *into the house.*

Demea

[*Slowly moves toward the forum.*] It wasn't because I didn't tell them that these things happened. If this were only the end of it! Truly, too much wild living will ultimately wind up in some great catastrophe or other. I will go find my brother that I may disgorge this mess on him.

[DEMEA *leaves, and* HEGIO *backs out of Sostrata's door.*

Hegio

Keep your chin up, Sostrata, and do what you can for your daughter. I will see if Micio is in the forum and will tell him how the event occurred. If he wants to do what he should, then let him do it; but if he is disposed otherwise, then let him answer me so I'll know at once what I have to do.

[HEGIO *goes off in the direction of the forum.*

Act Four

[CTESIPHO *and* SYRUS *come out of Micio's house.*

Ctesipho

You say that my father has gone to the farm?

Syrus

A while ago.

Ctesipho

Please tell me what he's doing there.

Syrus

He's at his country place, and I suppose he's just about ready now to do some job or other.

Ctesipho

If only he is! Although I hope he keeps his health, I wish he'd get so tired that he can't get out of bed for the coming three days straight.

Syrus

May it happen as you say, and more than that if it is possible.

Ctesipho

Right, for I want too desperately to spend the rest of today as I have begun it—in merriment; and I hate that farm so violently for no other reason than that it is close by. Thus, if it were farther away, night would fall before he could get back here again. When he doesn't see me there now, he'll hurry back here, I'm certain. He will question me as to where I've been: "I didn't see you all day today." What am I to say?

Syrus

Haven't you any idea?

Ctesipho

Not a thing at all.

Syrus

That makes it all the worse. Don't you have some client, some friend, someone here on a business trip?

Ctesipho

Sure, what about it?

Syrus

Weren't you busy with them?

Ctesipho

When I really wasn't? It won't work.

Syrus

It will work.

Ctesipho

In the day, yes; but if it's at night, what excuse am I to make, Syrus?

Syrus

Gosh, how I wish it were our practice to conduct business with friends at night, too! But just relax: I understand his thoughts precisely. When he is roaring at his best, I am able to make him calm as a lamb.

Ctesipho

How?

Syrus

He enjoys hearing you praised; I turn you into a very god; I describe your virtues.

Ctesipho

Mine?

Syrus

Yours. It makes his tears fall at once for joy, just as if he were a boy. But see there!

Ctesipho

Now what is it?

Syrus

The old boy himself.

Ctesipho

It's father?

Syrus

No one else.

Ctesipho

What will we do, Syrus?

Syrus

Hurry inside; I'll see him.

Ctesipho

If he questions you, you never saw me; do you hear?

Syrus

Can't you keep quiet?

[CTESIPHO *runs into the house, and* DEMEA *enters from the country.*

Demea

[*Aside.*] I'm really an unfortunate fellow: I can't find my brother anywhere at all, and furthermore, while I was looking for Ctesipho, I met a laborer from the farm. He told me that my boy is not out in the country. I do not know what I should do.

Ctesipho

[*Softly from within.*] Syrus.

Syrus

[*To* CTESIPHO.] What is it?

Ctesipho

[*To* SYRUS.] Is he seeking me?

Syrus
[*To* CTESIPHO.] Yes.

Ctesipho
[*To* SYRUS.] I'm ruined.

Syrus
[*To* CTESIPHO.] Oh, cheer up.

Demea
[*To himself.*] What miserable misfortune! I can't figure it out unless I am to think that I was born just to put up with suffering. I am first to be aware of our troubles, first to learn the whole story, and first to pass on the bad news. If anything is done, I alone take the trouble to do it.

Syrus
[*To* CTESIPHO.] He's a panic! He says he's first to know, but he's the only one who doesn't know all about it.

Demea
[*To himself.*] I'm returning now to see whether my brother has come home.

Ctesipho
[*To* SYRUS.] Please, Syrus, see that he doesn't rush headlong in here.

Syrus
[*To* CTESIPHO.] Now you be quiet. I'll watch out.

Ctesipho
[*To* SYRUS.] I can't possibly trust you with that today. I'm going to lock myself with her in some room—that's safest.

Syrus
[*To* CTESIPHO.] Do it, but I'll chase him away anyhow.

Demea
[*Finally seeing* SYRUS.] Look, here's that scamp Syrus.

Syrus
[*Acting as if he has not seen* DEMEA.] Golly, if matters keep on this way, no one will be able to remain here. I'd like to know how many of them are my masters. What a mess this is!

Demea

What is he whining about? What's his problem? [*To* SYRUS.] What do you say, good sir? Is my brother in the house?

Syrus

Why in tarnation do you say "*good sir*" to me? I'm ruined.

Demea

What's your trouble?

Syrus

"Trouble" you ask? Ctesipho has beaten that cithara girl and me almost to death.

Demea

Huh? What are you telling me?

Syrus

Just look how he split apart my lip.

Demea

Why?

Syrus

He claims that I instigated her purchase.

Demea

Didn't you tell me that you just saw him to the farm?

Syrus

Yes, but he came back again raving: nothing moved him to mercy. He wasn't ashamed to thrash me, an old man! I used to carry him around in my hands when he was just a little fellow.

Demea

I approve! Ctesipho, you're a chip off the old block. Now I consider you a man.

Syrus

You approve? He'll certainly keep his hands to himself hereafter if he's intelligent.

Demea

Courageously done!

Syrus

Yes, it's very courageous to beat up a poor woman and

me, a little slave who was not able to hit back. Yes, courageously done!

Demea

It couldn't have turned out better. He realized just as I so that you are the cause of this affair. But is my brother in?

Syrus

He's not in.

Demea

I wonder where I can find him.

Syrus

I know where he is, but I am never going to show you today.

Demea

Now, what are you saying?

Syrus

Just what I said.

Demea

You want your head really bashed in now.

Syrus

I know the place where the man is, but I don't know his name.

Demea

Tell me the place then.

Syrus

Do you know the portico near the meat shop down the street?

Demea

Why shouldn't I know it?

Syrus

Go past it right on up the street. When you have arrived there, a hill slopes downward before you; you go down that. After that there is a shrine on this side; there is a little side-road nearby.

Demea

Where's that?

Syrus

There, where the big fig tree is.

Demea

I know.

Syrus

Go that way.

Demea

But that side-road is a dead-end.

Syrus

By Hercules, that's right. You must think I've lost my senses; I was wrong. Go back again to the portico again. You can really go a much shorter way, and you can't go wrong so easily. Do you know the home of the rich Cratinus?

Demea

I know where it is.

Syrus

When you've passed it, go left and walk straight down that street until you've arrived at the Temple of Diana. Then go right. Before you come to the gate to the city by the lake, there is a little corn mill and a woodshop opposite; he's there.

Demea

What is he doing there?

Syrus

He has put in an order for benches to be built with oaken legs to withstand the sun.

Demea

Where you can do your drinking: that's great! But I must find him.

[DEMEA *goes down the street.*

Syrus

[*To himself.*] Yes, go; today I'll give you the workout that you deserve, you bag of bones. Aeschinus is inexcusably late: the dinner is ruined. Since Ctesipho is head over heels in love, I'll go in now and provide for myself. I'll take the most delicious bit for myself, and then I'll spend the rest of the day leisurely sipping drinks.

[SYRUS *goes in the house.*
[HEGIO *and* MICIO *enter from the forum.*

Micio
I can't find any reason in this for so much praise, Hegio.
I am simply doing my duty by straightening out the
wrong which we did; unless you considered me one of
those men who believe that you do them a wrong and
who blame you if you ask restitution for the wrong they
did. Are you thanking me because I haven't done this?

Hegio
Oh, not in the least: never have I thought you to be
anything other than what you are, but I beg you, Micio,
go with me to the girl's mother and inform her of the
things you said to me, that this suspicion is because of
his brother Ctesipho and his cithara singer.

Micio
If you think I should and if it ought to be done, let's go.

Hegio
You're doing the right thing, for this way you will ease
the mind of a woman who languishes with sorrow and
misery, and you will have performed your duty; but if
you think differently, I shall tell her myself what you
said to me.

Micio
No, I shall go.

Hegio
You're doing the right thing—everyone who has not been
so fortunate is somehow more likely to be suspected:
they interpret everything as an insult and think they
are more ludicrous because of their own insecurity. For
this reason you will be more easily forgiven if you
explain yourself personally.

Micio
You offer excellent advice.

Hegio
Then follow me inside.

Micio
By all means.
[*They go into the home of* SOSTRATA. AESCHINUS *enters.*

Aeschinus

I'm very worried. I have come upon such great diffi-
culties suddenly that I'm not sure what I should do for
myself or how I should act. My limbs are weak from
fright. My courage has left because of fear. My heart
cannot formulate a course of action. Gosh, how shall I
ever extricate myself from this confusion? So much
suspicion has fallen on me now, and for good reason.
Sostrata thinks that I bought this cithara girl for myself.
The old lady informed me of this; for, as chance would
have it, she had been sent for a midwife when I saw
her. I went right up to her and inquired how Pamphila
was doing, whether she was about to give birth and
if on that account she was summoning the midwife. The
old lady shouted, "Off with you, off with you, now,
Aeschinus! You have fooled us long enough. We have
had enough of your poor faith up to now." I said, "Well,
I beg you, tell me what is all this about?" "So long," she
said; "you may keep your favorite girl." I realized
immediately why they were suspicious, but nonetheless,
I contained myself so that I should not say anything
about my brother to that blabbermouth and make the
whole affair common knowledge. Now, what should I
do? Should I say that the girl is really my brother's?
That secret must certainly not be allowed anywhere in
the open. But I shall pass over that as we can see that
it doesn't leak out. I'm afraid they would not believe
the real truth with so much circumstantial evidence
against me. I seized the girl myself; I was the one who
paid the money; she was carried off to my home. I
confess that I am to blame for all this by not having
informed my father of this matter and of how it was
being conducted. I might have begged to marry her.
I've been doing nothing thus far: so now, Aeschinus, be
alert. This is the first step now: I shall go to the ladies
to explain myself. Let me step to the door. Confound
it! I always shudder when I start knocking here. [*Knocks
and yells to those within.*] Hello there! This is Aeschinus.
Somebody open the door quickly! [*To himself.*] Someone's coming out. I'll stand here at the side.

[MICIO *comes out of Sostrata's house.*

Micio

Just do as I said, Sostrata; I will have a talk with

Aeschinus so that he'll know how matters stand. But who knocked on the door?

Aeschinus

[*Aside.*] It's Father, by Hercules. I'm ruined.

Micio

Aeschinus!

Aeschinus

[*Aside.*] What business has he here?

Micio

Did you knock at this door? [*Aside.*] He doesn't say anything. Why shouldn't I have some sport with him for a little while? It is more than right since he never wanted to tell me about it. [*To* AESCHINUS.] Aren't you going to give me an answer?

Aeschinus

I don't think it was that door.

Micio

Really? I just wondered what business you might have here. [*Aside.*] He's blushing. It's all right.

Aeschinus

Please tell me, Father, why are you there?

Micio

Oh, not for myself. A friend just led me here from the forum to give him some legal advice.

Aeschinus

What advice?

Micio

I'll tell you. Some very destitute women live here. I don't believe you know them—in fact, I know you don't, for they have moved here just recently.

Aeschinus

What about them?

Micio

A girl lives here with her mother.

Aeschinus

Continue.

Micio
This girl is without a father; this friend of mine is her closest relative, and he has to marry her by law.

Aeschinus
[*To himself.*] Confound it!

Micio
What's that?

Aeschinus
Nothing; all right. Continue.

Micio
He's come to fetch her away with him, for he lives in Miletus.

Aeschinus
Oh, no! To fetch the girl away with him?

Micio
That's the way it is.

Aeschinus
And all the way to Miletus?

Micio
Yes.

Aeschinus
I'm going to faint. And the women? What do they say?

Micio
What do you think they would say? Nothing, of course. The mother gave out a story that a boy was born to her daughter and some man or other; she didn't name the fellow, but she said that he was first and that the daughter should not marry my friend.

Aeschinus
Really, wouldn't you say she was justified in asking this?

Micio
No.

Aeschinus
Why not? And he will take her off, Father?

Micio
Why shouldn't he take her off?

Aeschinus

You and your friend behaved harshly and mercilessly, and even, if I may say so openly, Father, inconsiderately.

Micio

Why?

Aeschinus

You ask me that? What do you imagine it is like for that wretched, unhappy fellow who loved her first, and who, perhaps, may now yet love her madly, when standing right there he sees her snatched away from him and removed from his sight? A disgraceful thing, Father.

Micio

Why is that? Who offered her hand to him? Who gave her away? To whom was she married and when? Who gave her hand away? Why, has he married a woman promised to someone else?

Aeschinus

Or ought such a mature girl to have sat in her house waiting until her relative should arrive here? You should have said that, Father, and argued for it.

Micio

What foolishness! Was I to argue against the welfare of the man whom I had come to advise? But what do we care about that, Aeschinus? Or what do we care about these people? Let's be off. [*Turns to go.*] What's this? Why the tears?

Aeschinus

Father, I beg you, listen.

Micio

Aeschinus, I have heard and know all about it; for I love you, for which reason I care all the more what you do.

Aeschinus

My wish is that I deserve your love as long as you live, Father, and so I am very sorry that I made this blunder and I'm ashamed of it before you.

Micio

I believe it, by Hercules, for I know your considerate

nature; but I'm afraid that you are over-reckless. In what state do you think you live? You have violated a young woman whom it was not right for you to touch. Now, this is your first really big sin, but it was only human: other good men have often done likewise. But, I ask you, after it had occurred, didn't you think about it? Didn't you look ahead as to what should be done? Or how it should be done? If you were embarrassed to confide it to me, how was I ever to learn it? While you were wondering what to do, nine months passed. You have been as false as you could be to yourself and to that poor girl and to your son. What about it? Were you thinking that the gods would resolve your problems for you when you were asleep and that she would be brought to your bedroom at home without any action on your part? I wouldn't want you to be so lax about your other affairs. Cheer up. You'll marry her.

Aeschinus
What!

Micio
I say, "Cheer up."

Aeschinus
Father, please; you're not teasing me now?

Micio
I tease you? Why?

Aeschinus
I don't know, but I hope so passionately that this is true, that I'm even more afraid it isn't.

Micio
Go on home and pray to the gods to let you fetch a wife. Go on!

Aeschinus
What? A wife now?

Micio
Now?

Micio
Now, as soon as you can.

Aeschinus
May all the gods detest me, Father, if I don't love you more than life itself.

Micio
What? More than you love her?

Aeschinus
Just the same.

Micio
How very kind!

Aeschinus
Well, where's that Milesian fellow?

Micio
He disappeared, took off, got on a ship. But why are you still here?

Aeschinus
Father, you go. It is better for you to ask the gods, for I know they would rather listen to your requests since you are a much better man than I.

Micio
I'm going inside to make the necessary arrangements. You'll do as I have said, if you are sensible.

[MICIO *goes in.*

Aeschinus
[*To the audience.*] What's going on? Is he my father or my son? If he were a brother or a close pal, how could he do more? Is he not worthy of love and adoration? Sure enough! But his complaisance has given me still another great worry, that accidentally I might do something foolish which he wouldn't like; I will have to watch out. But I'll go in now so I won't be the one to delay my own wedding.

[AESCHINUS *enters the house.*

[DEMEA *enters.*

Demea
I'm weary from so much walking. Syrus, may great Jupiter damn you and your directions! I have crept over the whole city: to the city gate, to the lake; where didn't I go? And no woodshop was there, nor did anyone say he had seen my brother. Now I know I'll wait at his home until he comes back.

[MICIO *enters.*

Micio

[*Talking to* AESCHINUS *inside.*] I'll go to tell them that we'll be on time.

Demea

But here he is. I've spent some time looking for you, Micio.

Micio

What for?

Demea

I bear reports to you of other monstrous deeds of that "good" young son of yours.

Micio

Come now!

Demea

New and very serious ones.

Micio

Oh, really!

Demea

You don't know what kind of fellow he is.

Micio

I do know.

Demea

You stupid fellow; you suppose I'm talking about the cithara girl. This is a crime against a young woman, a citizen.

Micio

I know.

Demea

Oh, you know and you permit it?

Micio

Why shouldn't I permit it?

Demea

Tell me, aren't you raving? Aren't you beside yourself?

Micio

No. Indeed, I should rather . . .

Demea

A baby boy has been born.

Micio
May the gods bless him!

Demea
The girl is destitute.

Micio
I've heard.

Demea
She's to be wed with no dowry.

Micio
To be sure.

Demea
Now what's to happen?

Micio
Whatever the circumstances require: the girl will be conveyed here from her house.

Demea
Oh Jupiter! Is that the manner in which you should handle it?

Micio
What else ought I do?

Demea
What ought you do? If this whole affair doesn't bother you, you might at least make believe it does as a decent fellow would.

Micio
But I have already promised him the girl; the marriage is arranged; the wedding will go on. I dispelled their fears. This is more like what a decent fellow would do.

Demea
Are you happy about the whole affair, Micio?

Micio
Not if I were able to change it. But since I'm not able, I take care of it with a level head. A man's life is like a dice game: if that throw which you needed most doesn't fall, you must with your ingenuity make the best of that throw which by chance did fall.

Demea

Make the best! By your great ingenuity you lost the twenty minas paid for the cithara girl, whom you'll have to give away if she can't be sold.

Micio

I neither want to sell her, nor is she for sale.

Demea

What are you going to do, then?

Micio

She will stay in my house.

Demea

Heavens! A mistress and wife together in one home!

Micio

Why not?

Demea

Do you think you're all there?

Micio

I think I am.

Demea

May the gods look after me! Considering your foolishness, I think you plan to take lessons from her.

Micio

Why not?

Demea

And the bride can take these lessons, too!

Micio

Naturally.

Demea

You will play up to both of them?

Micio

Right.

Demea

Right?

Micio

And you along with us if the occasion arises.

Demea

Oh, me! Don't these things cause you any shame?

Micio

Now just bridle that temper of yours, Demea, and be joyous and gay, as you should, at your son's wedding. I'll meet the ladies; I'll be back after that.

[MICIO *goes into Sostrata's home.*

Demea

Oh, Jupiter, this is some life! What morals! What asininity! A wife is arriving without any dowry; a cithara girl is inside; the house is expensively laid out; a young man is ruined through luxury; an old man is raving mad. If the goddess of deliverance herself wanted to, she could not possibly save this family.

Act Five

[SYRUS *comes out of the house. He is drunk.*

Syrus

[*To himself.*] Golly, old Syrus, you did right well for yourself and you fulfilled your office magnificently. Good! But after I am sated with everything inside, I feel like taking a walk out here.

Demea

Look at that product of his discipline, if you will!

Syrus

Well now, our old man is here. What's up? What makes you sad?

Demea

Oh, you rascal!

Syrus

Hey, now! You're too free with your words, wise guy!

Demea

If you were a slave of mine . . .

Syrus

You would be really wealthy, Demea, and well off financially.

Demea

I'd make sure that you set an example for all others such as you.

Syrus

Why? What did I do?

Demea

You ask me that? In all this confusion and in this very worst of sin, when the matter is hardly even settled, you, you rascal, go drinking as if things couldn't be better.

Syrus

[*To himself.*] I wish to hell I hadn't come out.
[DROMO *sticks his head out of the door.*]

Dromo

Ho there, Syrus! Ctesipho asks that you come back.

Syrus

Beat it!
[DROMO *pulls his head in.*]

Demea

What did he say of Ctesipho?

Syrus

Nothing.

Demea

You rogue! Is Ctesipho inside?

Syrus

No, he's not.

Demea

Why did he give his name?

Syrus

This is another fellow, a contemptible little parasite. Do you know him?

Demea

I will now.
[*Steps toward the door.*]

Syrus

What are you doing? Where are you going?
[*Grabs hold of Demea.*]

Demea

Hands off me!

Syrus

Don't go, I say.

Demea

Will you keep your hands to yourself, you wretch, or would you prefer that I splatter your brains here?

[DEMEA *breaks away and runs into the house.*

Syrus

He's going. What a helluva drinking buddy he'll be, especially for Ctesipho. What'll I do now? But I should go off in a corner somewhere until these messes blow over and I sleep off my wine. I'll do that.

[SYRUS *staggers into the house.*

[MICIO *comes out of Sostrata's house.*

Micio

We have made the preparations, as I told you, Sostrata; whenever you want . . . Now who's knocking so hard on my door?

[DEMEA *comes out of Micio's house.*

Demea

Oh me, what am I to do? How am I to contend with this? Shall I rave or just complain? Oh sky, oh earth, oh oceans of Neptune!

Micio

[*To the audience.*] Look there! He's learned the whole truth; that's what he's yelling about, of course. A quarrel is in the making; I have to help out.

Demea

See, there's the one who corrupts both of our sons.

Micio

Just control your temper and be sensible.

Demea

I have controlled it; I am sensible; I'm not saying any naughty words. Let's consider the whole affair. Did we not agree (*and it was all your idea*) that you would not interfere with my son, nor I with yours? Answer me.

Micio

That's so, I admit it.

Demea

Why is he drinking now in your house? Why have you been keeping my boy as a guest? Why are you buying him a girlfriend, Micio? It isn't right for me not to have complete control over my son as you do over yours, is it? Since I'm not concerned over your son, don't concern yourself over mine.

Micio

You're not speaking fairly.

Demea

No?

Micio

There is an old saw that what belongs to one of two friends belongs also to the other.

Demea

That's just great! Why didn't you think of it before this?

Micio

Unless you object, Demea, hear these few words of mine. First, if the boys' extravagance bothers you, I ask you to consider this side of the matter. You were once going to raise the two boys with such money as you had because you thought that your wealth would be sufficient for them both, and because you believed that I would naturally take a wife. You continue that same old system as before: hoard it, look for more, be stingy, do what you must to leave them as much as you can—you revel in that. Let them spend my money which none of you expected. You lose none of your wealth. Whatever they get from me can be considered pure profit. If you would consider these things from this point of view, Demea, you would save yourself, them and me much grief.

Demea

I'll forget the squandering; what about their behavior?

Micio

Hold on; I know; I was coming to that. There are many indications in a man, Demea, from which one can easily draw conclusions; when two men do the same thing, often you can say, "It can hurt this one, that one it won't hurt." The things they do are not different, but the natures of the men who do them are. Those things which I see in those sons of ours will be, I am sure, just what we want. I see that they have sense, intelligence, proper respect, and a love for each other. You know they have noble characters and temperaments. You can lead them back to the right way any time you wish. But you may be worried that they'll be somewhat careless with money. Oh, Demea, we have a better understanding of everything as we get older; old age gives men just this one vice: we are more interested in financial matters than is necessary. They will become keen enough in these as they grow older.

Demea

Just so those good plans of yours and that good-natured character of yours don't cause the destruction of us both, Micio.

Micio

Be still: it won't happen. Now, let's forget it. Let me be your host, and stop worrying.

Demea

I admit the occasion demands it; I'll have to do it. But tomorrow at daybreak I'll go with my son to the country.

Micio

I don't care if you go tonight; just live it up today.

Demea

And that cithara girl I'll take along there with me.

Micio

That way you'll come out on top and you'll have your boy bound to the farm. But be sure you keep her.

Demea

I'll see to that, and in the country I'll force her to do the cooking and the corn-grinding so she's full of smoke, ashes and corn dust; furthermore, I'll have her bringing in straw in the midday sun: I'll cook her black as coal.

Micio

That's it. Now I think you're getting wise. And I'd make the boy share his bed with her, even if he doesn't like it.

Demea

Are you mocking me? You're fortunate to have such a disposition. I believe . . .

Micio

Oh, aren't you through yet?

Demea

I'm about to stop now.

Micio

Then go in and let's pass today as the occasion demands. [*They enter Micio's house.*

[*A short time later* DEMEA *comes out of the house.*

Demea

[*To himself.*] Never has anyone spent his life in such a well-balanced manner but that situations, maturity and experience always contribute a new point of view or advise him in some way; the result is that you don't know what you believed you knew and that in practice you disregard that which you once considered to be of importance. This just happened to me, for though I have now nearly spent my life, I am giving up the strict life which I have lived hitherto. What for? I have discovered that a man can have nothing better than a kind and merciful disposition. From the example of my brother and me, it is simple to see that this is true. He has always lived a life of leisure and parties; he's kind-hearted and calm, never talks roughly to anyone, and is pleasant to all. He has enjoyed himself and spent his money; everyone likes him and talks well of him. I, the crude, strict, grasping, cruel, frugal rustic, got married; have I seen misery as a result of that! There were two sons born—more worries. Now look how, in my eagerness to make as much money as possible for them, I squandered my life and vitality. Now when my life is about over, the only fruit I can show for my labor is their hatred; that other fellow has a father's enjoyment without doing any work. They love him and stay away from me; they make him a party to their plans; they rave about him; they both stay at his house; I am left by myself; they wish him good health, but I'm sure they are just waiting for me to die. So the boys, whom I raised with a lot of work, he has made his own at very little expense: I have all the

misery, he has the enjoyment. Well, well now, let's try
the other way and find out whether I am able at all
to speak or to act generously, since he has dared me
to do it. I, too, ask to be loved by my sons and to
be highly regarded; if I can accomplish this by giving
gifts and obliging them, I shall do as much as my
brother does. My money will be gone, but I couldn't
care less since I am the older brother.

[SYRUS *comes out of Micio's house.*

Syrus

Ho there, Demea, your brother asks that you stay
nearby.

Demea

Who's this? Oh, hello, my dear Syrus. How are things?
How are you making out?

Syrus

Just fine.

Demea

[*To the audience.*] This is tops. Now for the first time I've
included these three phrases which are not in keeping
with my true nature: "Oh, my dear," "how are things?"
"how are you making out?" [*To* SYRUS.] You've proven
yourself to be a pretty noble slave, and I'd like to do
something for you.

Syrus

I am indebted to you.

Demea

This is really so, Syrus; you'll soon see.

[SYRUS *stands to the side as* GETA *appears from Sostrata's
house.*

Geta

[*To* SOSTRATA *inside.*] Mistress, I'll find out here at our
neighbors how soon they will come for the girl. But
Demea's here. How do you do?

Demea

Oh, what is your name?

Geta

Geta.

Demea

Geta, I have concluded today that you are a man of
very great value, for in my opinion, the slave who
takes good care of his master demonstrates his real
worth. I know you do, Geta, and for that reason I'd
like to do something for you if you ever need a favor.
[*To the audience.*] I'm practicing how to be friendly and
getting on pretty well.

Geta

It is good of you to think this of me.

Demea

[*Aside.*] I'm doing this gradually, beginning with the
lower element.

[AESCHINUS *comes out of Micio's house.*

Aeschinus

[*To himself.*] They are really killing me in their desire to
make the wedding so formal: they're taking up the
whole day to get ready for it.

Demea

How are you making out, Aeschinus?

Aeschinus

Oh, Father, you are here?

Demea

Indeed, in spirit and by blood it is your father, who
has more love for you than for his own eyes. But why
don't you take your wife home?

Aeschinus

I'd like to, but I have to wait for the flutists and
vocalists.

Demea

Well now, would you heed the words of an old man
such as I?

Aeschinus

What words?

Demea

Don't have any vocalists, crowds of people, torches or
flutists, and have the garden wall torn down as soon
as possible: take her through there; make the two

homes into one; take the mother and everyone else in the house to our place.

Aeschinus
I like that idea; what a very nice father!

Demea
[*To the audience.*] Splendid! Now I'm called "nice." My brother's home is made into a thoroughfare; he'll bring a mob of people there and will have a big expense—I should worry? I'm nice and I'm popular. [*To Aeschinus.*] Now, tell that old moneybags to count out twenty minas.[11] Syrus, aren't you going to do it?

Syrus
Do what?

Demea
Tear down the wall. [SYRUS *departs; to* AESCHINUS.] You go to the women and conduct them.

Geta
Heaven bless you, Demea, for I see you have really the best interests of our family at heart.

Demea
I think they merit it; [*to* AESCHINUS] wouldn't you say so?

Aeschinus
I think so, indeed.
[GETA *goes inside.*

Demea
It is much more fitting than that this young mother who is weak from childbirth be conducted here through the street.

Aeschinus
I have never seen anything done better, Father.

Demea
I always do things well; but look, Micio is coming out.
[MICIO *enters, speaking to men inside.*

Micio
My brother bids you? Where is he? [*To* DEMEA.] Are you bidding them do this, Demea?

Demea
Yes, I'm bidding that we, in this and in all other affairs, make ourselves into one family as far as possible, to love, to help, and to join together.

Aeschinus
Please do it, Father.

Micio
I wouldn't have it otherwise.

Demea
In fact, we are obliged to do it. First of all, his wife has a mother.

Micio
True. What about it?

Demea
A good and virtuous woman.

Micio
That's what they say.

Demea
A little old.

Micio
I know.

Demea
She hasn't been able to have a child for some years now, and there is no one to watch over her. She's by herself.

Micio
What's his point?

Demea
It's only right that you marry her, and [*to* AESCHINUS] that you see that he does.

Micio
Right that I marry her?

Demea
You.

Micio
Me?

Demea
  I said you.

Micio
  That's foolishness.

Demea
  [*To* AESCHINUS. If you're a man, he'll do it.

Aeschinus
  Father!

Micio
  Why do you listen to this, you jackass?

Demea
  You can't avoid it; it must be done.

Micio
  You're crazy.

Aeschinus
  Let me beg you, Father.

Micio
  Go on, you're out of your mind.

Demea
  Come, grant your son's request.

Micio
  Are you sane? Should I finally become bridegroom in my sixty-fifth year and take a broken-down old lady for a wife? Is this what you suggest I do?

Aeschinus
  Do it; I assured them you would.

Micio
  Did you, now? Speak for yourself, boy!

Demea
  Now, what if he should beg something more of you?

Micio
  As if this were not the ultimate!

Demea
  Grant the request.

Aeschinus
  Don't be a crank.

Demea
Do it, assure me that you will.

Micio
Won't you give up?

Aeschinus
No, not until I persuade you.

Micio
This is high-handed, indeed!

Demea
Come, be a sport, Micio!

Micio
Although I think this whole thing is improper, foolish, absurd and contrary to my way of life, I agree if you two wish it so ardently.

Aeschinus
You're acting nobly.

Demea
You have earned my respect; but . . .

Micio
What?

Demea
I'll tell you, since I have what I wished.

Micio
What more is left?

Demea
Hegio, a close relative of theirs (and now of ours), is a poor fellow; we should do him a favor.

Micio
Do what?

Demea
There's a little farm in the suburbs which you lease. Let's give him the benefits of it.

Micio
That's a little one?

Demea
Even if it is a big one, you should do it anyway. He's a

good fellow, one of our kind, a father to her. He should
have it. Now I'm finally following that adage which
you, Micio, spoke wisely and well a little while ago:
"Man's most common vice is that, in his old age, he
cares too much for wealth." We should avoid this fault;
your words are right, and it is only fitting that we act
accordingly.

Aeschinus
Father!

Micio
Now, now! Because Aeschinus wants it, I'll give Hegio
the farm.

Aeschinus
I'm overjoyed.

Demea
Now we are brothers in body and soul alike. [*Aside.*]
I'm giving him a dose of his own medicine.
[SYRUS *enters.*

Syrus
I did what you said, Demea.

Demea
You're a worthy man. That's why I think that today
Syrus should be given his freedom.

Micio
Him free? Whatever for?

Demea
Lots of things.

Syrus
Oh, dear Demea, you're really a gentleman! I have cared
for your two sons with diligence since their childhood;
I have instructed them, advised them, and always
taught them well in everything I could.

Demea
We can see that. These are not the duties of an ordinary fellow: to be honest in the matter of buying
food, to procure a mistress, and to arrange for a banquet
at noon.

Syrus
Oh, you nice fellow!

Demea

And now, he helped me to buy the cithara girl today. He arranged it: it is right to pay him. The others will be better slaves. Furthermore, Aeschinus wants it.

Aeschinus

Yes.

Micio

If you really want it . . . Syrus, come here to me. [*Strikes* syrus *a light blow.*] [12] Be free.

Syrus

You are very kind; I thank all of you, and especially you, Demea.

Demea

I'm delighted.

Aeschinus

I, too.

Syrus

I feel that way, too. If only this joy of mine were complete, by seeing my wife Phrygia free with me!

Demea

A very good woman, to be sure.

Syrus

Yes, she's the first to give her breast today to your grandson, her master's son.

Demea

Well now, if she's really the first to give it to him, there is little question but that she should be freed.

Micio

What for?

Demea

For this. I'll pay you later whatever she cost you.

Syrus

May all the gods shower you always with the things you ask for, Demea!

Micio

Syrus, you have made out beautifully today.

Demea
Of course, now, Micio, if you will fulfill your obligations and lend him a little cash for expenses, he'll give it back in a little while.

Micio
[*Snapping his fingers.*] Not even that.

Aeschinus
He's a hardworking fellow.

Syrus
I'll return it, I promise; just give it to me.

Aeschinus
Come, Father.

Micio
I'll worry about it later.

Demea
He will do it.

Syrus
Oh, you are the best of men!

Aeschinus
Oh, what an agreeable father!

Micio
What is all this? Why have you changed your ways so suddenly? Because of a fancy? How come you are suddenly so generous?

Demea
I shall tell you, to show you that your boys think you are easy and agreeable not because of your righteous mode of life, nor even because you are fair and good, but because you give in, because you indulge them and because you are generous, Micio. Now then, Aeschinus, if you hate my way of life for this reason, that I don't let you have everything you wish whether it is right or not, I'll forget the whole thing. Squander, buy, do what you like; but since you understand less because of your youth and since your passions may more easily overcome your reason, if you would prefer that I scold and correct and hearten you on occasion, you see me ready to do these things.

Aeschinus

Father, we give in to you completely. You know what must be done. But what will you do about my brother?

Demea

I'll let him have her; but she is to be the end of his foolishness.

Micio

That's fine.

Cantor

[*To the audience.*] Applaud.

Notes

1. A four-stringed musical instrument.

2. *The Dying Friends.*

3. Probably a slave who had been sent to meet Aeschinus the evening before.

4. The Roman marketplace.

5. Sannio was once a slave and has been set free.

6. About $450.

7. Sannio would have to pay a stiff fine if it were proved that the girl was actually a citizen and made a slave illegally.

8. Hegio is Pamphila's legal guardian, since her father, Simulus, is dead.

9. Syrus deliberately mocks Demea's words above.

10. All Athenians belonged to one of ten tribes. See J. B. Bury. *A History of Greece* (New York, 1900), pp. 162–3. Current editions are available from Modern Library (Random House) and St. Martin's Press, both in New York.

11. Micio had paid this much for the cithara girl. Demea is obviously alluding to this former transaction.

12. The act necessary to make Syrus legally free.

Seneca

MEDEA

Translated by Moses Hadas

Characters *Medea, daughter of King Aeetes of Colchis, wife of Jason*

Jason, prince of Iolcus, sometime commander of the Argonauts

Creon, king of Corinth, father of Jason's bride Creusa

Nurse, confidante of Medea

Messenger

Two sons of Medea and Jason (mutes)

Chorus of Corinthians

Guards, servants, Corinthian crowd

SCENE: *the front of Jason's house in Corinth.*

Act One

[*Enter* MEDEA.

Medea

Ye Jupiter and Juno, patrons of wedlock; thou Lucina,
keeper of the conjugal couch; thou Minerva, who didst
teach Tiphys to bridle a novel craft that would master
the seas; thou Neptune, savage lord of Ocean's depths;
thou Sun, who dost apportion bright light to the globe;
thou triform Hecate, whose radiance serves as accom-
plice to silent sacraments—ye deities by whom Jason
swore to me, yea, and ye deities whom Medea hath better right to invoke: thou Chaos of endless night; ye
realms opposed to the upper world's; ye impious
ghosts; thou Pluto, lord of the gloomy demesne; thou
Proserpina, ravished with more honorable intentions
than was I—all you I invoke, but not for blessing. Attend, ye goddesses who avenge crime, attend, your unkempt hair foul serpents, your bloody hands grasping
the ominous torch; attend now in such dread presence
as once ye showed when ye stood posted at my bridals.
Make your gifts death for the new bride, death for the
father-in-law and the royal stock.

But for the husband I have a worse gift to beg: let
him live. Let him wander through cities he knows not, a
needy vagabond, a trembling alien, hated and homeless.
Let him beg at a stranger's threshold, now a recognized
cadger. May he wish I were his wife. May his children
—I can think of no worse imprecation—be like their
father, yes, and like their mother. Born is my vengeance,
already born; I have given birth.

But idle are the plaints I broadcast, mere words. Shall
I not march against the enemy? I shall wrest the wedding torches from their hands, the very light from
heaven. Can Sun, founder of my race, look on? Can he
let himself be looked at as he sits upon his chariot and
drives his customary course in untainted air? Will he

not return to his rising and retrace the day's course?
Grant me to ride through the air in my father's chariot,
do grant it; hand me the reins, sire, assign me to steer
that fire-bearing car with blazing traces. Corinth with
the obstruction of its twin shores shall be burned down
and its two seas joined.

Only this remains, that I myself serve as matron of
honor and carry the flambeau into the bridal chamber!
—and after sacrificial prayers slaughter the victims on
the appointed altars. Through the vitals find a path for
punishment, my soul, if you still have feeling; if a spark
of your old energy is left, banish womanish timidity
and put on the temper of stranger-hating Caucasus.
Whatever crime Phasis and Pontus have seen, Corinth's
Isthmus shall see. Savage and unexampled enormities,
horrifying to heaven and earth alike, my mind within
me is churning up, wounds and murder and death that
slithers along the limbs. Too trivial are the deeds I
recall—those things I did as a girl. 'Tis time for deeper
passion; now I am a mother, more impressive crimes
are expected. Gird yourself in fury, with all your frenzy
ready yourself for destruction! Let the tale of your
divorce be as memorable as that of your marriage: how
did you leave your husband?—by the methods by which
you won him. Away with laggard lethargy; the bond
concluded by crime must by crime be severed.

[MEDEA *withdraws to one side as the* CHORUS *enters in procession, chanting the epithalamium for the marriage of*
JASON *and* CREUSA.

Chorus

With divine benison attend ye the marriage of princes,
ye heavenly gods and ye that govern the sea; and in
manner ordained show your good will, ye people.

First, to the scepter-bearing Thunderers a bull of
gleaming white shall raise his lofty neck. To Lucina a
heifer of snowy body, untried by the yoke, shall be
offered. Venus, who restrains rough Mars' bloody hands,
who offers terms to warring peoples and holds plenty in
her rich horn, will be presented, for her gentleness, with
a tenderer victim. And thou, Hymen, patron of legiti-
mate marriage, who dost disperse night's darkness with
the torch in thine auspicious right hand, come thou
forward wth languorous step wine-drenched, thy brows

bound with a chain of roses. And thou, star of the evening, twilight's herald, whose slow coming makes lovers impatient, whom eager matrons and brides long for, quickly as may be spread thy clear rays.

Our maiden's comeliness surpasses far the beauty of Athenian brides, and those of unwalled Sparta who exercise like boys on the ridges of Taygetus, and those on the banks of Theban Aonia or Elis' sacred Alpheus. If our Jason, Aeson's scion, would display his beauty, then would the wicked lightning's offspring yield to him, even Bacchus, who harnesses tigers to his chariot. Yield, too, would Apollo, who shakes the tripod, severe Diana's brother; Pollux, adept in boxing, would yield, along with his brother Castor. So, I pray you heaven-dwellers, so may our lady transcend all wives, the husband far surpass all husbands.

When our lady takes her stand in the maidens' choir, her sole beauty outshines them all, as when comeliness fades from the stars when the sun rises, or the dense crowds of Pleiades hide when Phoebe completes her wonted orb with her circling horns of borrowed light. As snowy whiteness blushes when tinged with scarlet, so the dewy shepherd beholds the shining beam of fresh dawn.

Delivered from the wedlock of uncouth Phasis, schooled fearfully and with unwilling hand to fondle the bosom of an incontinent mate, now, happy groom, take unto yourself an Aeolian maid, only now can you marry with the blessings of the bride's kin.

Come, lads, banter is seasonable: take your fun. From this side and then from that discharge your barbed verses; license to chaff nobles comes rarely.

Flawless Hymen, noble offspring of thyrsus-bearing Bacchus, now is your time to kindle the torch of splintered pine: wave the ritual blaze with drunken fingers. Let the fescennine patter pour out its festive banter, let the crowd chaff and jest. In silence and darkness depart the woman who surreptitiously marries a foreign husband.

Act Two

[As the CHORUS *retires backstage,* MEDEA *steps forward.*

Medea

Lost! The wedding chant has beaten on my ears. Even I can hardly believe, even now, so total a calamity. Could Jason do this? He robbed me of father, country, kingdom: can he cruelly desert me, all alone and in a foreign place? Is he scornful of my services when he has seen fire and ocean vanquished by my crime? Or does he believe that all my uncanniness is used up? Without resolution or decision or rational wit, I am tossed about in all directions. In what quarter can I take vengeance? I wish *he* had a brother! But he has a wife: against her shall my sword be driven. But is this satisfaction for my abuses? If cities Pelasgian or cities barbarian have learned any enormity of which your hands are ignorant, now is the time to study them. Your own crimes should urge you on; recall them all: the glorious symbol of royalty stolen away; the impious girl's little brother dismembered with a sword, his death thrust upon his father, and his body scattered over the sea; the limbs of aged Pelias boiled in a brass cauldron. How often have I perpetrated bloody murder! Yet no crime have I committed in anger; it was ill-starred love that impelled me.

But what could Jason do, subject as he was to another's decision and authority? He should have bared his breast to the sword—more kindly, mad grief, speak more kindly! Let Jason live, if possible, my own as in the past, but if not, let him live nevertheless, and remember me, and cherish the life I gave him. The whole fault is Creon's; with capricious lordliness he dissolves marriages, tears mothers from children, and severs loyalties cemented by the most intimate of pledges. It is he that must be attacked; he alone shall pay the score he owes. His house I shall heap high with ashes.

As his roofs are blackened with flame they shall be
conspicuous at Malea, which enforces long delay on
shipping.

[*As* MEDEA'S *tirade reaches a crescendo, enter the* NURSE,
hurriedly.

Nurse

Silence, please! Muffle your complaints, confide them to
secret sorrow. One who is mute under hard blows, and
keeps patient and collected, can requite them: wrath
concealed can inflict injury, but hatred professed for-
feits opportunity for vengeance.

Medea

Light is the grief which can take counsel and dis-
semble; great ills cannot take cover. I choose open
hostility.

Nurse

Halt this passionate offensive, my darling; passive defense will scarcely save you.

Medea

Fortune fears the brave, the cowardly crushes.

Nurse

Valor is admirable when it has a place.

Medea

It is impossible valor should ever have no place.

Nurse

No hope points a path in your prostrate position.

Medea

Who has nothing to hope should despair of nothing.

Nurse

The Colchians have deserted you, your husband is gone,
of all your resources nothing is left.

Medea

Medea is left. Here you see sea and land, steel and
fire and gods and thunderbolts.

Nurse

A king is to fear.

Medea

My father was a king.

Nurse
Are you not afraid of soldiery?

Medea
No! though they sprouted from earth.

Nurse
You will die!

Medea
So I desire.

Nurse
Flee!

Medea
I have regretted flight.

Nurse
Medea—

Medea
—will I prove myself.

Nurse
You are a mother.

Medea
You see by whom.

Nurse
Then do you hesitate to fly?

Medea
I shall fly, but first take my vengeance.

Nurse
The avenger will track you.

Medea
Perhaps I shall contrive to delay him.

Nurse
Restrain your words, have done with threats, mad
woman, bate your temper. One must adjust oneself to
the situation.

Medea
Fortune can cancel my resources, not my spirit.—But
who is that knocking at my palace door? It is Creon himself, swollen with Pelasgian lordship.
[*As* CREON *enters,* MEDEA *moves to the rear. Exit* NURSE.

Creon

Has Medea, Colchian Aeetes' cankerous growth, not yet carried herself off from my kingdom? She is working some mischief: I know her guile, I know her power. Whom will that woman spare, whom will she leave in peace? For my part, I was ready to eradicate that dangerous plague with the sword, but my son-in-law begged her off. I have granted her life, but she must free my realm from fear and go elsewhere for her safety.

Beetling she strides toward me, her expression is menacing as she approaches nearer to address me. Keep her off, slaves!—far off from touch or access; bid her be silent. It is time she learned to accept a king's edict. [*To* MEDEA.] Go, fly headlong! Take your monstrous, savage, repulsive self away at once!

Medea

What is the charge? What offense brings sentence of exile?

Creon

An innocent woman asks why she is expelled!

Medea

If you are judge, examine the case; if king, issue your orders.

Creon

Just or unjust, a king's orders you must accept.

Medea

Unjust rule is never lasting.

Creon

Go, complain to the Colchians.

Medea

I go, but he who carried me from Colchis should take me back.

Creon

Speech comes late when the decree is fixed.

Medea

Whoso passes sentence with one party unheard—even though the sentence be just, not just was the judge.

Creon

Did you hear Pelias before he received his doom? But

speak on; for your excellent case a place shall be made.

Medea

How difficult it is to sway an excited temper from
anger, how royal the man whose proud hands have
touched the scepter regards it to persist in a course he
has begun, I have learned in my own experience of
royalty. Yes, though I am overwhelmed with wretched
ruin, expelled, a beggar, forlorn, forsaken, afflicted on
every side, once I shone brilliant in my father's high
birth and traced glorious lineage from my grandfather,
the Sun. Whatever lands the Phasis waters with its
placid bends, whatever Scythian Pontus sees at its back,
where the seas grow sweet with the waters of the
marshes, whatever lands live in fear of the manless troop
armed with shields bounded by Thermodon's banks—
all this broad domain my father holds under his sway.
Nobly born, blessed, royalty and power made my life
a shining splendor. Then did nobles sue for my hand
—now I must be the suitor. Rapid is fortune and
fickle. Headlong it has swept me from royalty and
delivered me to exile.

Trust kingship when the slightest accident plays havoc
with its mighty state! But there is a glorious and in-
calculable possession in the power of kings which time
can never snatch away: to protect the downtrodden,
to shelter suppliants with a hearth they can trust. This
alone have I brought with me from my Colchian realm,
that myself I saved that magnificent and illustrious
flower of Greece, bulwark of the Achaean race, progeny
of gods. Orpheus is my gift, who enchants stones by
his song and draws the forests to hear; my gift, too,
are Castor and Pollux, and Boreas' scions, and Lynceus,
whose sharp sight perceives things beyond Pontus, and
all the Minyans. Of the leader of leaders I say nothing;
for him there is no debt, him I charge to no one's account. The others I brought back for you, Jason for
myself.

Proceed now and pile your indictments high; I shall
confess all. The sole charge to which I am liable is the
return of the *Argo*. Suppose my choice had been
maidenly modesty and my own father: then all the
Pelasgian land would have collapsed along with its
leaders, and first of all would this son-in-law of yours

have succumbed to the fiery breath of that fierce bull.
Fortune may overwhelm my case as it will: I am not
sorry I saved that numerous band of glorious princes. It
is in your power to fix the reward I receive for all my
transgressions. Condemn the defendant, if you like, but
give me back the source of my sin. I am guilty, Creon,
I confess it; but so you knew me to be when I touched
your knees as a suppliant and begged the solemn
protection of your hand. Again I beg for some little
corner, some repose, for my miseries, some humble
hovel to hide in. If the decision is to drive me from
this city, let me have some faraway cranny in your
kingdom.

Creon

I think I gave sufficient evidence that I am not a man
who is overbearing in wielding the scepter or who
tramples upon misery with proud foot when I chose
for my son-in-law an exile helpless and haunted by
pressing fear, inasmuch as Acastus, who holds the
Thessalian realm, is demanding his person for capital
punishment. Acastus' complaint is that his aged father,
palsied and heavy with years, was murdered and that
the limbs of the aged victim were dismembered when
his dutiful sisters, deceived by your cheat, ventured on
an undutiful enormity. Jason can defend his case if
you separate yours from it. No blood has tainted his
innocence, his hand plied no sword, he has detached
himself from complicity and kept himself undefiled. It
is you, you, who are the architect of odious crime. You
have a woman's irresponsibility for reckless daring and
the strength of a man, with no thought of reputation:
begone, purge my realm, take your lethal herbs with
you, free my citizens from terror, settle in some other
land and there trouble the gods!

Medea

Is it flight you enforce? Then for flight give me back
my ship, give me back my shipmate. Why do you order
me to flee alone? I was not alone when I came. If it is
fear of war that impels you, eject us both from your
realm; why do you differentiate between a pair equally
guilty? It is for him Pelias fell, not for me. Add to your
indictment elopement and theft, a deserted father and
a butchered brother—all the crimes that bridegroom

teaches his new wives: the sin is not mine. Many times have I been made guilty, but never for myself.

Creon

You should have been far away by now. Why do you purposely delay matters with speechmaking?

Medea

I am going; this is my last humble petition: let the mother's guilt not drag her innocent children down.

Creon

Go, I will take them into my fatherly embrace as if they were mine.

Medea

By the blessed bed of this royal marriage, by your hopes for the future, by the continuance of kingdoms, which is subject to the vicissitudes of variable fortune, I pray you: bestow the largesse of a brief stay upon the refugee mother, until I imprint what may be my dying kiss upon my sons.

Creon

It is for a trick you want time.

Medea

What trick is there to fear when the time is so slight?

Creon

For the wicked no time is too scant to work harm.

Medea

Will you deny a poor creature a tiny respite for her tears?

Creon

Though inveterate fear opposes your plea, one day shall be given you to prepare for exile.

Medea

Generous, even if you curtail it a bit; I, too, am impatient.

Creon

But you will pay with your head if you have not cleared the Isthmus before Phoebus raises bright day.

But the marriage rites summon me, the festive day of Hymen calls me to prayer.

[*Exeunt* CREON *and* MEDEA *severally.*

Chorus

Too bold the man who first ploughed the treacherous sea with frail bark, who saw his familiar mainland receding behind him and entrusted his life to the fickle winds; slicing through the unbroken surface in his uncertain course he dared put his faith in a thin board which drew too tenuous a line between the paths of life and death.

No one as yet knew the constellations nor understood the use of the stars which spangle the ether. Not yet could craft avoid the rainy Hyades; unnamed as yet were the lights of the Olenian Goat, or the Attic Wain which creeping old Boötes follows and guides, or yet the North Wind, or yet the West.

'Twas Tiphys who ventured to spread sail over the vast main and to write new laws for winds: now to stretch canvas to belly out full, now to haul the sheet forward to catch cross winds from the south, now to set the yards safely in the middle of the mast, now to make them fast to the very top, when the too eager sailor is greedy for every gust and the ruddy spinnaker flutters aloft.

Stainless the ages our fathers saw, when trickery was far distant. Every man trod his own shore free of ambition and waxed old on his ancestral health; rich on a pittance, he knew no wealth but what his native soil produced. Worlds well and lawfully dissevered that Thessalian timber forced into one; it bade ocean endure lashes and the hitherto isolated sea to be reckoned among human fears.

Upon that wilful boat a severe penalty was inflicted after it had made its way through far-off perils when two mountains, barriers of the abyss, were driven together from this side and that by a sudden thrust and roared as with heaven's thunder and the trapped sea splattered their peaks and the very clouds. Bold Tiphys blanched and his faltering hand relaxed its hold upon all the reins; Orpheus fell mute, his lyre stunned to silence; and Argo itself lost its god-given voice. And what panic was there when the maid of Sicilian Pelorus, Scylla, girt about her waist with rabid hounds, opened all her gaping maws at once! Who would not quake in every limb when so many simultaneous barks issued from a single monstrosity? What turmoil when the

Sirens, those deadly plagues, mesmerized the Ausonian sea with their melodious chant, when Thracian Orpheus responded to their song on his Muse-given lyre and almost forced the Siren, whose habit it was to hold ships back, herself to follow! And what was the prize of this voyage? The Golden Fleece and Medea, an evil worse than the sea and an appropriate cargo for the first of ships.

Today the sea has capitulated and submits to human terms. There is no need for a famed *Argo* fashioned by Pallas' hand and manned by princely oars: any skiff may wander at will over the deep. All boundaries have been abolished, cities fix their walls in new lands, nothing is left where it had always been, the whole world may be freely traversed. Indian quaffs cold Araxes, Persians drink Elbe and Rhine. An age shall come in latter years when Ocean shall relax nature's bars, when the whole wide surface of earth shall be open and Tethys shall uncover new worlds; Thule shall no longer be land's end.

Act Three

[*Enter* MEDEA, *her movements showing her distraction, followed by the* NURSE, *whom she ignores and who proceeds to describe her movements.*

Nurse

Darling, where to abroad in such haste? Stop, control your emotion, bridle your impetuosity.

Like a maenad crazily bounding when she is possessed by the god and beside herself, on the snowy peak of Pindus or Nysa's ridges, so is Medea coursing from this side to that, her movements undirected and signs of frantic fury in her face. Her cheeks are hectic, her breath a deep panting, she shouts, she floods her eyes with a gush of tears, she beams with ecstasy, she passed through the gamut of every passion. She is frustrated, she threatens, she seethes, she complains, she groans. How will her mind's weight veer, how will her threats be directed, where will that surging wave break? Her fury spills over its bounds. It is no slight or ordinary crime she is brewing; she will outdo herself. I recognize the symptoms of her old intensity; something big is afoot, something monstrous, huge, godless. [MEDEA'S *paroxysm subsides and she pauses to speak.*] It is the visage of a madman I see: may the gods disprove my fear!

Medea

If you ask, poor creature, what limit you should place on your hatred, copy your love. Can such as I tolerate this wedding without vengeance? Can this day, campaigned for with such ado and with such ado granted, drag idly by? So long as earth's core shall bear heaven in balance, so long as the bright universe shall unroll its sure alternations, as sands are numberless and day follows sun and stars night, so long as the pole rotates the waterless Bears and rivers fall into the sea, my passion to exact punishment shall never falter, but ever wax greater. What savagery of wild beasts, what Scylla, what Charybdis, sucking up Ausonian sea and Sicilian, what Aetna resting heavily on heaving Titan shall boil with threats so dire? No rushing torrent, no storm-tossed sea, no Pontus whipped to fury by the north wind or fire sustained by its violent gale could match my drive and my intensity. I shall overturn everything, flatten everything to ruins.

Was Jason afraid of Creon and the saber-rattling Thessalian chief? True love can fear no one. But suppose that he gave in under duress and yielded his hand: at least he could have come for a last conversation with his wife. Even this he was afraid to do, for all his fierceness. Surely a son-in-law could procure a postponement for the harsh sentence—one single day was given me for two children. But I do not complain of the shortness of time; it shall stretch far. This day shall bring to pass a deed, aye, it shall bring to pass a deed which no other day can overlook. I will assail the gods, I will make the universe totter.

Nurse

Master your heart, mistress, which your woes have set in turmoil; mollify your spirit.

Medea

I can be quiet only if I see everything overwhelmed along with my ruin. As you go down it is a satisfaction to drag others with you.

[*Exit* MEDEA.

Nurse

See how much we have to fear if you persist. No one can attack the powerful and remain safe.

[*Exit* NURSE; *enter* JASON.

Jason

Ah, fate always hard and fortune harsh, malignant alike when she rages and when she forbears. How often does the god find us remedies worse than our perils! If I should choose to keep faith with my wife's deserts, I should have to yield my head to death; but if I should choose not to die, I must, poor wretch, prove faithless. Yet it is not fear that has vanquished faith, but the apprehension of a conscientious father, for surely the children would follow their parents to death. Hallowed justice, if thy seat is in heaven, I invoke thy divinity to witness: the sons have prevailed over the father. Nay, I do believe that fierce as she is in heart and impatient of the yoke, she would herself be more concerned for her children than for her marriage. Angry though she be, I am determined to ply her with prayer. [*Enter* MEDEA.] And look, at sight of me she bridles, shows her fury, makes her hate plain to see; all her passion is in her face.

Medea

I am on the run, Jason, on the run. That is nothing new, to scurry from shelter to shelter; it is the cause of my running that is new: it was *for* you I used to run. You force me to fly from your house—I leave it, I go away; but where are you sending me? Shall I make my goal Phasis and the Colchians, my father's kingdom and the fields drenched with my brother's blood? What country do you direct me to? What seas do you point out to me? Shall it be the jaws of the Pontic strait through which I carried back that noble band of princes when I followed an adulterer through the Symplegades? Shall I make for little Iolcus or Tempe in Thessaly? Every road I opened up for you I closed for myself. Where would you have me go? You decree expulsion for the refugee, but assign no place of exile. But I am on my way; a king's son-in-law has issued his orders, and I accept them. Heap cruel tortures upon me! I have deserved them. Let regal wrath crush your concubine with bloody torments, load her hands with chains, bury her in the rocky dungeon of eternal night: my sufferings will be less than I deserve.

Ingrate! Let your mind dwell on the fiery puffing of that bull; on the blazing crew in Aeetes' arms-sprouting field amidst the wild terror of that untamed race; on the weapons of the instantaneously ripened enemy, when, at my bidding, the soldiery born of earth fell at each other's hands. Recall, too, the spoil of the ram of Phrixus; the sleepless dragon compelled to close his eyes in unprecedented slumber; the brother done to death, and the compounding of the crime when he was dismembered; the daughters who minced the limbs of the old man, deceived by my trick into thinking he would be resurrected. By the hopes of your children, your secure home, by the monsters vanquished, by these hands which I have never spared in your service, by the perils we have passed through, by heaven and sea, the witnesses of my marriage, pity me. You are happy: give the suppliant her turn. Gaining kingdoms for others, I abandoned my own. Of all the wealth the Scythians accumulate, raided from as far afield as the sun-scorched folk of India and so abundant that our palaces are too full to hold more treasure and we decorate the woodland with gold—of all this I took nothing away with me except my brother's limbs, and those, too, I squandered for you. For you my country is lost, my father, my brother, my chastity; that was the dowry I brought when I married you: now that I am rejected, give me back my own.

Jason

When Creon was resolved to do away with you it was my tears that prevailed him to grant you banishment.

Medea

And I thought it was a punishment; I see now that exile is a favor.

Jason

Escape while you can still leave, get yourself away. The anger of kings always falls heavy.

Medea

So you urge me in Creusa's interest; you are trying to rid her of a paramour she loathes.

Jason

Is Medea taking exception to love?

Medea

And to murder, and to guile.

Jason

But what act of mine can you really take exception to?

Medea

Every act I committed.

Jason
That is all that is wanting, that I, too, should be guilty of your crimes!

Medea
They are yours, they are yours, indeed! The one who profits by a crime is guilty of it. Though the world should insist your wife is infamous, you alone must defend her, you alone declare her innocent. In your sight she should be guiltless if her guilt is for your sake.

Jason
Life is thankless when one is ashamed of having received it.

Medea
One should not cling to it when one is ashamed of having received it.

Jason
Nay, try to master your angry and excited heart, be reconciled for the children's sake.

Medea
I resign them, disclaim them, disown them! Shall Creusa bear brothers to *my* children?

Jason
A queen to the sons of aliens, a lady of position to the afflicted.

Medea
Never may so black a day befall the unhappy as shall adulterate a noble stock with a vile, the issue of Pheobus with the issue of Sisyphus.

Jason
Why, wretched woman, are you dragging us both down to destruction? Go away, please!

Medea
Creon listened to a suppliant.

Jason
Tell me what I can do.

Medea
For me? Crime.

Jason

On this side a king and on that—

Medea

—Medea, a greater terror. The two of us should compete, with Jason as the prize.

Jason

I give up, I am worn down by my troubles. But you had better be wary of tempting chance too often.

Medea

Fortune has always stood inferior to me.

Jason

Acastus is on the offensive.

Medea

Creon is a nearer enemy. Flee them both, Jason. Medea is not forcing you to take arms against your father-in-law or to pollute yourself with the murder of your kinsman Acastus; flee with me, free of guilt.

Jason

But who will defend us if twin wars assail us, if Creon and Acastus join forces?

Medea

Add the Colchians, too, add Aeetes to be their general, combine Scythians with Pelasgians: I will overwhelm them all.

Jason

I am terribly afraid of lofty scepters.

Medea

Are you sure you do not covet them?

Jason

Our long colloquy will arouse suspicion; cut it short.

Medea

Now, supreme Jupiter, thunder in all heaven, stretch forth your right hand, prepare your avenging flames, cleave the clouds and set the whole world atremble. Poise your weapons, with hand indifferent, against me or him; whichever of us falls, a criminal will perish. Against us your bolt cannot misstrike.

Jason

Do begin to think rationally and speak sanely. If any consolation from my father-in-law's house can ease your flight, ask for it.

Medea

You know that my spirit is able and accustomed to despise royal riches. All that I ask is that I may have my children as companions in my exile, so that I can pour my tears into their bosom. *You* can expect new sons.

Jason

I confess I should like to comply with your request, but paternal obligation forbids. Not even king or father-in-law could compel me to agree to their leaving. They are my reason for living, the solace of a heart burned black with cares. Sooner would I be deprived of breath, of limbs, of light.

Medea

[*Aside*]. Has he such love for his children? Fine! I have him, the place to wound him is uncovered. [*To* JASON.] At least allow me to give them my last injunctions, allow me a final embrace; even that will be appreciated. This is my last plea: I beg you, if my despair and grief have overflowed, do not let what I have said stick in your mind. I would have you retain a better memory of myself; ascribe the other to my passion and blot it out.

Jason

All that I have put out of my mind. And I, too, pray that you govern your hot temper and cultivate placidity. Calm mollifies misery.

[*Exit* JASON.

Stoic

Medea

He has gone. Is this how it is? Do you walk away forgetful of me and all I have done? Have I become a cipher to you? I shall never be a cipher. To work! Summon all your powers and skills. The profit of your crimes is to count nothing a crime. For guile there is no chance; fear has alerted them. Attack where no one could fear. Oh, now, be bold, venture what Medea is capable of, and what she is not capable of. [*Enter* NURSE. *To* NURSE]. You, my loyal nurse, companion of my sorrow and my changing fortunes, help my poor schemes. I have a robe, a divine heirloom which is the glory of our house and kingdom, bestowed on Aeetes by the Sun as a pledge of his fatherhood. There is also a necklace woven of shining gold, and a gold band for binding the hair set with brilliant gems. These things my sons shall take as a gift to the bride, but first they must be smeared and steeped with baneful art. Invoke Hecate and prepare the lethal rites. Have altars set up, and let their flames crackle inside the house.

[*Exeunt.*

Chorus

No force of fire or of whistling wind or of hurtling spear is so violent as a wife's blazing hatred when she is robbed of her marriage—not when cloud-laden South-wind brings wintry rain and the Danube in spate sweeps bridges apart and wanders unchanneled; not when Rhone pounds the sea or when invigorated Sun melts the snows into torrents as Haemus dissolves in mid-Spring. Blind is love's fire when goaded by anger; it scorns guidance, will not tolerate checkreins, has no fear of death; it strains to advance upon ready swords. Spare him, ye gods; we pray your indulgence for the man who subdued the sea. Let him live unhurt, though the lord of the deep resents the conquest of the realm second to heaven's. The youth who made bold to drive the Sun's immortal chariot disregarded the limits his father had set, and was himself victim of the sparks he so madly scattered over heaven's vault. High is the price of the pioneer path; walk where former generations have found it safe, nor breach, wilful man, the hallowed covenants of the universe.

All who laid hand to the noble beams of that audacious ship and despoiled Pelion of its sacred woodland's thick shade, all who passed between the wandering rocks and traversed the sea's many perils, who tied hawser to barbaric shore to ravish and bring back the prize of foreign gold, expiated the violated rights of the sea by some dire doom.

Challenged, the sea exacts its penalty. First of all Tiphys, who tamed the deep, left his rudder to a novice pilot. Dying on a foreign strand, far from his ancestral kingdom, he lies covered in a contemptible grave, among alien shades. Aulis remembered the king it had lost, and its windless harbor holds the Greek fleet, which chafes at standing still.

Orpheus born of the melodious Muse, whose plectrum evoked chords at which torrents halted and winds fell silent, at whose music the birds left off their song and with the whole woodland attending followed the singer —Orpheus lies mangled over the Thracian plains while his head floats down mournful Hebrus. He reached Tartarus and the Styx he already knew, but this time never to return.

Hercules laid North Wind's sons in the dust and slew Neptune's scion whose habit had been to transform himself into numberless shapes. But Hercules himself, after he had brought peace to land and sea, after he had forced open the realm of cruel Dis, laid him down on blazing Oeta while he was yet alive, and to the pitiless flames gave his limbs eroded by his wife's gift, mingled of the gore of Nessus and the Hydra.

Ancaeus was laid low by the fierce charge of the bristly boar, whereat, Meleager, you impiously slew your mother's brother and yourself died at your angry mother's hand. All these deserved the punishment which tender Hylas incurred, the lad Hercules could not find because he had been ravished away amidst waters which held no dread. Then proceed, my stalwarts, to plough the sea whose waters are full of dread!

Idmon, though clairvoyant of other's fate, was despatched by a serpent in the sands of Libya. Mopsus, truthful to others but to himself false, succumbed far from his Thebes. If Mopsus prophesied truly, Thetis' husband Peleus shall be a roaming exile. Nauplius shall fall headlong into the deep as he seeks to wreck the Argives with spurious beacons, and his son Palamedes shall pay with his life for his father's voyage in the Argo. Ajax died by lightning and the sea. Alcestis ransomed her husband and paid her life for Admetus'. Pelias himself, by whose orders the prize of the golden spoil was fetched back on that first ship, was boiled in a hot cauldron, in whose narrow waters he, too, was a wanderer, and so burned to death. Enough, ye gods, have you avenged the sea: spare him who was ordered to his deed.

Act Four

[*Enter* NURSE.

Nurse

My spirit quakes and shudders; great calamity looms near. Her passion grows prodigious; it stokes its own fires and keeps its violence undiminished. Often have I seen her in a frenzy, assailing the gods and pulling heaven down; but this is bigger. Medea is preparing some bigger monstrosity. With step distraught she strode forth to gain her deadly shrine. There she is pouring forth all her stock; phials she herself had feared she now broaches. She is unwrapping her whole baneful pharmacopeia, specifics arcane, occult, uncanny. With her left hand she conjures her baleful witchery and invokes her pestilential powers—all that the burning sands of Libya bring forth and all that frozen Taurus, stiff with Arctic cold, holds imprisoned in everlasting snow, and everything that is monstrous. Drawn by her magic chants the scaly throng leave their lurking and stand at attention. Here a savage serpent drags its huge length along, darts out its forked tongue, and asks to whom it shall deal death; when it hears the chant it yields its own will, twines its swelling mass into piled folds, and shapes them into coils. "Puny the evils and paltry the weapons which lowly earth begets," says she; "from heaven will I seek my drugs. Now is the time, now, to transcend common trickery. Hither descends serpent Draco, who stretches over heaven like a torrent, whose enormous knots the two Bears feel— the Greater used by Pelasgians, the Lesser by Sidonians; let Ophiuchus at last relax his tight grip and pour his virus forth. Come Python to my chant, who dared assail Apollo and Diana. Let Hydra, which renewed its heads as Hercules lopped them off, and every snake that Hercules scotched come back. Even you, wakeful dragon, first lulled by my incantations, leave the Colchians and come to serve me."

After she had conjured up the whole tribe of snakes, she heaped together the virulence of her noxious herbs. Whatever impassable Eryx produces on its rocky heights; whatever the ridges of Caucasus, swathed in endless winter and spattered with Prometheus' blood, bring forth; tinctures which the rich Arabs apply to their arrows, or the Mede, whose prowess is in his quiver, or the nimble Parthians; the extracts which Suebian ladies collect under the wintry sky in the Hyrcanian forests; whatever earth produces in the nesting season of spring or when stiff winter has shaken off the woodland's crowning glory and has congealed all things with flaky frost; every shrub whose burgeoning bloom is lethal or which generates noxious juices in its twisted roots—all these she is manipulating. These poisons Haemonian Athos contributed, those towering Pindus; that surrendered its tender foliage to the ruthless sickle on the ridges of Pangaeus; these Tigris checked its deep eddies to nurture, those the Danube, those the gem-bearing Hydaspes whose warm waters course through stretches of desert, and the Baetis, after which the Spanish province is named, whose slow waters batter the western seas. This plant suffered the knife while Phoebus was readying the day, that growth was culled in deepest night, and this was harvested with fingernail and incantation.

These death-dealing herbs she grasps, squeezes over them the venom of serpents, and adds obscene birds to the brew—the heart of a hoot-owl, and the vitals cut out of a living screech-owl. Other properties that artificer of wickedness arranges in separate heaps; some hold within them the tearing violence of fire, others the frigid stiffness of inert cold. To her witch's brew she adds mutterings no less formidable.—But look, hear the mad beat of her footsteps, the sound of her chant. At her opening lines the whole world shudders.

[*Enter* MEDEA, *chanting.*

Medea

I conjure the mob of the silent, and you, deities of the dead, and blind Chaos, and the opaque dwelling of shadowy Dis, and the enclaves of foul Death fixed to the banks of Tartarus. Leave your torments, ghosts, and hie you to the new marriage. Halt the wheel that whirls Ixion's limbs and let him touch ground; let Tantalus quaff Pirene's waters unfrustrated; come you, too, Danaids, mocked by the vain task of fetching water in perforated pitchers: this day requires the service of your hands. Let only Sisyphus, father of my husband's father-in-law, stay back for a heavier punishment: let the slippery stone carry him with it as it rolls back down the rocks.

Summoned now by my sacraments, thou luminary of night, come clothed in thy most baneful visage, thy three forms all threatening.

For thee, after the manner of my race, I have loosed my hair from its band and paced the mystic grove with bare feet. I have evoked water from dry clouds; I have driven the seas back to their depths; Ocean has bestowed his mighty waves deep within, his tides defeated. Heaven's law, too, have I confounded: the world has seen sun and stars together, and the Bears have touched the sea forbidden them. The order of seasons I have rearranged: by my witchcraft earth has blossomed in summer, and at my bidding Ceres has seen harvest in winter. Violent Phasis has turned its waters back to their source, and Hister, divided into many mouths, has constricted his truculent billows and fallen spiritless in all his banks. Waves have crashed and the sea has raged and swelled, though the winds were still. The home of the ancient woodland lost its shadows when daylight returned at my imperious voice. Pheobus has halted in midcourse, and at my incantation the Hyades totter and collapse.

It is time, Phoebe, to attend to thy rites. [*She holds her offerings up in turn as she presents them to Hecate.*] For you these wreaths woven with bloody hand, each knotted with nine serpents; for you these members which the fractious serpent Typhoeus bore when he shook Jove's throne. In this is the blood of Nessus which the perfidious ferryman presented to Alcmena when he gasped his last. These ashes are the residue of the pyre on Oeta which consumed Hercules and the venom that afflicted him. Here you see the brand Althaea burned when she proved a dutiful sister but undutiful mother. These feathers the Harpy abandoned in her trackless covert when she fled from Zetes. With them are the quills of the Stymphalian bird, whom the darts of Hercules, steeped in the Lernaean Hydra's venom, wounded.

You have rumbled, my altars; I perceive my tripods are stirred by my divine patroness.

Trivia's nimble car I see, not as when she drives it with full face lighted all through the night, but with the livid and gloomy aspect she bears when she is assailed by Thessalian witchcraft and skirts heaven with a nearer rein. Such a gloomy night do thou now diffuse through the heavens with thy pallid torch; terrify the peoples with a new horror, and make them sound costly Corinthian bronzes, Dictynna, to relieve thine eclipse. To thee we offer our solemn rites on bloody turf: for thee a torch snatched from a burning funeral pyre heaves its blaze up in the night; for thee I toss my head and writhe my neck and utter incantations; for thee a fillet flattened in the funereal fashion binds my loosened locks; for thee I brandish this mournful branch from the Stygian pool; for thee I bare my bosom like a maenad and strike my arms with ritual blade. Let my blood drip upon the altars; inure yourself, my hand, to draw sword and endure shedding dear blood—I have struck, I have supplied the hallowed liquid.

But if you complain that you are too often summoned by my petitions, forgive me, I pray; the reason for my too frequent invocation of your aid, Hecate, is always one and the same—Jason. [*She takes up various flasks and caskets as she addresses them.*] Do you tinge Creusa's robe, so that as soon as she puts it on, the creeping flame shall burn her inmost marrow. In this golden casket lies hidden a fire given me by Prometheus, who expiates its theft from heaven with the new growth of his vitals; he taught me how to keep its force safe stored. Mulciber also gave me fire, concealed in powdered sulphur; and from my kinsman Phaethon I received bolts of living flame. I have gifts from Chimaera's fiery middle section, and I have flames snatched from the scorched gorge of that bull; these I have mixed with Medusa's gall, and so enjoined them to keep their evil power in silence.

Sharpen my poisons with thy stings, Hecate, and preserve the seeds of fire which I am hiding in my presents. Let them deceive sight and endure touch till their heat penetrates heart and veins. Let her limbs ooze and her bones smoke; let her blazing hair outshine the new bride's wedding torches.

My prayers have been received: thrice has bold Hecate uttered her bark, and her luminous torch has spurted its mystic flames.

All my power has now been exercised. Call my sons here to carry these costly gifts to the bride. [MEDEA's *sons are led in.*] Go, my sons, go. The mother that bore you is unlucky; placate your mistress and stepmother with presents and humble prayer. March, now, and quickly come home again, to give me the pleasure of a last embrace.

[*Exeunt,* MEDEA *into the house, the children toward Creon's palace.*

Chorus

Wither is savage love sweeping this bloody maenad headlong? What crime is she preparing in her unbridled frenzy? Her expression is rigid with stark passion, her head she weaves with gesture fierce and proud, and threatens even the king: who would believe her an exile?

Her cheeks burn red, then ruddiness makes way for pallor; her aspect is changeable, she keeps no complexion long. She dashes to this side and that, just as a tigress bereft of her cubs scours the jungles of the Ganges in frenzied arcs.

The curbing of neither anger nor love does Medea understand; and now that anger and love are joined in their suit, what will the issue be? When will that unspeakable Colchian rid Pelasgian fields of her presence and liberate king and kingdom from terror? Do give your team their head, Phoebus, spare the reins; let welcome darkness shroud the light, let night's herald Hesperus sink this terrifying day!

Act Five

[*Enter* MESSENGER *at a run.*

Messenger

Ruin, total ruin! Our royalty is annihilated. Daughter and father are one low heap of ashes.

Chorus

How were they trapped?

Messenger

As kings regularly are, by gifts.

Chorus

But what trap could those gifts entail?

Messenger

I, too, wonder, and though the evil deed is accomplished, I can scarcely believe it could have been. The disaster is endless; through every part of the palace the fire rages as if it were under orders. Now the whole structure has collapsed, and the city is feared for.

Chorus

Water can quench flames.

Messenger

This is another strange aspect of that disaster: water *feeds* the flames. The more it is fought, the harder the fire burns; of itself it seizes upon its adversary.

[MEDEA *and* NURSE *enter as the* MESSENGER *completes his speech; exit* MESSENGER.

Nurse

Out of the Peloponnese at the double quick, Medea! Go anywhere, but make haste!

Medea

I retreat? Even if I had already fled I would have come back for this. It is a novel wedding I witness. [*Solilo-*

quizing.] Why, my soul, do you falter? Exploit your successful sally. How small a fraction of your revenge elates you! You are still in love, madwoman, if you are satisfied with Jason celibate. Find some species of punishment wholly unexampled; this is how to make yourself ready: away with every scruple, out every trace of conscience! Paltry the punishment which innocent hands inflict. Put your weight into your passion, goad your lethargy, from deep down in your heart force up your elan of old. Give the name of piety to what you have perpetrated up to this point. Put forth your efforts to make them realize how trifling and of what common brand were the crimes I obliged him with. Those were merely school exercises for my passion; could prentice hands achieve a masterpiece, could a girl's temper? Now I am Medea; my genius has matured with evils.

A fine thing that I wrenched off my brother's head, it is a fine thing! A fine thing that I minced his body and robbed my father of that mystic symbol; a fine thing that I instigated the daughters to arm themselves for the destruction of their old father. Find fresh scope, my passion; there is no crime for which your hand is not sufficiently schooled.

What then is your objective, my anger, with what weapons will you ply your treacherous foe? The fierce spirit within me has determined upon a measure, but does not yet dare acknowledge it to itself. I have been foolish in my breathless haste—my enemy should have had a few children by his bedfellow. But your children by him have Creusa for mother. On that mode of punishment I am resolved, and rightly resolved. I must prepare my temper, I realize, for the ultimate crime. Children once mine, you must pay the price for your father's wickedness.

Horror has knocked at my heart, my limbs are numb with cold, my breast is atremble. Anger has yielded place; the wife in me is banished, the mother wholly returned. Shall I slaughter my own children, my own flesh and blood? Forfend it, mad passion! Far be a crime so unprecedented, an enormity so accursed, even from me! What sin have the children to atone? That Jason is their father is a sin, but that Medea is their mother, a greater sin. They are not mine, let them die. Shall they indeed perish? They are mine. They are without crime

or fault, they are innocent—true enough, but so was
my brother. Why, soul of mine, do you teeter? Why are
my cheeks flooded with tears, why do I waver and let
anger now jerk me this way and now love that? I am
buffeted by a riptide, as when rushing winds wage
ruthless war and from both sides opposing waves lash
the seas and the cornered surface seethes; just so does
my heart oscillate: anger routs affection and affection
anger. Yield, anger, to affection.

[*Enter* MEDEA's *sons.*] Here, dear children, sole solace
of a house overthrown, come here and fuse your limbs
with mine in close embrace. Your father may have you
unharmed, provided your mother, too, may have you.
But exile and flight press hard; any moment they will
be torn from my bosom, weeping and sighing amidst
their kisses as they are snatched away. They are lost to
their mother; let them be lost to their father. Again my
passion waxes and my hatred boils; the old Erinys
reaches for my unwilling hand. Where you lead, wrath,
I follow. Would that proud Niobe's brood had issued
from my womb, that I had given birth to twice seven
sons! I have been too sterile for vengeance, but two I
did bear, enough for a brother and a father.

That unruly crowd of Furies—where are they rushing, whom are they seeking, for whom preparing their
flaming strokes? Against whom is that hellish band
stretching forth their bloody torches? A whip cracks
and a monstrous snake hisses. Whom is Megaera attack-
ing with her menacing beam? Whose ghost is that
approaching? Its limbs are scattered and it is hard to
recognize; it is my brother, and he is demanding vengeance. I shall pay, the whole account. Thrust your
torches into my eyes, mangle, burn; see, my breast is
bared to the Furies.

Tell the avenging deities to leave me, brother, tell
them to return content to the ghosts below. Leave me
to myself, brother, use this hand of mine; it holds a
drawn sword. With this victim I placate your ghost.

[*She kills one son.*] What is that sudden tumult? Arms
are brandished, they are seeking me to destroy me. I shall
mount the lofty roof of our palace; my slaughter is in-
complete. [*To the living son.*] You come along with me;
[*to the murdered son*] your corpse also I will carry away

with me. Now to work, my soul: your prowess must not be wasted in obscurity; demonstrate your handiwork for popular approval.

[*Exit* MEDEA, *carrying the body of one son and leading the other by the hand; presently she appears on the roof. Enter* JASON *at the head of an excited crowd.*

Jason

Here, quickly, every loyal subject who grieves over royalty's ruin! Let us seize the author of this horrible crime herself! This way, aim your weapons this way, stout soldiers, turn the house upside down!

Medea

[*From the rooftop.*] Now, now have I recovered my scepter, my brother, my father; again the Colchians hold the prize of the gilded ram; my royal state is restored, my virginity returned. O divinities complaisant, at last, O festive day, O joyous wedding! Onward, the crime is consummated, but not yet vengeance. Finish the task while your hands are at it. Why delay now, my soul? Why hesitate when you have the power? But now wrath has subsided. I am sorry for my deed, ashamed of it. What, poor wretch, have I done? Poor wretch? Though I am sorry, I did it; a delicious pleasure steals over me, without my will, and look, it is growing: all that was missing was yonder man to be spectator. What I have done so far I count as nothing; any crime I committed without his seeing it is wasted.

Jason

Look, there she is, leaning over the steep part of the roof! Bring fire, someone, quickly! Let her burn and fall in her own flames!

Medea

For your sons, Jason, you must heap a funeral pyre and build a tomb. Your wife and father-in-law have already received the rites of the dead; it is I that buried them. This son has met his fate; this other shall be delivered to like destruction as you look on.

Jason

By every deity, by our shared flights and shared bed, which my faith has not violated, spare the boy. If there is any crime it is mine. I devote myself to death; immolate my guilty head.

Medea

Nay, *here* will I drive my sword, where you like it least, where it will hurt you most. Go now, proud man, find maids to marry and abandon mothers.

Jason

One is enough to punish me.

Medea

If this hand of mine could be satisfied with one death it would have sought none; even though I slay two, the number is too petty for my passion. If any pledge of yours is lurking in my womb, even now, I shall rummage my vitals with a sword and with iron drag it forth.

Jason

Presently carry out what you have begun, I will not beseech you further; only give me a respite for my punishment.

Medea

Enjoy your deliberate revenge, my grief, do not hurry. This day is mine, and I am using the time allotted me.

Jason

'Tis me you loathe: kill me.

Medea

You bid me be merciful; [*she kills the boy*] very well, it is finished. I have nothing more to offer you for atonement, my passion.

[*A car drawn by dragons appears at* MEDEA's *side.*] Lift your swollen eyes this way, ingrate Jason. Do you recognize your wife? This is how I am accustomed to flee. A path is opened in the sky and twin serpents submit their scaly necks to the yoke. Take your sons back now, father. [*She throws the bodies down to him.*] On my winged chariot I shall ride through the air.

Jason

Ride through the lofty spaces of high heaven, and wherever you go bear witness that there are no gods.

Horace

ARS POETICA

Translated and Introduced by Norman J. DeWitt

I have elected to stand by a prose version because the Horatian expository hexameter seems to come off somewhat better in English prose. One sacrifices something, to be sure; Horace did write in regular meter; but one gains, I feel, by avoiding the temptation which presents itself to the translator in verse: to be either cute or frisky. Horace, after all, was a classical poet.

As for the essay-letter itself: the reader who is not addicted to classical philology need be advised only that the substantive aesthetic and dramatic theory set forth by Horace was not quite original with him: he derived some of it from the general critical lore of the Hellenistic schools and found it intellectually congenial. But like Cicero, who also relied on the learning of the Greeks, Horace added something of his own, something Roman.

In point of originality, two aspects of the Ars Poetica should be noted.

First, the student who comes to the Ars Poetica in the course of readings in Horace (rather than directly from Aristotle's Poetics in a course in literary criticism, ordered chronologically) will observe that the beginning and the end of the work (and some of the middle) have the technique of satire: there are the exaggerated examples of artistic incongruity at the beginning, and at the end Horace loses his temper and lays about him with quite as much zest as Juvenal ever does in his passages of highest indignation.

Second, it is a fairly sound principle in examining satirical writing that there is an implicit norm or standard of propriety which can be inferred and stated explicitly by the student. (Very often the norm of satire is simply "common sense, common honesty, common decency," as H. L. Mencken once put it.) In the case of the Ars Poetica, the norms are stated explicitly. There are the substantive academic materials, which Horace dutifully sets forth; there are also the literary standards and procedures which reflect the serious thought and discourse of the intensely earnest literary group often called the "Augustan circle." These standards and procedures Horace commends to his young literary advisees.

Vergil and Horace became, of course, the immortals of the circle. With the encouragement of Augustus and the patronage of Maecenas, they supported the official policy of making Rome a cultural center that would equal Athens and Alexandria in accomplishment and prestige. Latin had to have its epic, its history, its lyric poetry and, of course, its drama.

But while the Ars Poetica is ostensibly directed to the standards and procedures to be observed in the writing of poetry, with such recognition of dramatic theory as may be appropriate, the satirical vehemence of the work is directed against all less than first-rate poetry. Anything but the best is insufferable. Literature is a severe discipline; it requires strict intellectual honesty, rigorous self-criticism, submission to competent criticism from others, indefatigable industry, infinite pains, driving ambition, absolute dedication: all imposed on natural talent. These are the conditions of classicism.

The formal theories set forth by Horace, we have seen, are not original. Most readers, one suspects, find them somewhat unexciting after reading Aristotle's Poetics. There is no terse, compelling, logical analysis; and worst of all, no fear, no pity, no high sense of cosmic fate and human error.

But Aristotle and Horace present two entirely different ways of thought. Both are commonly used.

The two ways may be illustrated by an analogy from botany. Imagine that we have a raspberry, a bean pod, a Winesap apple, a cocklebur, and an acorn. These are all fruits, as far as the botanist is concerned. Let us also imagine that we have come by these five fruits by accident or by random selection, rather than by any deliberate choice of ours. The two ways of thought then present themselves.

We may decide that the Winesap apple is the fruit, by definition ideally representative of the general class of fruit.

We may decide that a fruit, by definition, must embrace the common properties of all specimens of fruit.

Our modern concept of tragedy, reinforced by Aristotle, is based on the first procedure. But it may be observed that the primacy of the Winesap apple as a fruit depends upon criteria exterior to the natural order of presentation. It may also be observed that our concept of tragedy relies on a very few surviving plays plus extensive but unrecognized commitments to some of Aristotle's major concepts, e.g., the inevitable historical development of an organism, an organization, or an institution (e.g., drama) toward a pre-existent ideal form in a managed universe (i.e., the organization of the universe itself as an administrative enterprise).

The Greeks (and Romans), by and large, appear to have followed the second procedure: taking tragedy simply as it came, they thought of tragedies, by general definition, simply as plays about the legendary aristocracy of Greece. Plato, whose youth fell within the fifth century, viewed tragedy with very grave misgivings; its emotional appeal for the Athenian audience, one may venture to infer from Plato's comments, was comparable to that of Stella Dallas combined with The Thing from the Asteroid Belt. And while Aristotle's influence in general has been profound ever since his day, his specific influence in the Hellenistic world (the third century B.C. and thereafter) tended to disperse into one or another special field of inquiry; his views of the managed universe, as well as our view of tragedy, cannot fairly be said to represent "Greek thought" or "the Greek point of view" other than by our own contemporary fiat, i.e., the Winesap apple method.

Horace, on the other hand, follows the general or non-idealizing concept of tragedy. He is telling the two young Pisones how to write good plays about tragic characters, i.e., late Bronze Age personages. And it may be added that the critical tradition which he follows does not use the structural, whole-and-parts, technique so common in Aristotle's writings (e.g., tragedy, as a whole, has six parts). The veteran professor, when dealing with almost any work of Aristotle, will feel an urge to reach for the chalk and diagram the current structure on the board; to illustrate the Horatian concept of unity, the professor would have to make drawings on the board with, one assumes, pastel crayons.

(The numbers inserted in the translation give the approximate location of every tenth line in the Latin text; the original translation was made from Bennett and Rolfe's annotated text; the revision presented here has been checked against F. Klingner's Teubner text of 1950.)

Suppose a painter meant to attach a horse's neck to the head of a man, and to put fancy-work of many-colored feathers on limbs of creatures picked at random; the kind of thing where the torso of a shapely maiden merges into the dark rear half of a fish; would you smother your amusement, my friends, if you were let in to see the result?

Believe me, Pisones, a book will be very much like that painting if the meaningless images are put together like the dreams of a man in a fever, to the end that the head and the foot do not match the one body.

"Poets and painters have always enjoyed their fair privilege, of experimenting however they will." [10]

I know it; and I claim that privilege as a poet and, as a poet, I grant it to the painter; but not to the extent that vicious creatures mate with gentle ones, that snakes are paired with birds, lambs with tigers.

When a poem has a pretentious introduction, promising great themes, a bright red patch or two is usually stitched on, to achieve an expansive, colorful effect, as when a sacred grove and an altar of Diana are described, or a hurrying rivulet of water wandering through the lovely meadows, or the river Rhine, or a rainbow. All very well; but there was no place for these scenes at this point in the poem.

And perhaps you know how to represent a cypress tree: what good is this when the client who has paid your fee in advance is swimming for his life in the picture from the wreckage of his ship? [20] I have started to mould a two-handled jar to hold wine: why does a pitcher come off the potter's turning wheel? What I am getting at is this: let the work of art be whatever you want, as long as it is simple and has unity.

To you, Piso senior, and to you sons worthy of your father, I admit that the majority of us poets are tricked by our own standards. I work hard to be brief; I turn out to be obscure. When I try to achieve smoothness and polish, I lose punch, the work lacks life; the poet who proposes grandeur is merely pompous; the poet who tries to be too conservative creeps on the ground, afraid of gusts of wind; if he is anxious to lend marvellous variety to a single subject, he paints a dolphin in the forest, a boar in the breakers. [30] The avoidance of mistakes leads to serious defects if one is lacking in artistic sense. The sculptor in the last studio around the [gladiatorial] school of Aemilius will mould fingernails and imitate wavy hair in bronze, but the net effect of the work will be unfortunate because he will not know how to represent the whole. If I wanted to make a comparison, I would not care to be like him any more than to go through life with an ugly nose but good-looking otherwise, with dark eyes and dark hair.

If you plan to write, adopt material to match your talents, and think over carefully what burdens your shoulders will not carry and how strong they really are. When a writer's chosen material matches his powers, the flow of words will not fail nor will clarity and orderly arrangement. [40] This is the virtue and charm of such arrangements, unless I am mistaken: that one says now what ought to be said and puts off for later and leaves out a great deal for the present. The author of a poem that has been [asked for and] promised likes one thing and rejects another, is sensitive and careful in putting words together.

Again, you will have expressed yourself with distinction if a clever assocation gives an old word new meaning. If it turns out to be necessary to explain recent discoveries with new terms, you will be allowed to invent words never heard by the Cethegi in their loin-cloths; [50] and licence will be given if you exercise it with due restraint; and new words, recently invented, will win acceptance if they spring from a Greek source with a minor twist in meaning. For that matter, what will a Roman grant to Caecilius and Plautus that he takes away from Vergil and Varius? As for me, why should I be criticized if I add a few words to my vocabulary, when the language of Cato and Ennius enriched the speech of our fathers and produced new names for things? It has always been permissible, and always will be, to mint words stamped with the mark of contemporary coinage. [60]

As the forests change their foliage in the headlong flight of years, as the first leaves fall, so does the old crop of words pass away, and the newly born, like men in the bloom of their youth, come then to the prime of their vigor. We and our works are mortgaged to die. It may be that the land embraces Neptune and diverts the north wind from our navy, the engineering of a king; or a swamp, long unproductive, and good only for boating, now feeds nearby towns and feels the heavy burden of the plow; or it may be that a river, a ravager of fruitful fields, has changed its course, has been taught to follow a better channel: no matter, human accomplishments will pass away, much less does the status of speech endure and popular favor persist. Many things are resurrected which once had passed away, and expressions which are now respected in turn will pass, [70] if usage so decrees—the usage over which the authority and norm of daily speech have final jurisdiction.

The careers of kings and leaders, and sorrow-bringing battles: the meter in which to compose these, Homer has shown us. Laments were first expressed in couplets of unequal lines; later, sentiments of vows fulfilled were included [in this verse] as well. However, what author first published dainty elegiacs, the philologists are arguing, and up to now the dispute rests unresolved. A nasty temper armed Archilochus with his specialty, iambic lines; the sock of comedy and the elevated boot of tragedy took on this meter [80], just the thing for on-stage conversation, to rise above the noisy audience and quite natural for relations of events. The Muse gave men of wealth and sons of gods, and the victor in the boxing ring and the horse first in the contest, and the heartaches of youth and relaxing wine, to lyric poetry to sing about.

The standard distinctions and overtones of poetic forms: why should I be addressed as a poet if I cannot observe and know nothing about them? Why should I, with a feeble sense of shame, prefer to be ignorant rather than learn them? A comic situation does not want to be treated in tragic verse forms; in the same way, the banquet of Thyestes repudiates a telling in the lines of everyday affairs, close to the level of comedy. [90]

Let each form of poetry occupy the proper place allotted to it.

There are times, however, when comedy raises its voice and an angry Chremes scolds in fury with his swollen cheeks; and, in tragedy, Telephus and Peleus very often express their pain in prose, when the penniless hero and the exile both project inflated lines and complicated compound words, if they are anxious to touch the hearts of the audience with their complaints of deep distress.

It is not enough for poems to be pretty; they must have charm and they must take the heart of the hearer wheresoever they will. [100] Just as the faces of men smile back at those who smile at them, so they join with those who weep. If you want me to weep, you must first feel sorrows yourself; then your misfortunes, Telephus or Peleus, hurt me, too. If you speak your lines badly, I'll go to sleep —or laugh out loud. Sad words fit a mournful face, words full of threats an angry face, playful words a face in fun, words seriously expressed, a sober face. I mean that Nature has already shaped us inwardly for every phase of fortune: fortune makes us happy, or drives us into anger or brings us down to earth with a burden of grief and then torments us. [110] Afterwards it brings out our emotions and our tongue acts as interpreter. If the lines do not correspond to the emotional state of the speaker, the members of the Roman audience will burst out laughing, regardless of their income bracket.

It will make a great deal of difference whether a comedy slave or a tragic hero is speaking, or a man of ripe old age, or a hothead in the flower of youth, or a great lady, or a worrying nursemaid, or a traveling merchant or the farmer of a few flourishing acres, a character from Colchis or an Assyrian, a native of Thebes or of Argos.

You have two choices: either follow the conventions of the stage or invent materials that are self-consistent.

If, as a writer, you happen to bring back on the stage an Achilles [120] whose honor has been satisfied, energetic, hotheaded, ruthless, eager, let him claim that laws were not made for him, that there is nothing not subject to possession by force. Let Medea be wild and untamed, Ino an object of pity and tears, Ixion treacherous, Io a wanderer, Orestes depressed.

If you risk anything new and original on the stage and have the courage to invent a new character, let it maintain to the very end the qualities with which it first appeared—and let it be self-consistent.

It is difficult to develop everyday themes in an original way, and you would do better to present the *Iliad* in dramatic form than if you were the first to produce unknown materials never used before on stage. Material in the public domain will become your private property if you do not waste your time going around in worn-out circles, and do not be a literal translator, faithfully rendering word for word from Greek, and do not be merely an imitator, thereby getting yourself into a hole from which either good conscience, or the laws of the work itself, will forbid you to climb out.

And do not start off like this, the way a cyclic poet once did: "I shall sing of the fate of Priam and a war of renown." What did this promise produce to match such a wide-open mouth? The mountains will go into labor and deliver a silly mouse! How much more properly this poet began who undertook nothing in poor taste: [140] "Sing to me, Muse, of the man who, after the time of the capture of Troy, saw the ways of numbers of men and their cities." He gives thought to producing a light from the smoke, not smoke from the gleam of the firelight, so that he may bring forth beauty thereafter, and wonder, Antiphates and Scylla and with the Cyclops, Charybdis; nor does he in detail relate the return of Diomedes after the passing of Meleager, or the story of the Trojan War, starting with the twin eggs. He speeds always on to the outcome, and rushes his hearer into the midst of the action just as if the setting were known, and the events that he cannot hope to treat with brilliance, he omits. [150] And then, too, his inventions are such that fiction is mingled with fact to the end that the middle may match with the start and the end with the middle.

Listen to me: here is what I look for in a play, and with me, the public.

If you want a fan in the audience who waits for the final curtain and stays in his seat to the very end, when the singer says, "Give us a hand," you must observe the habits and manners of each period in men's lives, and the proper treatment must be given to their quickly changing characters and their years. The little boy who already knows how to talk plants his feet firmly on the ground, and is eager to play with boys of his own age, and loses his temper and for no good reason gets it back, and changes his disposition every hour. [160]

The adolescent boy with no beard as yet, when [to his relief] he at last is on his own, has fun with hounds and horses and the turf of the sunny Campus, soft as wax to be moulded to folly, resentful of advice, slow to anticipate what is good for him, throwing his money around, high-spirited and eager, quick to change his interests.

The age of maturity brings a change of interests, and the manly character seeks influence and friends, becomes a slave to ambition and is wary of commitments that he will soon have to break off with great difficulty.

Many disagreeable circumstances surround the old man; for example, he still seeks for wealth and, poor fellow, shrinks from spending it [170], or, again, his management of everything is overcautious and without any fire, he is indecisive, hopeful wthout reason, slow to act, grasping for time, hard to get along with, always complaining, always praising the way things were when he was a boy, scolding and correcting the young generation. The years as they come bring with them many advantages, and as they go, take many things away.

Do not by any chance let the character of the elderly be assigned to a younger man, or a man to a boy; we shall always insist upon the qualities of character joined and fitted to the proper age of man.

An event is either acted on the stage or is reported as happening elsewhere. [180] Events arouse our thoughts more slowly when transmitted through the ears than when presented to the accuracy of the eye and reported to the spectator by himself. On the other hand, do not bring out on stage actions that should properly take place inside, and remove from view the many events which the descriptive powers of an actor present on the stage will soon relate. Do not have Medea butcher her sons before the audience, or have the ghoulish Atreus cook up human organs out in public, or Procne turn into a bird, Cadmus into a snake. If you show me anything of this kind, I will not be fooled and I shall resent it.

Do not let a play consist of less than five acts or be dragged out to more than this length, if you want it to enjoy popular demand and have a repeat performance.

Do not have a god intervene unless the complication of the plot turns out to be appropriate to divine solution; and do not have a fourth leading character working hard to get in with his lines.

Have the chorus carry the part of an actor and take a manly role in the play, and do not let them sing anything between the acts which does not contribute to the plot and fit properly into it. The chorus should side with the good and give friendly advice, curb those who are angry and befriend those who fear to do wrong; the chorus should praise a dinner which has but few courses, healthy legal processes and law, and the conditions of peace when the gates of the city stand open; the chorus will keep secrets, entreat the gods and pray that good fortune will come back to the afflicted and desert the overconfident. [200]

The pipes (not, as now, displaced by the brass and their rival the trumpet, but slender in tone and simple, with only a few stops) used to be helpful in accompanying and supporting the chorus and in filling the auditorium (which was not, in those days, overcrowded) with its music—the audience in which the entire community gathered was then such as one could count, what with its small size; it was thrifty, moral and proper.

After the community began to win wars and extend its domain, and the walls of the city enclosed a wider area, and one's guardian spirit was appeased on holidays without reproach with wine in the daytime [210], greater license in meters and modes came to the theater. This is to say: what critical sense could an ignorant community have when freed from work, the farmer mingling with the townsman, the commoner with the gentleman? And so the flute player added movement and display to the old-fashioned art and trailed his costume about on the platform. And so, again, they invented special notes for the once sober lyre, and the unrestrained speech of the chorus gave rise to a new kind of eloquence, wise in advice on matters of state, and its divine utterances of things to come were quite in the oracular manner of Delphic ambiguities.

The writer who entered the contest for a common goat [220] in tragic verse soon added rustic satyrs with scanty clothing, and crudely tried his hand at humor without loss of tragic dignity, for the reason that the member of the audience had to be kept in his seat by the enticements of novelties, because after taking part in the Bacchic rituals, he was drunk and rowdy. But it is expedient, nonetheless, to sanction the merry, impudent satyrs, to turn solemnity into jest, so that whatever god, whatever hero, may have been but now presented on the stage in gold and royal purple, shall not move into the slums, use vulgar speech, or, while avoiding the ground, grasp at verbal clouds and empty words. [230]

Tragedy is above spouting frivolous lines, like a modest matron told to dance on festive days; she [tragedy] will have little to do, as a respectable woman, with the boisterous satyrs.

As a writer of satyr-plays, my Pisones, I for one will not favor the commonplace and current nouns and verbs, and I shall not try to differ in vocabulary, from the speech that gives tragedy its color; it will make a difference whether Davus is speaking and the saucy Pythias who has swindled a talent out of Simo, or Silenus, the guardian and attendant of a divine foster child.

I shall follow a poetic style from well-known material, just the same as anyone may expect to do himself; [240] and just the same, if he tries it, he will perspire freely and make little progress: that's how difficult the order and connections of words are: that's how much distinction is attached to our everyday vocabulary.

Fauns imported from the woodlands, in my opinion, should be careful not to carouse around in polished lines, like boys reared at the four corners and practically brought up in the Forum, nor shout out dirty words, make scandalous remarks. I mean, they will offend members of the audience who have a house, a distinguished father, and wealth, who will not accept calmly and give the prize to entertainment that pleases the purchaser of dried peas and nuts. [250]

A long syllable following a short is called "iambic," a rapid foot; for this reason, it had the name "three-measure iambic" [trimeter] applied to itself although the beat, the same from first to last, adds up to six per line. Not so very long ago, so that the line might come to the ear more slowly and with a little more weight, the iambic shared its traditional privileges with the steady spondee, accommodating and tolerant, with the reservation that the iambic foot would not, as a partner, move out of its first and fourth position. The spondee, I may add, rarely appears in Accius' "noble" trimeters; and it burdens Ennius' verses, sent ponderously out on the stage [260], with the charge of overhasty work and the lack of care and attention, or shameful neglect of the principles of art.

No critic whom you may name in Rome can see that a

poem is unmusical; and Roman poets have been given un-warranted freedom. Because of that, am I to wander around and write free verse? Or am I to assume that everyone will see my mistakes and play it safe and stay cautiously within the limits of the license I may be granted? No; what I have been saying simply amounts to this: I have merely managed to escape criticism; I have not earned praise.

You—turn our Greek models in your hands at night, turn them in the daytime. But, you say, your forefathers praised the lives and jokes of Plautus; [270] they were much too tolerant of both; they admired him, if I may say so, stupidly, assuming that you and I know how to tell the difference between expressions in poor and good taste, and have had enough experience to tell, on our fingers and by ear, when a sound has been produced ac-cording to the rules of meter.

Thespis is said to have discovered the form of tragic poetry and to have hauled his plays around on carts: plays sung and acted by those who had smeared their faces with sediment from wine jars.

After Thespis: the discoverer of the mask and color-ful costume, Aeschylus, also constructed the stage on a limited scale, and taught how to speak in lofty style and to walk in the high boots of tragedy. [280]

After these came old comedy, not without considerable popular approval; but its freedom of speech fell off into license and a violence that deserved restraint by law: law was acknowledged and the chorus was disgraced into silence when its right to libel was removed.

Our Roman poets have not failed to try all forms of drama; they deserve no honor whatsoever for venturing to desert the trail blazed by the Greeks and attempting to give fame to Roman events—those who presented serious history or comedies of daily life. Nor would the land of the Latins be more mighty in valor and glory in war than in words, if the toil of time and polish did not discourage our poets, every one of them. [290] As for you, who represent the bloodline of Pompilius, see that you are severe in your censure of a poem that many a day and many an erasure has not trimmed down, and not corrected ten times by the test of a newly-cut finger-nail.

Because Democritus believed natural talent to contri-

bute more to success than pitiful technical competence,
he barred from Helicon all poets who were mentally well-
balanced; most poets do not bother to trim their nails,
their beards, they look for out-of-the-way places, steer
clear of the baths. I mean, one will acquire the title of
poet and the reputation, if he never entrusts his head—
too crazy to be cured by medicine even from three
Anticyras—to Licinus the barber. [300]

Oh, how inept I am! I have myself purged of bile as
the spring season comes on! Otherwise no man could
write a better poem. But it isn't worth the trouble. I'll
play the role of whetstone, which is good enough to put
an edge on iron but is out of luck when it comes to
cutting. While I write nothing myself, I'll teach the gift,
the business of the poet, where he gets his material, what
nourishes and forms the poet, what is appropriate, the
way of right and wrong.

The origin and source of poetry is the wisdom to write
according to moral principles: the Socratic dialogues will
be able to clarify your philosophy [310], and the words
themselves will freely follow the philosophy, once it has
been seen before you write. The man who has learned
what he owes to his country, what he owes to his friends,
what love is due a father, how a brother and a family
friend are loved, what the duties of a senator are, what
the duties of a judge, what roles a leader sent to war
should play: he knows, as a matter of course, how to
assign to each character what is appropriate for it.

I shall tell you to respect the examples of life and of
good character—you who have learned the art of imitation
—and from this source bring forth lines that live. Quite
often a play which is impressive in spots and portrays
good character, but with no particular charm, without real
content and really good writing [320], will give the public
more pleasure and hold them better than lines without
ideas and with resounding platitudes.

To the Greeks, genius, the gift of speaking in well-
rounded phrases—these the Muse presented. The Greeks
are greedy for nothing save acclaim. The Roman boys
learn to calculate percentages of money by long divi-
sion. "Let the son of Albinus tell me: if one-twelfth
is taken from five-twelfths, what's the remainder? You
should have been able to tell us by this time." "One-
third." "*Très bien!* You'll make a good businessman. Add

a twelfth, what happens?" "One-half." [330] When this smut, this worrying about business arithmetic, has permeated our minds, do you think we can expect to put together poems to be treated with oil of cedar and kept in cypress-wood cases?

Poets aim either to help or to amuse the reader, or to say what is pleasant and at the same time what is suitable. Whatever you have in the way of a lesson, make it short, so that impressionable minds can quickly grasp your words and hold them faithfully: every unnecessary word spills over and is lost to a heart that is already filled up to the brim.

Whatever you invent to please, see that it is close to truth, so your play does not require belief in anything it wants; do not have it pull a living child from Lamia's insides just after she has eaten lunch. [340]

The centuries of elders in the audience cannot stand a play that has no moral; the noble young gentlemen ignore an austere composition; but the writer who has combined the pleasant with the useful [*miscuit utile dulci*] wins on all points, by delighting the reader while he gives advice. This kind of book makes money for the Sosii [publishers], this kind of book is sold across the sea and prolongs the famous writer's age.

There are, however, faults which I should like to overlook: I mean that the string, when plucked, does not give forth the sound that heart and hand desire; it very often gives back a high note when one calls for a low; and the arrow does not always hit precisely the mark at which it aimed and threatened. [350] So, when most of the passages are brilliant, I am personally not bothered by blots, which are spattered here and there by oversight or those which human nature failed to guard against enough.

Well, what's the point?

If a library copyist keeps on making the same mistake, even though he has been warned about it, there is no excuse for him, and a lyre player who always strikes the same sour note is laughed at; so a writer who is consistently sloppy is in a class with Choerilus—you know who I mean—whom I regard with amused admiration if he happens to write two or three good passages. Similarly, I think it's too bad whenever good old Homer dozes off, as he does from time to time, but when all is said and done, it is natural enough for drowsiness to creep up on a long job of writing. [360] A poem is like a painting: you will find a picture which will attract you more if you stand up close, another if you stand farther back. This picture favors shadow, another likes to be viewed in the light—neither has apprehensions about the keen perceptions of the good critic. Here's one that pleases you only once; here's another that you'll like if you come back to it ten times.

And now to address the older of the two of you: ah, even though your tastes have been formed to appreciate the right things by your father (as well as by others), and you have much good sense of your own, acknowledge what I am going to say and remember it: perfectly proper concessions are made to second-raters in certain fields. A second-rate legal authority and member of the bar [370] can be far from having the qualities of Messala, a very able speaker, and not be as learned as Cascellius Aulus, but still he hs a certain value—*a second-rate poet gets no advertising posters from either men, gods, or booksellers.*

You know how music off-key grates on your nerves at an otherwise pleasant banquet, and greasy ointment for your hair, and bitter honey from Sardinia mixed with poppy seeds, because the banquet could be carried on without them. That is how it is with poetry: created and developed to give joy to human hearts; but if it takes one step down from the very highest point of merit, it slides all the way back to the bottom.

The lad who does not know how to take part in sports keeps out of the cavalry exercises in the Campus; and if he has not learned how to work with the ball, the disc or the hoop [380]—he sits where he is because he is afraid that the spectators, jammed together, will laugh at his expense—there will be nothing he can do about it. For all of that, the man who has no notion of how to compose poetry has the nerve to go ahead anyhow. Why shouldn't he? After all, he's a free man and born free and what's more to the point, his income is in the top brackets—which puts him beyond criticism.

As for you, my boy, don't do or say anything that Minerva would not approve: that's your standard of judgment, that's your philosophy. However, if you ever do write something, see that it comes into court—to the ears of Maecius as critic, or your father's, or mine,

and also see that it is weighted down in storage, put
away between the leaves of parchment for revision in the
ninth year; you can always edit what you haven't published: the word that is uttered knows no return. [390]

Orpheus, a holy man and spokesman for the gods,
forced the wild men of the woods to give up human
killing and gruesome feasting; he is said, because of these
powers, to soothe tigers and the raging of the lion; yes,
and Amphion, the builder of the city of Thebes, is said
to move rocks with his lyre and with the softness of song
to lead them where he will.

I will tell you what was once the poet's wisdom: to
decide what were public and what were private suits at
law, to say what was sacred and what was not, to en-
join from sexual license, provide a code of conduct for
marriage, to build up towns, and carve the laws on wooden
tablets. This was the way honor and renown came to
god-like poet-preachers and their songs. [400]

After these, Homer gained renown, and Tyrtaeus with
his verses whetted the spirits of males for Mars and war;
oracles were given in the form of poems and the way of
life was shown; the favor of kings was sought in Pierian
strains; and dramatic festivals were invented and thus
the end of a long task [of development]—in case the
Muse in her lyric artistry and Apollo with his song embarrass you.

The question has been asked: is good poetry created
by nature or by training?

Personally, I cannot see what good enthusiasm is or un-
cultivated talent without a rich vein of genius; [410] each
requires the help of the other and forms a friendly com-
pact. The would-be poet whose passion is to reach the
hoped-for goal in this race for fame, has worked hard in
boyhood and endured a great deal, has sweated and
shivered, abstained from women and wine; the artist who
plays the pipe at the Pythian games has first learned his art
and lived in terror of a teacher. Nowadays it's enough to
have said, "I beat out wonderful poems; the hell with the
rest of the mob; it's a dirty deal for me to be left at the
starting line and admit that I obviously didn't know what
I never learned."

Like a huckster who collects a crowd to buy his wares,
the poet with his wealth in land, with wealth resting on
coin put out at interest, tells yes-men to come to his

readings for gain. [420] Yes, indeed; if there is a man who can set out a really fat banquet, and co-sign notes for irresponsible paupers, and save the neck of the client tangled in a murder trial, I'll be surprised if, for all his wealth, he can tell the difference between a liar and an honest friend! Whether you have aready given someone a present or only expect to do so, don't let him near your verses when he's full of joy: I mean, he'll gush "Lovely! Great! Swell!" On top of this, he'll turn pale, he'll even squeeze drops of dew from sympathetic eyes, leap to his feet and stamp on the ground. [430]

The way hired mourners wail at a funeral and—so they say—carry on more painfully than those who sorrow quite sincerely, thus the critic with his tongue in cheek is more deeply moved than the ordinary flatterer. Rich men are said to keep pushing glasses of wine at, and to torment with wine poured straight, the man whom they are trying hard to see through—to see if he is worthy of friendship. If you will put together poems, motives disguised with a foxy expression will never deceive you.

If you were to read anything to Quintilius, "Change this, please," he kept saying, "and this." If you said you couldn't do better, you'd tried twice, three times, with no success [440], Quintilius used to say to rub it out and put back on the anvil the lines that were spoiled on the lathe. If you preferred to defend your mistake, not revise it, he would not waste another word or go to more useless trouble to keep you from being your only friend, with no competitors.

A true critic and a wise one will scold you for weak lines, blame you for rough ones, he'll indicate unpolished lines with a black cross-mark made with his pen, he'll cut out pretentious embellishments, make you clarify obscure phrases, remove ambiguities, mark things to be changed, he'll turn into an Aristarchus, and he will not say, "Why should I hurt the feelings of a friend over these trifles?" [450] Well, these trifles will get you into serious trouble once you have been laughed down and given a poor reception.

As in the case of a man with a bad attack of the itch or inflammation of the liver or one who's offended Diana —he's moon-struck—everyone with any sense is afraid to touch the madman and keeps out of the way of the poet; small boys pester him and don't know any better than

to follow him around. If, while burping out his lines and
thinking they're sublime, he goes off the roadway, falls
into an excavation or a well, like a hunter intent on his
blackbirds—he can yell—so you can hear him a mile
away, "Help! Hey, neighbors!"—no one would be worried
about fishing him out. [460] If someone should get excited
about rescuing him and let down a rope, I'll say, "How
do you know that he didn't do it on purpose when he
threw himself down there, and doesn't want to be res-
cued?" And I'll tell the story about the death of the
Sicilian poet.

While he had a yearning to be regarded as an immortal
god, Empedocles was cool enough to jump down into the
red-hot crater of Aetna. Let poets have the right to perish;
issue them a license! When you rescue a man against his
will, you do the same as kill him. This isn't the first time
he's done it, either; and if he's hauled out, he still won't
behave like a human and give up his love of dying for
publicity. And it isn't very clear, either, why he keeps on
grinding out his verses [470], whether he's used his
father's funeral urn as a pisspot or whether he's tampered
with the boundary markers of a holy plot of ground—an
act of sacrilege. He's crazy, that's sure; and like a bear
that's powerful enough to break the bars at the front of
his cage, this dedicated elocutionist puts to flight the
scholar and the layman without discrimination. Yes, and
when he catches one, he'll hold on to him and recite him
to death. You can be sure he won't let go of the hide of
his victim until he's as full of blood as a leech.

NOTES